CALLAS

Portrait of a Prima Donna

BY GEORGE JELLINEK

With a New Preface
and Epilogue by the Author

Dover Publications, Inc.
New York

To the memory of *Charles Dicker,*
and to a life devoted to kindliness, geniality,
and music, which he personified

Published in Canada by General Publishing Company, Ltd., 30 Lesmill Road, Don Mills, Toronto, Ontario.
Published in the United Kingdom by Constable and Company, Ltd., 10 Orange Street, London WC2H 7EG.

This Dover edition, first published in 1986, is a slightly corrected republication of the work originally published by the Ziff-Davis Publishing Company, New York, in 1960. A new Preface and Epilogue have been prepared specially for this edition. The Discography, and the references to recordings in the Repertoire section, have been omitted.

Manufactured in the United States of America
Dover Publications, Inc., 31 East 2nd Street, Mineola, N.Y. 11501

Library of Congress Cataloging in Publication Data

Jellinek, George, 1919–
    Callas : portrait of a prima donna.

    Includes index.
    1. Callas, Maria, 1923–1977.   2. Singers—Biography.   I. Title.
ML420.C18J4   1986   782.1'092'4   [B]   85-24572
ISBN 0-486-25047-4

Preface to the Dover Edition

Although Maria Callas lived for seventeen more years, her artistic career virtually came to an end in 1960, when the first edition of this book was published. What followed were, for her, periods of superficial glitter, with many frustrations and personal crises underneath, and the steady and heartbreaking process of artistic decline. She learned no new roles, indeed appeared in very few staged performances after 1960, and the few recordings she made survive as vivid documentations of an artist past her peak.

What I related as contemporary events twenty-five years ago are now history, and the Maria Callas so vibrantly with us then has assumed a legendary stature. In all likelihood she will remain the most controversial and most influential operatic personality of our era, and will be so remembered by a generation that was too young to witness her rise and stormy path firsthand.

For that generation, the recordings of Callas—with possibly some video cassettes to come—are already available in a profusion undreamed of in 1960. As a result of a significant change in the Italian copyright law, just about every performance described in this book—whether in Milan, Rome, New York, or Mexico City—is now available to the public in recorded form, if at times through channels of dubious legitimacy. Callas has become a cult figure—her revelatory, multidimensional art has been perpetuated to enthrall and to instruct; her stormy and ultimately tragic life may do the same.

When the first edition of this book appeared, Callas was embarking on a new life of exciting adventures that eventually led to tragedy. What happened *before* 1960—her artistic life with its struggles, storms, and triumphs—is chronicled here with as much objectivity and insight as circumstances then permitted. I am grateful to be able to witness the book's republication with the addition of an Epilogue.

GEORGE JELLINEK

New York, N.Y., 1985

Preface to the First Edition

Tonio
*L'autore ha cercato invece pin-
gervi uno squarcio di vita. Egli
ha per massima sol che l'artista
è un uom . . .*[*]

LEONCAVALLO — I PAGLIACCI

By common consent, Maria Callas is an artist of the first magnitude. Even her detractors recognize in her one of the most exciting musical figures of this generation. Her admirers are huge in number and uncompromising in their devotion.

But Maria Callas is far more than an extraordinary opera singer. She is also an accredited member of the international set, a "celebrity" whose every move rates

[*] A translation of this quotation, together with translations of the quotations to be found at the beginning of each chapter, will be found on page 347.

headline attention. Her character, her personality, the company she keeps are constantly commented upon, and most frequently by journalists whose interest in opera stops at Sherry's Bar. Consequently, she has become a continuous topic of conversation. Day after day she is violently attacked and powerfully defended all over the world by people who have never seen her perform, nor even heard her sing on records. Undoubtedly, she is one of the world's most talked-about personalities. It is the aim of this book to show why this is so.

This is not a "tell all" book—a scandal-sheet exposé. Its premise is, rather, that the true significance of Maria Callas lies in her contribution to opera. The reader will become acquainted with the background essential to an understanding of her personality; the influences that have shaped her art will be explored; and a chronicle of her extraordinary career will be unfolded, illuminated by many heretofore unpublished details.

The world of opera is evocative of strong passions, and Maria Callas has been known throughout her entire career to inspire strong opinions. It was my primary purpose to rise above these currents and to present the events related here with a detached, dispassionate outlook, particularly in the light of so much previously published material of a partisan and contradictory nature.

This book is the result of careful research and extensive interviews, an objective book, allowing for an admitted sympathy for the subject, without which no biography should be undertaken. Finally, and this should be stressed, it is an independent effort, written with the knowledge and cooperation, but entirely without the participation, of its stimulating subject. As a matter of fact, Maria Callas has not read any part of the book prior to its publication.

Because some of the events related here are of a

personal and controversial nature, a certain amount of reluctance to interviews on the part of some key personalities was understandable. As it turned out, this reluctance
assumed considerable proportions. The fraternity of
American opera managers, for example, joined in an im-
penetrable phalanx of secretiveness. All the more appreciated, therefore, was the interest and kind cooperation
shown by Henry Koerner, Giacomo Lauri-Volpi, Walter
Legge, Nicola Rescigno, Tullio Serafin, and Dario and
Dorle Soria, to whom I am indebted for much valuable
information.

In the chronicle of past Callas performances, I have
quoted critics from a dozen different countries. The translations are mine, but the original sources are always identified. Because so much of the artist's career centered on
Italy, I feel particularly fortunate in having had access
to the excellent and extremely informative writings of
Messrs. Teodoro Celli, Eugenio Gara, and Emilio Radius
of Milan, and Giorgio Vigolo of Rome.

I am indebted to Miss Nancy Duryee and Miss Trudy
Goth of New York and Miss Teresa D'Addato of Milan
for valuable research assistance, to Miss Frances Moore
and Mr. Gerald Fitzgerald of New York for help in the
compilation of photographic material, and to Mr. Jack
Romann of Angel Records, New York, for his assistance
with disc data. My special thanks go to Earl Swick, a tireless and understanding editor.

Finally, I thank my wife, Hedy, for her constant encouragement, patience, and, above all, incalculable professional help. Without her, this book could not have been
written.

GEORGE JELLINEK

Contents

CHAPTER 1

Where It All Began

Manon
*Non ho sul volto luce di beltà,
regna tristezza sul destino mio.*

PUCCINI — MANON LESCAUT

All day long an air of excitement pervaded the corridors of Public School 189 at Amsterdam Avenue and 188th Street in the Washington Heights area of Manhattan. It was January 28, 1937, and graduation day for another eighth-grade class. The festive spirit of the occasion was reflected on the beaming faces of the students and their parents who filled the assembly hall to witness the commencement program.

The graduating class was of average size, some one hundred and forty students. Except to their parents, none of the youngsters appeared to be in any way unusual. Nor was the graduation program, with its well-rehearsed march, the obligatory hymn and pledge of allegiance, the national anthem, and several orations, any more than might be expected on similar occasions in any school in the country.

Then came the portion of the program for which students and parents alike had been waiting, the operetta. Based on the melodies of Gilbert and Sullivan, it was arranged to permit scores of youngsters with various degrees of talent to participate. The tall, bespectacled, earnest-looking girl, moving about the stage with no more and no less than the expected adolescent awkwardness, sang the tunes of *Pinafore* in a pleasant soprano voice and received a warm round of applause. She left the stage seemingly pleased, with a restrained little smile on her lips.

After the program came the joyful good-byes. As the graduates went about exchanging the usual good wishes, they scrawled the time-honored compliments and witticisms in each other's autograph books amidst lively discussions of future plans and ambitions. A goodly share of the heartfelt compliments, full of the innocent optimism of the young, went to the tall girl with the glasses, whose singing was greatly admired by her classmates.

Her own feelings seemed to reflect little optimism at the moment. She had done well at the graduation performance of P.S. 189. But her future was uncertain, perhaps more uncertain than that of any of her classmates. In the autograph book of one of her fellow students she wrote:
"Being no poet, having no fame,
permit me just to sign my name."
And she signed it "Mary Anna Callas."

A few days later, thirteen-year-old Mary Anna Callas said good-bye to her father and to her native New York. Turning her back on what had been a bleak and cheerless childhood, she was truly "embarking on the journey of life," as they said in the graduation ceremonies. She and her mother were sailing to Greece, to a hopeful but unknown future.

Mary Anna was an American, but she had been born in the United States almost by accident. Both her parents were Greek. Her father, George Kalogeropoulos, was a student of pharmacy at the University of Athens when he met Evangelia Dimitriadu, daughter of an Army officer. After a brief romance, they were married, in August, 1916, shortly after he was graduated from the university, and settled in the little town of Meligala in the Peloponnesus. There, George Kalogeropoulos, as the owner of a thriving pharmacy, became one of the town's most affluent and respected citizens.

Their first child, a daughter who was christened Cynthia, was born in 1917. A boy, Basil, came three years later. As is frequently true with some families, particularly in Europe, the son was especially dear to the parents. Then, when life seemed most beautiful, and Basil was a handsome child of three, typhoid fever appeared in Meligala. The little boy was among the first victims of the epidemic. The tragic blow had such shattering consequences that its shadow seems still to hover over the Callas family.

George and Evangelia were disconsolate. Life seemed to have lost all meaning. Meligala, despite their former happiness there, would always remind them of their crushing loss. It seemed best to husband and wife, as they talked it over night after night, to leave this region. To go to Athens or to another part of Greece was not enough. They wanted a new start in life. They wanted to forget the past and think only of the future. America, the land of promise to generations of striving, frustrated, and saddened Europeans, seemed to offer the greatest promise. Perhaps there they might be able to mend their broken lives.

So the pharmacy, George Kalogeropoulos's proud achievement, was sold. Fortunately, the proceeds were considerable, and the family could leave for the New World in reasonable comfort. That summer of 1923, little Cynthia was six years old and Evangelia was expecting another child. With the budding life they carried toward America, George and Evangelia desperately hoped that they would somehow regain their lost happiness.

Four months after the family arrived in New York, Evangelia gave birth to her child in Flower Hospital (now called Fifth Avenue Hospital) on the corner of Fifth Avenue and 106th Street. Both parents had hoped for a son to replace their beloved Basil. But the fates decreed that a daughter should be born to them on December 4, 1923.

The voice that was to launch a thousand controversies first issued from a twelve-and-a-half-pound body on that day. It was the name day of St. Barbara, a heroic martyr and patron saint of the artillery, for whom Maria Callas was to profess fond affection in her later, more combative, years. At her baptism, the infant's name was recorded in its full Hellenic glory as *Maria Anna Cecilia Sofia Kalogeropoulos*.

In the new world, George Kalogeropoulos had to face, first of all, the problem of earning a livelihood. Since he was a skilled pharmacist, he soon obtained employment with a drug store chain. His earnings enabled him to furnish a little apartment in Astoria, Long Island, without depleting the family's funds. Thus life started auspiciously for the new Americans.

A year later, they moved to the West Side of Man-

hattan. About this time, George Kalogeropoulos, in keeping with the inescapable experience of many Greek
Americans, felt the need to streamline his resounding sur-
name to a more succinct and pronounceable form. He chose
Callas.

George Callas, an earnest and meticulous man, took
his work very seriously. He made several friends, gained
much valuable experience, and, in time, felt encouraged
to open his own drug store. In 1927 he found a location
in midtown Manhattan, a neighborhood in which many
Greek Americans had settled. The new drug store did not
measure up, of course, to the one he had left behind in
Meligala. Neither did the social position it brought with it.
He had been one of the town's leading citizens there; in
New York he was still a dot in the faceless crowd. But he
worked at his profession, and he had the means to pro-
vide a good income for his family, an obligation which
had become the main purpose of his life.

In the tradition observed by European families, the
upbringing of the children was the mother's domain.
As her daughters grew up, Evangelia Callas was delighted
to discover that both Cynthia and Maria showed considerable musical talent. Music had always fascinated her.
She had vivid memories of her father, whose resounding
tenor voice had been widely admired by family and
friends. However, hers had been a family of army officers
—she and her sisters could admire artists from afar, but
musical or theatrical careers for themselves would have
been unthinkable. Besides, apart from this fascination
for music, Evangelia had not shown any real musical
talent. But now, as she came to realize the unusual gifts
of her children, the schoolgirl's fascination became a
mother's ambition. Cynthia and Maria could and would
have musical careers. She would see to that.

A pianola was added to the household to stimulate the children's interest. Maria was not three years old when she began to amaze her parents and to delight acquaintances by picking out the melodies of songs and arias she had heard on the family radio.

Then the family acquired a phonograph. Evangelia bought as many records as she could afford. Her choices were mainly operatic. With the children sitting next to her, she would play these records over and over again. Soon Cynthia and Maria were singing along with the performers. Maria's singing, in particular, became the talk of the neighborhood. There was a child-prodigy in the making, and Mama was determined to encourage her development.

After a few years, music turned out to be a source of tension and quarrels for the Callas family. Evangelia, an aggressive, strong-willed woman, was determined to seek musical careers for the children. Piano lessons were arranged for both girls, and at seven Maria began her formal study of music. George Callas had agreed to the piano lessons, but to Evangelia, they were just a beginning. When the talk turned to artistic careers, his conservative continental nature rebelled.

"It's too soon," he told her. "Let the children grow up, get through school. Let them, by all means, enjoy music, but not at the expense of serious studies."

By this time, the effects of the Depression were being felt by the Callas family. From 1929 to 1932 they moved yearly to a less-expensive apartment. Eventually the drug store had to be sold, and George Callas's dreams of re-creating his bygone business status were ended forever. But he was not defeated. He became a traveling salesman of pharmaceutical products. The salary was not much, but it was steady, and it allowed them the basic necessities. To

Evangelia, the children's music lessons were a necessity. They were continued at considerable sacrifice.

Today, George Callas, a solemn, lonely man, surrounded by memories and by countless pictures of his famous daughter, thinks back on these years with a good deal of satisfaction. In many ways, he has retained his Old World outlook. He takes special pride in having supported his family through those trying times—without ever allowing his wife to go to work.

But his efforts were not always appreciated. Evangelia could not forget the comfortable life in Greece, nor could she understand or cope with the sudden shock of economic hardships. There were many bitter reproaches and recriminations. Her husband, straining under his economic burdens and the constant tensions of an uncertain future, also grew more and more irritable.

It was not enough that his efforts and worries were being met with reproaches. On top of this he had to endure what he considered to be flimsy fantasies of musical and theatrical fame. Weary of her interminable talk and grandiose dreams of artistic life, he accused his wife of seeking to further their daughters' careers so that she might shine in their reflected glory. Such arguments became more and more frequent and could not be kept from the children.

Maria Callas today recalls her childhood with little pleasure. Not for her the memories of childish dreams and fancies, of toys and dolls, or even playmates. She enjoyed her singing, but eventually even music became a chore under the crossfire of her mother's demanding and unyielding drive and her father's continual objections. The stronger will of the mother prevailed. Maria was soon to experience the anxieties and frustrations that harass every talented child who has an ambitious parent.

At the age of eleven, urged on by Mama, Maria began to appear at childrens' contests and on radio programs. At first she found the atmosphere of these shows oppressive. She was frightened by crowds, lacked confidence, and, when the moment came to perform, often had the panicky sensation that no sound would leave her throat. However, her mother insisted that these appearances were important in building a career.

With experience and the as-yet-unrealized desire to succeed, Maria overcame her feelings of fright and insecurity well enough to eventually win a prize on Major Bowes's amateur hour. On one occasion, she even traveled to Chicago to take part in a children's show, where the second prize was awarded to her by comedian Jack Benny.

She was a moody child. There were moments when the temper that many years later was to explode into headlines would manifest itself.

One Saturday afternoon, her father recalls, the family was gathered around the radio, listening to a performance of *Lucia di Lammermoor*. The soprano, one of the Metropolitan's brightest stars, was singing the famous "Mad Scene." Suddenly, with the frank directness of a ten-year-old, Maria shouted that the diva had strayed off pitch.

A family friend who was present reminded the child that the singer was a great star and deserved more respect.

Maria erupted like a Greek volcano.

"I don't care if she *is* a star," she exploded, lightning flashing in her eyes, "she sings off-key! Just wait and see, one day I am going to be a star myself, a bigger star than she."

However, such shows of temper were exceptional. In these years, Maria was an extremely shy, quiet-spoken girl who, as she later confessed, was always able to conceal her anxieties beneath a calm exterior. She was a serious child, much too mature for her age. Like many other lonely children, she consoled herself with sweets, and her steadily growing fondness for delicacies began to have its effect on her figure. In her own eyes, she was "an ugly duckling, fat, clumsy, and unpopular."

Recollections by others do not go to such pitiless lengths; nor is this description fully justified by her photographs. True, her thick-rimmed glasses were no enhancement to her appearance. But, in all likelihood, she was no more than an ordinary girl driven by the self-doubts of adolescence, unmitigated by wise parental guidance, to a passionate and dramatic enlargement of her predicament.

It did not help matters that a lack of personal charm and an uninspired choice of clothing made her appear a poor second beside her sister Cynthia. Whether it was true or not, Maria was convinced that Cynthia (whose name had become "Jackie" in America) was their mother's favorite. Jealousy rankled in the adolescent, together with a dim awareness that she had been a disappointment to her parents from the beginning because she had been born a girl when they had so desperately yearned for a boy.

Maria's childhood insecurities were deep seated. Her anxiety to be loved by her parents, her premature exposure to the limelight, the constant bickering at home, the effects of the Depression—all these left their mark on the self-conscious child. "Even today," she wrote as recently as 1957 in the Italian magazine *Oggi,* reminiscing about the early thirties, "although I am generally regarded as a presumptuous person, I am never certain of myself, and I am frequently tortured by doubts and fears."

Her school years were relatively uneventful, except for the frequent changes in the Callas family's domicile to various points in Manhattan, which always meant changes in the children's schools. Maria's first four grades were completed in four different schools. Finally, she came to P.S. 189 for the fifth grade and stayed on until graduation.

Maria was a good student, with A and B-plus marks. Her father recalls that several teachers complimented him on his daughter's effort and behavior.

"A pleasant, well-behaved girl with no sign of temper." This was the 1960 recollection of Miss Jessie Sugar, one of Maria's teachers at P.S. 189.

During the last years of grade school, Maria gained in self-confidence. She was beginning to discover the extent of her talent. Gradually, appearing in public ceased to be a trial. The feeling of being lonely and friendless was at least partly dissipated in the sense of communication, in the response that greeted her whenever and wherever she sang.

Why *not* have a singing career? A really great career! She no longer doubted that she could develop into an outstanding artist. By listening to phonograph records, she learned a number of operatic arias—at first, the Habanera from *Carmen* and Titania's air from *Mignon;* later, several excerpts from *Aida* and the role of Carmen almost in its entirety. Rosa Ponselle, the Metropolitan diva who excelled in dramatic as well as florid parts, was a particular idol of the fledgling singer.

As the last term of Maria's public school drew to a close, Evangelia Callas decided to take her daughters back to Greece for an extended visit. George Callas protested. There were more arguments. But Evangelia was determined. She had a large family, many brothers and sisters, all well established. They would help her! The musical education of the girls could be continued more easily, and certainly with less financial strain, in the old country. To no one's surprise, her decision prevailed.

Jackie was sent to Greece first, just before Christmas of 1936. Evangelia and Maria followed in late February, 1937, shortly after the graduation ceremonies at P.S. 189.

George Callas was alone. He was prepared for a lengthy separation, but he had no way of knowing that it would take eight long years and a tragic World War before he would see his family again.

CHAPTER 2

War and Greece

Maddalena
*Fame e miseria! Il bisogno, il
periglio . . .*
Giordano—Andrea chenier

Their ship arrived at the port of Patras on a bright,
breezy March morning so typical of the early Greek spring.
Evangelia knew that at last she was home. Maria was fascinated by the old port city and would have liked to go
sightseeing. Evangelia would have none of that. They must
hurry to join Jackie in Athens and to begin the business
that had brought them there.

Mother and daughters moved into a pleasant two-
room apartment at Via Patission 61. Settled in Athens,
three-fourths of the Callas family soon reacquired the four
extra syllables that were rightfully theirs. Thus, Mary

Anna Callas became Maria Anna Kalogeropoulos—a name that had a euphonious ring to Hellenic ears.

George Callas cared for his distant family by regular monthly remittances of one hundred dollars, a considerable amount of money in Greece, so their support was assured. This allowed Evangelia to concentrate on what was now her life's mission: her daughters' careers.

A piano teacher was soon found for Jackie. Her lessons could now be continued to Evangelia's satisfaction. Next came Maria's turn. She presented more of a problem.

Maria was then in her fourteenth year. Tall, intense, and serious in demeanor, she could easily pass for sixteen or seventeen. Evangelia mobilized family, friends, and strangers. Maria's grandmother and numerous aunts and uncles were anxious to see and hear her, but they could offer no help.

Anyone who was presumed to have some influence was treated to an improvised audition. Everyone was pleased, though not everyone shared the mother's exalted hopes. Eventually, Nicola Moscona, the famous bass of the Athens opera, was consulted. He, too, commented on the girl's excellent potential, and he urged the most serious and concentrated study.

The logical place was the Conservatory of Athens, the best institution of its kind in Greece. However, its doors would not open to a fourteen-year-old, no matter how talented. In September, 1937, the determined mother succeeded in gaining admittance for Maria at the National Conservatory, this time giving her age as sixteen. The National Conservatory was less famous than the Conservatory of Athens, but it did offer the formal training that Maria needed.

Maria studied for nearly two years at the National

Conservatory. Her teacher was Maria Trivella, an Italian singer of no special fame, but a capable and considerate woman and a good judge of talent. Maria progressed to more and more demanding assignments under Trivella's guidance, and won several student prizes.

In late November, 1938, she made her first stage appearance as Santuzza in a full-scale student performance of Mascagni's *Cavalleria Rusticana*. She was then still a few days short of her fifteenth birthday.

The war broke out in Europe in the summer of 1939, but its effects were not immediately felt in Greece. However, it was as a direct consequence of wartime travel restrictions that the famous soprano Elvira de Hidalgo, then on one of her annual visits to Greece, decided to accept a permanent teaching post at the Conservatory of Athens.

A great favorite in Greece, the former diva of the Metropolitan and La Scala gave even brighter lustre to the distinguished faculty of the Conservatory. In addition to her teaching duties, De Hidalgo was also given the post of artistic advisor to the National Opera.

One afternoon, in the fall of 1939, Maria Kalogeropoulos, attracted by De Hidalgo's presence and prodded by the ever-urging maternal hand, presented herself before the Athens Conservatory's admissions board.

Elvira de Hidalgo, vividly remembering her first impressions of Maria, gave this account to the Italian magazine *Oggi* many years later: "The very idea of that girl wanting to become a singer was laughable! She was tall, very fat, and wore heavy glasses. When she removed them she would look at you with huge but vague, almost unseeing eyes. Her whole being was awkward, and her dress much too large, buttoned in front and quite formless. She wore crushed sandals. Not knowing what to do with her hands,

she sat there quietly biting her nails while waiting for her
turn.''

Maria's turn came, and she launched into the dramatic
"Ocean aria" from Weber's *Oberon*. De Hidalgo listened
in astonishment:

"I heard violent cascades of sound, not yet fully controlled but full of drama and emotion. I listened with my
eyes closed and imagined what a pleasure it would be to
work with such material, to mold it into perfection.''

The audition was over. After a brief conference, during which the young singer was waiting as if in a daze, the
members of the admissions board told her that she would
be admitted—free of tuition. For a moment, Maria was
speechless. At last she mumbled confused thanks, returned
to her chair, and resumed biting her nails.

So began five years of association during which
teacher and pupil were to become inseparable friends.
Maria threw herself into her vocal studies with extraordinary enthusiasm and an insatiable yearning for musical
knowledge. She had no other interests. From early morning until dark, even when formal instructions did not require her presence, she sought the company of her teacher.
In the evening, the two would walk together, discussing
their art and problems of repertoire and technique. De
Hidalgo reminisced about the glorious days of the past,
about Caruso, Chaliapin, and the other great singers with
whom she had sung. Maria never ran out of questions.

De Hidalgo was not only an exceptional teacher but a
thoughtful and perceptive woman. She understood by instinct the story behind the inward, retiring nature of her
pupil. Gradually, she began to occupy the place left empty
by a determined but insufficiently sympathetic mother.
She became the confidante Maria had always lacked.

Music was no longer being forced on an unwilling or hesitant youngster. Instead, it was carefully and judiciously imparted to give meaning to the present and to project bright hopes for the future.

During the long hours Maria spent with her teacher, whether at her own lessons or those of fellow pupils, she gradually became acquainted with a repertoire far beyond that of the average student. She had a phenomenal memory. One hearing was often enough to enable her to memorize an entire score page. She devoured every kind of musical knowledge and, without permitting herself the luxury of specialization, became familiar with an amazing wealth of the soprano repertoire.

The foundation of Maria Callas's versatility was established in those conservatory days. That she was able to master the celebrated coloratura parts was only a natural consequence of having had Elvira de Hidalgo, herself a famous coloratura, as a teacher. It was here, too, that Maria was first introduced to the little-known operas of Rossini, Bellini, and Donizetti. These were the works sopranos of two generations had steadily ignored and on which Maria Callas's worldwide reputation was to be built.

Thirst for knowledge, a fierce determination to succeed, and innate musicality were qualities any observer could readily detect in the Maria Kalogeropoulos of 1939. Her remarkable memory was a special blessing, particularly for a singer burdened with myopia. When she appeared without glasses she had to rely on her intimate knowledge of the scores, for she could barely see the conductor.

Maria's sister Jackie was an outgoing girl and had made many friends in Athens. She worked hard at her piano studies, but she also led an active social life, as would be expected of an attractive girl in her early twenties.

Maria had no social life. Music filled *her* life completely. She still enjoyed eating cake and confections, and the results continued to show on her figure. She was awkward in appearance, dressed carelessly, and had a bad complexion. These things nearly broke her teacher–friend De Hidalgo's heart. But Maria, far too engrossed in her work and ambition, did not seem to care about her appearance. As for her weight, she was going to become an opera singer, and what was so unusual about a corpulent diva?

There certainly could be no complaint about Maria's musical progress. Her vocal gifts were a cause of continual amazement to all who heard her. Under Madame De Hidalgo's excellent teaching, Maria's voice and singing technique were constantly improving. But there was something more. As if a well had been tapped within her, her singing was becoming infused with excitement and even passion. Her natural dramatic instinct and temperament had been unleashed.

Arda Mandikian, another pupil of De Hidalgo, who went on to a successful concert and operatic career in Europe, recalls that by 1940 Maria had all the earmarks of an unusually inspired musico–dramatic phenomenon. Both young artists made an outstanding impression at a student performance of Puccini's *Suor Angelica*, in which Maria sang the title role and Arda, that of the aunt.

With De Hidalgo's help, Maria was given a small part in the Royal Opera's staging of Suppé's operetta *Boccaccio*. This was her first professional appearance. Though her fellow students greeted her performance with raves, it attracted little general attention. But there was no question that the sixteen-year-old student carried herself with the bearing of a professional artist.

Maria's formal conservatory studies ended soon thereafter. There was no change, however, in the amount of time she spent with De Hidalgo learning parts, or in their devoted relationship.

Times, however, seemed hardly auspicious for long-range planning. Central Europe was in flames. The German army seemed invincible. Mussolini, not to be out-done by his Axis partner, became more menacing and pro-vocative toward Greece. By a dramatic turn of events, opera soon found itself caught in world history.

On October 26, 1940, the National Theater of Greece gave a gala production of Puccini's *Madama Butterfly*. In a gesture of friendliness, though not entirely without political overtones, the Greek government had invited the composer's son to attend the performance. Afterwards, there was a formal reception at the Italian embassy for the honored guest and dignitaries of both nations. Amidst the display of Greek and Italian flags, an enormous cake bearing the words VIVA LA GRECIA commanded par-ticular attention.

While the reception was in progress, the Italian Am-bassador, Grassi, received secret instructions from Rome. Twenty-four hours later he appeared before Premier Metaxas and, citing alleged ''provocations,'' demanded that Italian troops be permitted to occupy certain strategic points in Greece. Three hours later, at 6:00 A.M., October 28, 1940, war broke out between Italy and Greece.

What Mussolini had planned as a cheap victory turned into an ignominious fiasco. Italian troops were quickly repelled by the Greek army and forced into a disorganized rout. But the Axis could not afford defeat. Hitler's legions invaded Greece on April 6, 1941. After sixteen days of heroic but hopeless fighting, the Greek army was compelled to surrender unconditionally.

Greece is not a rich country. With vast areas laid

waste, roads and railways destroyed, her industries harnessed to the Axis war machine, and her merchant fleet either serving the Allies or at the bottom of the sea, the country faced economic and social ruin. The Germans entered Athens on April 27th. On this date began a rule of oppression that was to leave its mark on Greece for years to come, and on Maria Callas for life.

Famine and disease soon reduced the entire population to a chaotic existence. To make their hardships even more severe, the winter of 1941–1942 was the coldest in years.

With the outbreak of war, all contacts with New York came to an abrupt end. So did the monthly payments from George Callas. Evangelia Callas and her two daughters were now reduced to living in the day-to-day uncertainty shared by many thousands of their compatriots. Fortunately, by that time Jackie was engaged to a well-established Athenian named Milton Embirikos, who did his best to help his fiancée's family with occasional rations of food.

Living for months on a steady diet of tomatoes and cauliflowers, having to walk miles and miles to faraway farms for potatoes and greens, these are experiences one is not likely to forget. Even many years later, when she was surrounded by the luxuries of comfort and well-being, the specter of the war years still haunted Maria Callas. Not that she found it any more difficult than anyone else to adjust to luxurious modes of living. But she would never be casual about money, nor could she tolerate the sight or thought of wasted food.

During 1941, Italian troops came to share the occupational chores with the Germans, somewhat improving the lot of Maria and her family. Through friends they were able to obtain extra rations from an Italian army post.

And, Italians being a singing nation through thick and thin, an improvised concert of arias would always bring an additional supply of spaghetti, butter, and sugar.

The presence of Italian troops also made it possible for Maria to concentrate on learning their language. It was De Hidalgo's constant admonition that Maria's future lay in Italy. The sensation of hearing the language of opera around her served to remind Maria of her teacher's advice. With her unique powers of concentration and her special brand of fierce determination, she was able to converse in Italian with the utmost freedom within three months.

To further her protégée's career in every way she could, Elvira de Hidalgo succeeded in improving Maria's appearance by changing her hairdo and making her more clothes conscious. With her guidance, the timid and unassuming student was gradually transformed into a mature musical artist. De Hidalgo also arranged for her to become a permanent member of the Opera with a steady, though very modest, income of 1,300 drachmas. This at least ended her random singing for the troops.

In the interim, the war had taken a different turn. Italy capitulated to the Allies in September, 1943, and much of her military supplies fell into the hands of Greek resistance forces. The resistance movement gradually took on imposing proportions, forcing the Germans out of all but the major cities and industrial centers. By the summer of 1944, two-thirds of Greece was free. Athens, however, still remained under occupation. All administration was controlled by the Germans. The puppet government of John Rallis was entirely powerless.

During these chaotic years, the Athens Opera somehow managed to function. It even received the support and sympathy of the occupying army due to the artistic and musical inclinations of the military commander of Athens,

General Wilhelm Speidel, brother of today's leading German officer at NATO.

The career of Maria Callas took an upward swing in July, 1942, when she was catapulted into the title role of Puccini's *Tosca* when the Opera's leading soprano suddenly became indisposed.

In October, 1956, *Time* magazine reported on this war-time *Tosca* performance: "Backstage before the show, she overheard a male voice say, 'That fat bitch will never carry it off.' With a shriek of rage she leaped at the speaker, tore his shirt and bloodied his nose. Maria sang that night with a puffy eye. But she got raves from the Athens critics."

Maria remembers the raves, but roundly denies that there was a fight. Nor does Arda Mandikian, who was present, recall the incident. Had it occurred in the violent manner described, it would certainly have been difficult to keep secret. Another eyewitness, Dino Yannopoulos, the stage director, remembers only that Callas cut a mighty hefty figure as Tosca, and that her struggle with a middleweight Scarpia in the second act was a definite mismatch.

After *Tosca,* the young soprano was "discovered" by the Athens press. She was also "discovered" by the management and became one of the Opera's leading sopranos.

Maria soon found herself the center of backstage intrigues. Her rivals resented both her success and her all-too-obviously exceptional talents. There were many bitter moments in which Maria, by then no longer reticent but capable of standing her ground, proved equal to all attacks. Her temper was beginning to show itself.

With her gifts no longer under wraps, and in possession of an already considerable popular following, she had other important parts coming her way. Early in 1943, an opportunity presented itself to sing Santuzza again, this time as a member of the Athens Opera. Shortly thereafter, she was assigned the role of Marta in D'Albert's opera *Tiefland*.

The *Tiefland* performance, which was given in April, 1944, was the Greek première of the opera. Maria made a remarkable impression, not only by her vocal gifts but also by the compelling qualities of her acting. She was learning and growing in stature with every performance. Determined to master all phases of her art, she would never overlook an opportunity to improve herself.

Sharing her success in *Tiefland* was an artist of international experience, the eminent Greek baritone Evangelios Mangliveras. He was vocally past his prime but still an impressive singing actor. Contrary to other established artists at the Opera, Mangliveras was helpful to his young colleague. Maria's sharp powers of observation, her keen mind, and intuitive talent quickly responded to his guidance. She absorbed the many fine nuances of stagecraft that aspiring young opera singers often neglect to take seriously or are unable to assimilate at an early stage of their careers.

The interest of Mangliveras, a much older man, eventually transcended musical matters. He asked Maria to marry him. She declined. For her, no love existed aside from her love for music.

In September, 1944, the famous outdoor arena Herodes Atticus was to be the scene of a German-language performance of Beethoven's *Fidelio*. Preparations began during the summer. To assure a high level of production, Oskar Walleck, then director of the Prague Opera, was invited to stage the work.

The soprano who was to sing Leonora was unable to learn the part in time. Maria Kalogeropoulos was ready to take over, as she would be on many later occasions. She

had never sung in German before—in fact, all her previous
parts had been sung in Greek. However, this German-
language Leonora was, perhaps, her greatest triumph in
Athens.

Fidelio was an unusual opera to be staged before the
eyes of an occupying army and an oppressed people. The
majesty of Beethoven's music, its open glorification of
freedom and scornful condemnation of all forms of tyr-
anny found a powerful echo in the audience. The language
of the opera may have been German, but the all-pervading
joyfulness of the majestic finale, with Maria's jubilant
singing of "Oh, namenlose Freude," could only mean one
thing to the thousands who filled that marvelous theater
near the Acropolis, that the hour of liberation could not be
far away.

And it came within a few short weeks. On October 12,
1944, Athens and the port of Piraeus were liberated by the
Greek resistance troops. Two days later, British forces
landed to begin the work of consolidation.

At the urging of her mother, Maria accepted employment with an English army post to supplement the family's
income. She worked as an interpreter and clerk, handling
classified information.

Unfortunately, Greece's internal situation grew worse
instead of better. Early in December, civil war broke out
over the issue of Communist domination. Because of her
position with the British Army, Maria was in constant fear
of persecution for herself and her family by the Communist groups in the city.

Conditions in Athens were completely chaotic; there
were street fights, random gunfire, bombings. Communications were disrupted. Maria had to walk miles to work,
then walk home to share a meager meal with her mother
and sister, then back again.

Often the street fighting would come so dangerously near to the Via Patission that Maria could not even leave the house. At other times she had to make her way, always in haste, through fire-charred wood and shattered glass. The terrible days of late 1944 brought her never-too-robust health to its lowest ebb; the marks they left, physical and spiritual, cannot be discounted, even today.

With the appointment of General Plastiras as Premier on the last day of 1944, order began to be established, but hostilities continued for a long while until finally, mainly due to English intervention, the bloody civil war was brought to an uneasy end on February 13, 1945.

One war was over, and another about to start for Maria Kalogeropoulos. Plans were getting under way for the first theatrical and operatic season under a free government. A delegation of artists, composed partly of those who had refused to stay with the Opera during the occupation, brought pressure on the government against the continued presence of the young prima donna. The reasons behind their action were only in part political.

Maria had never been too popular with her colleagues. Some resented the fact that she was not really a Greek national; others considered her a young upstart, much too young for the roles she was singing and certainly much too young for the fame she had earned for herself. Nor did Maria behave like a novice, but rather as a star performer, insisting on the privileges and courtesies due a prima donna.

Faced with a number of disgruntled principal singers, the Opera's superintendent decided it was easier to dispense with the services of the young and troublesome artist. When Maria learned of his decision, she knew she was through with Greece.

The parting would have come anyway. She had been

advised by the American consulate that as an American citizen it would be best for her to return to the United States. When the Consulate assured her that it would assume her travel expenses, Maria immediately began to make preparations to leave Greece.

Her final appearance with the Athens Opera was in Millöcker's *Bettelstudent,* another operetta. No one could possibly foresee then that when she was to sing next under the auspices of that institution, some twelve years later, she would nearly provoke a government crisis.

Mother Evangelia was in complete agreement with her daughter's American journey. She, herself, had no desire at the time to return to New York—though her continued stay in Greece meant the loss of her own citizenship—but she was certain that Maria could pursue her career in the United States under more favorable circumstances. The only dissenting opinion came from Maria's beloved friend and teacher Elvira de Hidalgo.

"You should go to Italy, and not to America. You must make your career in Italy, and the rest will follow naturally."

Maria had always respected her teacher's advice, but this time she could not be swayed. They quarrelled, perhaps for the only time during their years of friendship. But, Maria went anyway. When she reached Piraeus, she called De Hidalgo to ascertain that they would part as friends, and to express her gratitude once more. They had a tearful farewell. The teacher's parting words were still, "You must not go to America."

With that, Maria Callas left behind the first architect of her unique career. She was never to forget what she owed Elvira De Hidalgo, nor has she missed an opportunity to express her gratitude, even at the height of fame: "I can repeat, with a heart full of emotion, devotion, and gratitude, that to this great artist I owe the formation of my artistic and musical life." (1957).

Maria left the port of Piraeus on the *S. S. Stockholm*. It was one of the first departures from the war-torn harbor. Neither mother nor sister accompanied her to Piraeus, only a few close friends were present to say good-bye. She was practically penniless and had almost no wardrobe. Yet, she experienced a feeling of relief and was filled with a hope that she was headed for a better future.

This hope was shared by Elvira de Hidalgo. She had a strong faith in her unusual pupil. In Italy, she felt, her success would have come sooner. But it had to come anyway. "She had a torrential force within her, and no one could restrain that torrent in its course," Madame de Hidalgo reminisced later.

There would be more trials, more frustrations, even suffering. But how could a great dramatic artist develop without the vital human experiences necessary to make her life complete as a mature woman?

CHAPTER 3

In Search of a Break

Butterfly
Ancora un passo, or via . . .
PUCCINI — MADAMA BUTTERFLY

George Callas had been completely out of touch with his family since the outbreak of the war. However, he followed events in Greece as closely as possible by religiously reading New York's Greek-language newspapers. It was there that he discovered, one September morning in 1945, the name of Maria Kalogeropoulos on the list of passengers on the *S. S. Stockholm* bound for New York.

Following her mother's advice, Maria had not tried to inform her father of her coming to New York. It was, therefore, a complete surprise to her when she saw him waiting at the dock. They had not seen one another for eight long years. Maria could not hold back her tears. With her father's arms around her, she stood weeping for several minutes before she could gain control of her emotions. George Callas, too, was in tears. His daughter had left a little girl; she returned a young woman.

The depression years were long forgotten. During his family's enforced absence, George Callas had returned to his profession as a pharmacist. He now lived in the comfortable apartment on Manhattan's upper West Side where he still resides. He was delighted to see his daughter again. Maria was happy beyond words.

The suffering and deprivations of the War seemed to belong to another world. New York, untouched by the conflagration, presented a sight of luxury. It seemed that she was now rewarded for the many years of fear, anxiety, and, above all, hunger. "When I got back to America I was hungry as you are hungry when you have not had enough to eat for a long, long time. I ate and ate..." she reminisced in a newspaper interview many years later.

The solicitude of her father and the security of home life were comforting in the difficult days of transition between war and peace, between one continent and another, between a state of constant emergency and sudden normalcy. Maria kept house and frequently visited her father in the drugstore. She became reacquainted with old friends of the family.

With travel conditions returning to normal, there were letters from Greece with fair regularity. Visitors would also drop in occasionally, carrying messages from Evangelia and Jackie and reminiscing with Maria about the days when she was the prima donna Kalogeropoulos of the Athens Opera. George Callas would listen to the stories with considerable pride, yet with some misgivings. The passing years had brought little change in his earlier opinions about the basic insecurity and tenuousness of a career on the stage.

For a while, reminiscing about her Athens career was

all Maria could, or wanted, to do as she concentrated on the new-found joys of family life. But it did not take long to rediscover that marking time was not for her. She was twenty-two, an artist conscious of her gifts and driven by a burning ambition. And here she was in the country of "golden opportunities."

Golden opportunities? Hardly for opera singers. No metropolis on earth harbors more talented singers at any given time—and fewer opportunities for their success—than New York, as Maria Callas was to find out after an initial round of discouraging explorations. No one seemed impressed with her record of accomplishments, with her studies with a world-famous diva, her former membership in the Athens Opera, her starring roles in *Fidelio, Tosca, Tiefland*. After all the bitter struggles, after all those years of dedicated study, frustrations, and successes, it looked as though she would have to start everything all over again.

Around Christmastime, 1945, an acquaintance referred Maria to E. Richard Bagarozy, a New York lawyer-turned-impresario, with a life-long interest in opera. Maria sang an audition—she was always ready to audition for anyone in those days who might eventually mean a step ahead—and Bagarozy liked what he heard. The voice was unusual in range, a little tight on top, a little rough in the bottom register, with noticeable breaks in between, but it was an unusually expressive instrument, nevertheless. "Reminiscent of Emmy Destinn," thought Bagarozy.

He was interested. But he told her that corrective studies would be needed before her talents could attract "Big Time" attention. Maria was somewhat disappointed at first. A few weeks later, however, she met Bagarozy again and agreed to start coaching with his wife, Louise Caselotti, a mezzo-soprano of considerable professional experience.

It was Madame Caselotti's opinion that Maria's voice

had suffered as a result of her operetta singing. She felt that it was basically a dramatic soprano voice which qualified for the heaviest, most demanding parts, but was harmed by any conscious "lightening" in an effort to encompass lyrical, coloratura, and operetta roles.

Caselotti was a serious student of the vocal art, quite persuasive and rock-sure in her convictions. Voice teachers, like physicians, hardly ever agree on diagnoses or cures, but never hesitate to voice their theories with conviction. At any rate, Maria was willing to listen.

A period of intensive study began. Maria was an almost daily visitor in the Bagarozy apartment. She startled her new friends with her intense, even furious dedication to work. She was unsparing with herself, practiced continuously, and subjected her voice to a far more rigorous training than any teacher would require. If, for any reason, she was unable to devote a good part of a day to her vocalizing, she would always work twice as hard the following day.

The Bagarozys were but one of several possible avenues to be explored. Maria also auditioned for Giovanni Martinelli, then at the end of his brilliant career but still very much in the operatic limelight. She hoped that Martinelli would recommend her to Edward Johnson, General Manager of the Metropolitan Opera. Instead, Martinelli, mindful of those "breaks" between registers, suggested further study. He strongly urged the young artist to do something about her figure, which by then had assumed proportions generally referred to in operaland as "Junoesque."

Another contact was Nicola Moscona, onetime pillar of the Athens Opera and by 1946 an esteemed member of the Met. Moscona had also enjoyed the rare privilege of being one of Arturo Toscanini's few personal choices for operatic concerts. Remembering Moscona's encouragement

back in Athens, Maria went to visit him and asked his inter-
cession for an audition with the Maestro. To this Moscona
would not consent. "Nobody can approach Toscanini with
a request like that!" Instead, he decided to put in a good
word with Edward Johnson.

Finally, the long-awaited Metropolitan audition materialized, though it was mainly the result of Maria's own
persistent efforts. It had taken several phone calls from the
drug store, accompanied by her father's dubious head-
shaking at what still seemed like hopeless chasing of the
operatic rainbow. But at last the answer was "yes."

By all indications, she must have made quite an impression. Maria's own account discloses that Johnson offered her a contract to sing two parts for the 1946/1947
season: Beethoven's *Fidelio* and Puccini's *Madama Butterfly*. Edward Johnson, interviewed by the New York *Post*
in 1958, recalled the incident.

"She was overweight, but that did not enter into our
thinking. The young ones are usually fat. We did offer her
the contract, but she did not like it and turned it down. She
was right. It was frankly a beginner's contract. But she was
without experience, without repertory...."

One could easily question Johnson's judgment about
the lack of experience in the light of Maria's Athens accomplishments. But this hardly matters since the Metropolitan
contract had, indeed, been turned down. Not for reasons of
money, but because Maria Callas, aged twenty-three, unknown, unaided, and determined to get ahead in the operatic world, would not sing *Fidelio* in English and would
not sing *Butterfly* at all with that un-Butterfly-like 180
pounds of hers.

Anybody who knows what a Met contract means to an
aspiring opera singer must throw up his hands in disbelief
at the very thought of this gesture! Would a journalism

school graduate refuse a job offer from the New York
Times? Would a raw bush-leaguer turn down the New York
Yankees? Anyone else in her shoes certainly would have
seized the opportunity. But this was Maria Callas, aware
of what she wanted. And, apparently, she did not want to
get ahead at *any* price.

In 1946, of course, such a decision was difficult to explain. Today, looking back on the number of times this
artist has shown her flair for the unconventional, the unexpected, and the unpredictable, it can be recognized as an
early manifestation of what eventually came to be established as the norm.

Maria did not join the Met in 1946. The part of Fidelio
in the Met's English production went to Regina Resnik
instead, then a singer with no more experience than the
Callas of 1946. To Miss Resnik, too, went the questionable
glory of critical comparisons between her performance and
the memories of Flagstad and Lehmann in the same role.

Maria also auditioned in 1946 for the late Gaetano
Merola, impresario of the San Francisco Opera. Nothing
came of this, either, except the kind of advice with which
aspiring American singers have been familiar for generations: "You are young. Go and make your career in Italy
and then I'll sign you up."

Hearing these words, Maria must have been reminded
of Elvira de Hidalgo's parting message in Athens, which
had expressed the same feelings. At any rate, she could not
resist telling Maestro Merola: "Thank you, but once I will
have made my career in Italy, I will no longer need you."

So passed the year 1946, with study, budding hopes,
disappointment, study, promises, and more study.

Evangelia Callas had also returned to New York.
Jackie remained behind in Greece. An attempt was made
to create, for the outside world, the appearance of a nor-

mal, every-day picture of mother, father, and daughter living a happy family life under the same roof. It was a futile effort. The Callas apartment on Manhattan's upper West Side was anything but a happy home. Maria spent most of her time, when not auditioning, in studying parts and coaching in the Bagarozy apartment on Riverside Drive.

Toward the end of 1946, there suddenly dawned a hopeful prospect. Bagarozy had always nurtured the hope of managing his own opera company some day. He now decided that the time was ripe to do something about his dream. The Metropolitan, he felt, was going nowhere under Edward Johnson's management. Europe, on the other hand, was virtually teeming with top-grade operatic stars who had no suitable opportunities in the war-torn countries and were eager to come to America. Here they could build new careers and get reacquainted with a world of luxurious living. An enterprising, alert impresario, Bagarozy thought, could do wonders with all that eager talent. And since European artists in 1946 were often thinking in terms of three square meals a day and comfortable living accommodations, not stellar salaries, the financial requirements did not appear forbidding.

Teaming up with a knowledgeable Italian impresario named Ottavio Scotto, Bagarozy went to work. In a short time their United States Opera Company managed to bring over a formidable array of European artists: Mafalda Favero, Cloe Elmo, Galliano Masini, Luigi Infantino, Nicola Rossi-Lemeni from Italy's leading theaters, Hilde and Anny Konetzny and Max Lorenz from the Vienna State Opera, and at least ten more stars of similar stature. To head the conducting staff, the team of Bagarozy and Scotto obtained the services of Sergio Failoni, a musician of vast experience in both the Italian and German repertoires.

The impresarios leveled their sights at Chicago, a metropolis with a great operatic past, and, for its opera-hungry audience, no present to speak of at that period.

Chicago papers soon began to herald the great operatic adventure. The roster of eminent artists, whose fame had preceded them via successful European recordings, caused great anticipation among cognoscenti. Soon the excitement extended over the entire musical United States, particularly since the new company was to make its entry with an ambitious program including, among other attractions, a revival of Puccini's *Turandot,* which had not been heard in the United States in nearly two decades.

Newspaper articles also hinted at a mysterious Greek soprano who was to make her Chicago debut in the spectacular title role of *Turandot.* She was identified as "Marie Calas." It was the Bagarozy plan to drop their artistic ward like a bombshell into this brilliant aggregation and have her explode over unsuspecting Chicago and the musical world.

But newspaper stories don't make an opera season. The opening date, confidently announced for January 6th, was postponed—first a week, then another week, then to January 27th, at which time the cast of *Turandot* was also made public: Turandot: Marie Calas; Liù: Mafalda Favero; Calaf: Galliano Masini; Conductor: Sergio Failoni.

The seeming optimism was entirely unwarranted. Although Bagarozy and Scotto invested heavily in the venture, they relied on outside backing to meet obligations. At the crucial moment, however, they had trouble lining up the "angels." To make the odds even more forbidding, the American Guild of Musical Artists insisted on a suitable deposit to assure payment to the members of the chorus. The impresarios were unable to satisfy the Guild's demands. Under the accumulating weight of obligations, the ambitious but recklessly planned enterprise collapsed into ignominious bankruptcy.

Strangely enough, January 27, 1947, did produce an operatic headline, but a shockingly tragic one:

GRACE MOORE AND 21 KILLED.

But there was no opening in Chicago and no debut for "Marie Calas."

The city was in an understandable uproar. The European singers, dazed by the effects of what may be considered a whirlwind course in United States operatic production methods, did not know what had hit them. Having come this far, and having lost the opportunity for financial rewards, they felt particularly concerned about the likelihood of leaving the country without being heard.

The management of the Chicago Opera House then came forward to rescue the city's good name. A benefit concert was hastily organized on February 5th. There was no orchestra—all proceeds were earmarked to finance the artists' homeward journey. Ottavio Marini, one of the conductors, officiated at the piano as Elmo, Lorenz, Rossi-Lemeni, and their distinguished colleagues proceeded to show the audience that, artistically at least, the defunct company had had the required foundation. The house was sold out and the concert netted $5,873 for the worthy purpose.

For some of the luckless imports the Chicago sojourn had produced other engagements. Cloe Elmo and Max Lorenz were signed up by the Metropolitan; Luigi Infantino by the New York City Opera. The others said good-bye to Chicago, richer by the experience but otherwise quite remarkably unprosperous.

Impresario Bagarozy's dreams vanished into air, and the mysterious Greek soprano, who had been preparing for

her debut with Sergio Failoni in New York with a concentration extraordinary even by her own standards, returned
to her vocalizing. Chicago was destined to be the scene of
one of her greatest triumphs, but not in 1947.

Nicola Rossi-Lemeni, a young bass of vigorous dramatic abilities, was in no immediate hurry to return to the
continent. With a contract for the open-air season in Verona in his pocket, he decided to remain in New York for a
while. He, too, was a frequent visitor in the Bagarozy
apartment, going over parts with Maria and Louise Caselotti. At his urging, Maria decided it was time for another
audition. This one was to be for the famous tenor Giovanni
Zenatello, a native son of Verona and artistic director of
that city's summer festivals.

The time was very appropriate. Zenatello needed a
soprano for the title role in Ponchielli's *La Gioconda*. It
was rumored that he had wanted Zinka Milanov and had
also considered Herva Nelli, but he was willing to hear a
new talent.

The audition took place at the Zenatello apartment on
Central Park West. To the accompaniment of her friend
Louise, Maria sang the aria *"Suicidio"* from *La Gioconda,*
then other passages from the opera. Zenatello grew excited,
dashed to the piano and turned a handful of score pages to
the passionate duet between Gioconda and Enzo, in the
third act.

"Enzo, sei tu!" Maria began, and Zenatello lunged
into his part of the duet with a fervor and vocal presence
belying his seventy years.

More than an audition, the event turned into a revela-
tion. The old maestro congratulated the Bagarozys for discovering such a great talent. They, in turn, congratulated
Zenatello for landing such a sterling prima donna for his
festival. And Maria had a contract.

Financially, it was nothing earth-shaking. Zenatello offered six performances of *La Gioconda* at 40,000 lire each (approximately sixty dollars). On the surface, it could hardly compare even with Edward Johnson's offer for the Metropolitan. But here was an opportunity to sing in plain view of all Italy, in a role she wanted, in the company of topflight artists. Maria Callas accepted without any hesitation.

Preparations then began for another transatlantic journey. Both Maria Callas and Nicola Rossi-Lemeni entrusted the management of their careers to E. Richard Bagarozy. Before this, with no income in sight, there had been no contractual agreement between them. Now, however, both artists appointed Bagarozy as "sole and exclusive personal agent for a period of ten years." Maria signed her contract on June 13, 1947, the day of her departure.

Maria agreed to pay "to said Personal Representative the sum equivalent to ten per cent (10%) of all gross fees earned by her in Opera, Concerts, Radio, Recordings, and Television. Said fee becoming due and payable upon receipt of monies earned by Artist."

On the other hand, Bagarozy agreed "to use his best efforts to further and promote the Artist's career. That he will, with due diligence, analyze and examine all offers received for the Artist's services, and in the interest of the Artist will use his best judgment accepting or rejecting such offers so presented."

Neither the Artist nor the Personal Representative had the funds for Maria's steamship tickets. Fortunately, Dr. Leonidas Lantzounis, a New York physician who was Maria's godfather and whose friendship with George and Evangelia Callas dated back to their youth in Greece, came to her aid with a loan. All George Callas could spare was fifty dollars, which made Maria fifty dollars richer than she had been on her westbound oceanic trip less than two years before.

But success now seemed closer, and that made all the difference. The ship on which Maria, Rossi-Lemeni, and Louise Caselotti, who accompanied them, embarked, was the *S. S. Rossia,* an erstwhile German freighter, and a rather battered specimen at that. It was anything but a pleasant journey. The ship was overcrowded, accommodations were poor, there were mice in the cabins, facilities for relaxation were meager. Her two companions took the inconveniences in their stride, but for Maria the end of the journey could not come soon enough.

On a hot day, as Mediterranean travelers will agree, the port of Naples is anything but an irresistible sight. But so it appeared to at least one weary and irritable passenger of the broken-down *S. S. Rossia* on the morning of June 27, 1947.

CHAPTER 4

Enter Meneghini

Elena
*Oh! fortunato il vincol che
mi prepara amore.*

VERDI—I VESPRI SICILIANI

The train trip to Verona proved to be no improvement on the transatlantic journey. Travel conditions in 1947 were a long way from peacetime normalcy. Seats were at a premium, and Maria and her friends had to take turns standing part of the way. Finally, Verona! A city immortalized, long before its famous summer festivals, by the most celebrated lovers in literature. But Romeo and Juliet could hardly have been of immediate concern to Maria Callas as she wearily checked into Verona's Hotel Accademia.

The thoughtful management of the Summer Festival had arranged a dinner in the new diva's honor. Two gentlemen from Verona, Gaetano Pomari, representing the

Arena, and Giuseppe Gambato, representing the city, called for her at the hotel. A few hours later, Maria was introduced to a third, a businessman by the name of Giovanni Battista Meneghini.

Meneghini was then in his early fifties, a short, dapper figure with graying and thinning hair, but wiry, alert, and dynamic. The eldest of six children, he managed the family business, a building materials plant. In these years of post-war reconstruction, the Meneghini enterprise had expanded tremendously. It was now worth several million dollars.

Giovanni Battista Meneghini was a member of Verona's elite. He lived the life of a wealthy small-town *bon vivant* and especially liked to be seen in the city's gay open-air caffés in congenial company. Although business was his main interest, he shared the natural Italian fondness for opera.

Both as an opera lover and as a city father he had followed the affairs of the Arena with personal concern. He also had a reputation for being a ladies' man, with a special predilection for the ladies of the stage. Altogether, Signor Pomari could not have made a better choice when he asked his longtime friend Meneghini to join the banquet and take personal charge of the "American" prima donna's entertainment.

"I knew he was *it* five minutes after I first met him," Maria reminisced some time later. Unquestionably, Giovanni Battista Meneghini must have done justice to his reputation that evening at Verona's Pedavena Restaurant. The following morning he escorted Maria on an excursion to Venice, and from that moment on they were inseparable.

Meneghini was instantly fascinated by Maria's youth, temperament, and individuality. For Maria, it may not have been the storybook "love at first sight," but something deeply satisfying, nevertheless. At the side of her quietly self-assured, courtly admirer, Maria's life was suddenly changed, and her days were spent in unaccustomed gaiety and ease.

There were only a few days of undisturbed idyll, however. Rehearsals began in mid-July, immediately following the arrival of the eminent conductor Tullio Serafin.

The very thought of working with such a musician thrilled Maria. Serafin was a conductor of immense experience, celebrated at the world's most famous operatic centers: La Scala, the Rome Opera, the Metropolitan. This was a man whose name had a magical ring in Verona ever since he had presided over the opening performance of the Arena, back in 1913.

Serafin radiated knowledge and authority, and he had a remarkable understanding of singers. Under his unostentatious but forceful leadership, Maria found the atmosphere of the rehearsals uncommonly exciting.

"As soon as I heard her sing," recalls Serafin, "I recognized an exceptional voice. A few notes were still uncertainly placed (especially for an Italian audience), but I immediately knew that here was a future great singer."

Everything clicked happily on the first day. Maria was in excellent voice, the Maestro beamed, and the amorous Meneghini was delighted. And so it went for several days as the Ponchielli opera was gradually whipped into shape under Serafin's baton. All were smiles until the dress rehearsal, when Maria, carried away by the realism of her acting, fell on the rocky stage and sprained an ankle.

Determined to continue, she somehow managed to last through the final act. A doctor was summoned immediately and Maria was carried from the Arena straight to her hotel. There she spent a sleepless, painful night before the performance, with Meneghini at her bedside, a fount of comfort and solicitude.

Recalling the occasion a decade later, Maria reminisced: "This was just one little episode that revealed my husband's character. I would give my life for him immediately and joyfully. From that moment on I understood that I would never find a more generous man... If Battista had wanted, I would have abandoned my career without regrets, because in a woman's life love is more important than artistic triumph."

The 25,000 spectators who filled the huge Arena to capacity on August 3, 1947, saw an exciting *La Gioconda*. Enzo was sung by Richard Tucker, who made his Italian debut that evening with great success. Maria's friend and travel companion, Rossi-Lemeni, sang Alvise. Elena Nicolai and Carlo Tagliabue rounded out the fine cast.

As for Maria Callas, who hobbled around with a bandaged leg on the enormous stage, her debut seemed only moderately auspicious. The reviews were polite, generally approving, but unenthusiastic. The "vibrant quality and easy production of her high notes" were praised by one newspaper, while a visiting English critic commented on a "metallic timbre of a most moving and individual quality."

The other featured opera of that Verona summer season was Gounod's *Faust*. Mephistopheles was sung by Rossi-Lemeni and Marguerite by Renata Tebaldi, the young soprano whom Arturo Toscanini's recommendation had placed at La Scala only the previous year. It was here that the paths of the two great rivals first crossed. But actually no real *crossing* took place. Absorbed in their own commitments and moving within their own circles, the two artists did not even meet face to face.

After six appearances in *La Gioconda,* the Verona season was over for Maria Callas. It had brought no sensations, no fame overnight. Yet Maria had good reason to believe that she was on her way. For the first time in her life she felt confident and secure. Now she could concentrate on her career while the devoted Meneghini was ready to remove all cares and responsibilities from her shoulders. Everything she needed, everything that had eluded her up to that moment—love, devotion, encouragement, and security—had suddenly become hers. In a happy frame of mind, Maria waited for the "big chance" that Meneghini and Serafin both felt imminent.

The first offer was a modest one, an invitation from Vigevano, near Milan, to repeat *La Gioconda*. Maria did not accept it for fear of missing a better opportunity. There was an important audition pending with Mario Labroca, artistic director of La Scala . . . .

The audition took place a few weeks later, but it produced nothing of immediate importance beyond the usual helpful criticism of certain vocal defects. Still, the doors were by no means closed. Maria received the assurance that she would be considered for La Scala's forthcoming production of Verdi's *Un Ballo in Maschera*.

Two months went by. Maria waited, first hopefully then tearfully. Much too impatient to sit around in Verona, she went from one theatrical agency in Milan to another, but they had nothing for her. Meneghini did all he could to keep her spirits high, but it was hard to fight off a growing feeling of dejection.

When an offer finally did come it was not from Milan but from Tullio Serafin, who had not forgotten his "American" Gioconda. The Maestro was planning to conduct *Tristan und Isolde* at the Teatro La Fenice in Venice. He had instructed a friend to sign up Maria for the part of Isolde.

The word reached her in Milan. She seized the offer

hungrily. Only afterwards did she realize that she had committed herself for a part she did not know.

Serafin arrived in Milan the following day. When Maria revealed her "secret," he reacted with the Italian equivalent of "So what!" He had an unshakable faith in his judgment and in Maria's talents. "One month of study and hard work is all you need," he told her. And, under Serafin's guidance, that was exactly how it turned out to be.

The contract with La Fenice called for several performances in two roles, Isolde and Turandot, at 50,000 lire per evening. Modest perhaps by American standards, but already 25 per cent higher than what she had earned in Verona. Things were looking up!

Venice holds its opera season during December and January. *Tristan und Isolde* was given on opening night, just before Christmas. In this great Wagnerian role Maria Callas achieved the first undisputed success of her new career. Venice, the city of her first idyllic days with Meneghini, became the scene of the happiest Christmas in her life.

Even years later, when she was already a reigning diva, she would remember that Christmas with special fondness. She had hungered long for this recognition, and she savored every moment of her new-found success. Overnight she regained her faltering self-confidence. She knew she was on the right road, and she knew she was not fighting her battles alone.

In January, her Turandot solidified the excellent impression she had made on the Venetian press and public. The lone dissenting voice came from her friend and business associate Louise Caselotti-Bagarozy.

"I was alarmed when I heard her Turandot," remembers Madame Caselotti. "The soaring high notes I admired when we were preparing the part for Chicago had lost their freedom, and wavered badly. Her low register was also weak. I knew that she was on the wrong track and told her so.''

Maria's reaction was bitter, and the friends soon parted, no longer friends. Louise Caselotti also had hoped to find engagements in Italy but was unsuccessful in her efforts. Convinced that neither Maria nor Meneghini were helping her, she returned to the United States shortly thereafter.

A more pleasant episode during the Venice engagement was Maria's first meeting with Renata Tebaldi, who was also a member of La Fenice that winter. The two young artists obviously enjoyed each other's company. Whenever they met they would discuss artistic matters of mutual interest in an atmosphere based on respect and admiration.

After Venice, their soaring careers made such meetings infrequent. But one evening, in early 1948, as she was singing her first Aida in Rovigo, Callas was delighted to discover her new friend in the audience, with the *Brava!* of Tebaldi's silvery soprano rising above the cheering audience.

As a result of the excellent press in Venice, other engagements followed in quick succession. Maria Callas's rare vocal gifts were no longer a secret shared between herself, Meneghini, and Tullio Serafin. Serafin, of course, was instrumental in these engagements. He never missed an opportunity to recommend his protegée.

Because his recommendation was backed up by an enormous reputation and fifty years of experience, important doors opened up, one after another, before the young singer. She went to Trieste to sing Leonora in Verdi's *La Forza del Destino* early in 1948. She was also offered a return engagement to Verona in *Turandot* and an invitation to Rome's open-air season in *Aida*. Then she went on to sing Isolde in Genoa, during May, 1948.

This Genoa performance of *Tristan und Isolde* turned out to be a memorable experience. It was held in a small theater, as the city's beautiful Carlo Felice was still lying in ruins. The stage was tiny, and the scenery consisted of ill-assorted odds and ends. Under the circumstances, dramatic illusion was almost nonexistent. When the action called for more than four performers on the stage at the same time, there was no room to move about.

The formidable line-up boasted of Max Lorenz, Raimundo Torres, and Nicola Rossi-Lemeni, robust six-footers all. Elena Nicolai, a tall and powerfully built mezzo-soprano, sang Brangäne. Isolde–Callas weighed in at approximately 180 pounds. It was praiseworthy, against such odds, to have even attempted a serious performance. The singers did their best. However, whether or not they were worth their weight in gold is an interesting speculation under the circumstances.

The early summer of 1948 went by with Maria in furious study with Tullio Serafin. She was concentrating on Norma—the heavenly part with the diabolical demands on the voice, the role that unites dramatic force with coloratura agility.

In July she returned to Verona for a series of Puccini's *Turandot*. She moved about the giant stage of the Arena like a seasoned veteran and this time there were no accidents. In August she sang Aida in Rome's famous open-air amphitheatre at the Caracalla baths. This was to be followed by an engagement in Florence, but Maria was forced to cancel because of an appendix operation.

It was a most unwelcome interruption in the accelerating pace of her career. While she basked in Battista's loving concern for her health, she was counting the days until she would be able to get back to work. Words of encouragement also came from Tullio Serafin, her artistic mentor, who urged Maria to take all the rest she could in preparation for what was shaping up to be a busy winter season.

The Maestro was as good as his word. He informed Maria shortly thereafter that he was preparing a new production of Wagner's *Die Walküre* for the 1948/1949 season of Venice's Teatro La Fenice. Maria Callas, the previous year's outstanding Isolde, was his choice as the Brünnhilde of the new production—at a fee of 100,000 lire per performance.

Whenever Wagner is given at one of Italy's major theaters, impresarios are often tempted to import a German or international cast in preference to searching for Wagnerian voices among Italian singers. But Serafin was convinced that in Maria Callas he had an artist who could sing any role. He saw in her the reincarnation of the fabulous singers of the early nineteenth century; singers who could rise to the vocal challenge imposed by *any* composer, without regard to such twentieth-century specializations and limitations as "lyric," "dramatic," and "coloratura."

With the encouragement and inspiration of her seraphic taskmaster, Maria threw her pent-up energies into this new and formidable challenge. She spent most of the fall and winter of 1948 in mastering Brünnhilde, her second Wagnerian role. Her enthusiasm was dampened only by the much-too-frequent absence from her beloved Titta (her nickname for Meneghini). By her own recollection, there were times she hated her career so much she dreamed of giving it all up.

In December, Maria was back in Venice, scene of her first triumph and city of happy holiday memories, where

Wagner's *Die Walküre* was to open the new season. But, as soon as she arrived, she found herself in the midst of an unexpected crisis.

Margherita Carosio, one of Italy's leading coloratura sopranos, had been scheduled to sing Elvira in Bellini's *I Puritani*. The day before Maria arrived, Carosio became ill with influenza and was forced to withdraw. There was no replacement available.

The following morning Maria was awakened by phone, and summoned before Tullio Serafin. Sleepy and disheveled, she ambled into the salon of the Hotel Regina to find herself surrounded by the sleepless Maestro and a group of desperate-looking La Fenice officials.

Almost like an operatic chorus, they demanded to hear one of the *Puritani* arias. For a moment Maria stood in disbelief. Then, realizing the seriousness of the situation beneath its comic guise, she sang. When the aria was over, she was given the part of Elvira in what may have been the most unanimous and certainly the quickest casting decision in La Fenice's long history.

The aria she sang was just about all she knew of the part at that moment. Thanks to her studies with Elvira de Hidalgo, she had accumulated a sizable repertoire of coloratura *arias*. But she had not the vaguest notion of the *rest* of Elvira's music, the duets and ensembles, or of the opera's plot, for that matter.

Six days remained before the first performance of *I Puritani*. Amid the frantic preparations for the unfamiliar role, Maria Callas could hardly stop to think that *Die Walküre,* too, was almost equally unfamiliar to her. If she could think at all, she preferred to remember that here was an opportunity seldom offered to an artist. No two parts in the repertoire could be more dissimilar. Imagine the idea of suggesting to Kirsten Flagstad a part left vacant by Lily Pons!

But the incredible happened. Callas sang the mighty dramatic utterances of Brünnhilde on Wednesday and Friday of the opening week, while spending the daytime with Bellini's trills and roulades. Sunday, she had Elvira's part under firm control for the dress rehearsal. That same evening, she intoned her final *Ho-jo-to-ho,* and divested herself of Brünnhilde's martial attire for the last time. Two days later she appeared in *I Puritani*—and scored a fantastic success.

This feat of virtuosity became the talk of musical Italy. No one could now deny Serafin's affirmation that Maria was a phenomenon destined to make musical history. True, the annals of opera recall the legendary Grisi and Malibran, who dominated the entire soprano repertoire of their age, embracing vocal writing of dramatic thrust as well as coloratura agility. But that kind of dramatic singing was not Wagner's kind of drama; its vocal line did not have to battle the Wagnerian orchestra. Connoisseurs with long memories could remember the fabulous Lilli Lehmann (1848–1929), a unique artist who could do Norma one evening and Isolde the next and was unforgettable in every one of her one hundred thirty roles. But even Lehmann was of the past, her matchless art, in 1949, only a distant memory.

Maria Callas was the present and the future. The days of waiting around for engagements were over. Palermo heard her in *Walküre* and Naples in *Turandot*—both "old" roles. Then, in March, 1949, she made her debut at the Rome Opera in *I Puritani*. Almost immediately thereafter, she dazzled the Romans with a repetition of her musical quick-change: she sang Kundry in Wagner's *Par-*

sifal. Maria learned the part in five days. The "impossible" had become the norm by then.

Before the Rome appearances, Maria had made her first radio broadcast in Turin. It was a program designed to exhibit her versatility before a large listening audience, and consisted of the "Casta Diva" from *Norma,* two arias from *I Puritani,* and Isolde's "Love Death." Cetra, one of Italy's most important recording firms, duplicated that program on three twelve-inch single records. These three records were to become the foundation of one of the most remarkable recording careers of our time.

Among the thousands who heard Maria Callas on the radio that day was Nazzareno de Angelis, La Scala's celebrated bass of a generation ago. Prompted by that remarkable recital, the old artist dashed off the following wire to Turin:

"After this radio concert I forecast that in Maria Callas the spirit of Maria Malibran will be reborn. My enthusiastic congratulations."

The septuagenarian De Angelis came to Rome to attend the performance of *I Puritani* and to pay his personal respects. Maria received him joyfully. By then his congratulatory telegram had been framed and was displayed in her dressing room. But De Angelis was not at all pleased with the performance and, mincing no words, proceeded to say what was on his mind:

"Signorina, if you will continue singing a repertoire that is not yours, I am sorry to say that within three or four years you will sing no more."

The old master proceeded to make himself clear. In his judgment, Callas was a lyric soprano who should not force her voice into parts not meant for her. Already, he added, the adverse effects of singing uncongenial roles were showing in her voice.

The Kalogeropoulos family, New York, 1924. Maria, an appealing one-year-old in her Mother's arms.

Members of the eighth-grade graduating class of P.S. 189. Mary Anna Callas (second row from the top, third from the right) poses with her fellow performers in the school operetta.

Elvira de Hidalgo, Callas's mentor, confidante, and only important
teacher, as she appeared in 1915 as Rosina in Rossini's *The Barber of Seville*.
(Courtesy of *Opera News*.)

The Herodes Atticus Theater in Athens where Maria Callas performed
during World War II and had her first triumphs. (Courtesy of Greek
Embassy Information Service.)

Maria Callas and Evangelios Mangliveras, famous Greek baritone, as they appeared in D'Albert's *Tiefland* in Athens, 1943. (Courtesy of Wildente, Hamburg.)

Callas, the young woman. Athens, 1944.

Louise Caselotti, Nicola Rossi-Lemeni, and Maria Callas in a gay mood
as they are about to sail from New York for Italy in July, 1947.

One of the first roles Callas sang in Italy was that of Abigaille in Verdi's *Nabucco* in Naples, December, 1949.

The great Italian maestro, Tullio Serafin, said that Callas could sing anything. Here they are discussing an artistic point at the recording session of Donizetti's *Lucia di Lammermoor* in Florence, February, 1953.

Recordings began to play an increasingly important part in Callas's career. At the recording session of Bellini's *I Puritani* in Milan, March, 1953, Callas relaxes for a few minutes with her poodle. (Courtesy of Angel Records.)

"Above all, take care of your health," were his parting words.

"Believe me, I will take good care of myself," replied
Maria.

Artists must learn to live with criticism. If only the
critics could agree among themselves on the one and only
path that artists should follow! The advice of a wise veteran like De Angelis could hardly have been ignored by a
conscientious singer. But was he really right? True, he had
decades of experience on his side, but what about Tullio
Serafin who was just as secure in *his* conviction that Maria
Callas could sing *any* role? What about Elvira de Hidalgo,
under whose guidance Maria had first discovered the glorious heritage of Vincenzo Bellini's operas?

Maria Callas was already a subject of controversy—a
prerequisite of stardom.

The spring of 1949 brought a contract for the Teatro
Colon in Buenos Aires. Maria was about to cross the ocean
again; but first a vital personal issue had to be settled.

During the past year and a half she and Meneghini had
been inseparable. Maria would have married him at any
time; it was Meneghini who did not wish to force the issue.
There was, first of all, the age difference. She was twenty-
six, he fifty-four. There were also strong objections from
Meneghini's family. His mother, his brothers, with their
conservative, provincial upper middle-class outlook, did
not approve of Battista's growing interest in operatic matters—which inevitably meant an ever lessening concentration on building materials—to say nothing of his courting
an opera singer. This was not *his* world, the family contended.

Nor were the letters from New York more approving.
Evangelia and George Callas seldom saw eye to eye, but
they did agree for once on the issue of their daughter's

marrying a man almost thirty years her senior. Two of Maria's good friends, however, assured her that she was doing the right thing for her future. One was Dr. Lantzounis, the old family friend in New York, and the other was Elvira de Hidalgo, her beloved teacher, whom she had kept informed about the major events of her life.

Never one to depend on others for making up her own mind, Maria Callas hardly needed reassurance that marrying Meneghini was the right decision. It seemed to be the *only* decision. With the South American trip hanging over them, Maria's mind was made up. She would travel as Signora Meneghini.

Meneghini, a Roman Catholic, required a dispensation to marry outside his faith. The couple would have settled for a civil ceremony, but, finally, permission was granted and nothing stood in their way.

Their marriage took place in the Chiesa dei Filippini in Verona, on April 21, 1949. There was no one there to represent the Meneghini family. The priest, the sacristan, and two witnesses were the only ones to hear the couple's eternal vows. None of this mattered. For Maria Callas, it was a happy day, a day of fulfillment, and, because nothing in life had ever come to her without a struggle, a day of victory.

"They said I had only come to Verona to marry a rich man," she was to tell Chicago newspaperwoman Claudia Cassidy five years later. "You know how women are about losing a bachelor. But there is justice. There is a God. I have been touched by God's finger."

That same evening the newlyweds departed for Genoa. The following day, Maria Meneghini Callas boarded the *S. S. Argentina* and embarked on a new phase of her career.

CHAPTER 5

Toward the Top

Tosca
*Vissi d'arte,
vissi d'amore . . .*
PUCCINI—TOSCA

The Italian contingent for the 1949 season of the Teatro Colón, Buenos Aires, was led by Tullio Serafin and the baritone Carlo Galeffi. Both men were longtime favorites of the Argentines and were remembered from previous appearances that spanned a whole generation. The other members of the group represented the finest crop of Italy's young singers, all at the beginning of their careers: Maria Callas, Fedora Barbieri, Mario del Monaco, and Nicola Rossi-Lemeni. Callas and Del Monaco headed the cast of *Turandot* which opened the season on May 20th.

"The title role was filled by a singer who is new to our public, the Greek soprano Maria Callas," commented *La*

Prensa the following day. "She was an expressive Turandot in acting, while judgment of her vocal rendition of this extremely difficult part should await another occasion. Evident nervousness and a slight vocal indisposition prevented a display of her full powers, though the facility of her middle and low registers was noteworthy."

Neither *Turandot* nor *Aida,* which she was to sing soon thereafter, turned out to be unqualified successes with the Argentine critics. Her best achievement, in unanimous opinion, was *Norma,* in which she appeared for the first time on June 17th, flanked by Barbieri, Rossi-Lemeni, and Antonio Vela. "Her dramatic interpretation was vigorous and human, she sang 'Casta Diva' with delicacy and fine musical feeling and was impressive in the remainder of her part" was the judgment of *La Prensa.*

Summing up the entire season, Roberto Turrò reported later in *Opera News*: "Though [Callas] possesses a voice of great range that allows her to sing with agility and power, some of her tones are dry and in general lack quality, except in the pianissimi, which are of amazing beauty."

Although the Buenos Aires season, which lasted until August 15th, was several degrees short of triumphant, Maria found loneliness far more painful to endure than the slight critical stings. She missed Battista's loving devotion, his calm and astute judgment, his constant attention to all matters, large and small, that assured her well-being. Above all, she was depressed to be alone again. She would frequently lapse into fits of moodiness and melancholy, from which her husband's constant stream of letters, telegrams, and occasional transatlantic telephone calls would bring only sporadic relief. When the four-month separation finally came to an end, Maria was happy beyond belief to return to a marriage which had hardly begun.

While his wife was away, Meneghini had busied himself with setting up their first home in Verona, a penthouse
apartment situated near his offices and overlooking the
Arena. The daily sight of this scene of her Italian debut
was now a pleasant reminder of the many obstacles overcome and the many goals achieved since those dreary days
of 1947. With a devoted husband, a comfortable home, and
absolute material independence, life could have been
utterly joyful to Maria. Actually, her happiness was far
from complete, for the harmony of her home life suffered
constantly from the discordant rumbles coming from the
Meneghini clan.

Battista was devoted to his mother, then in her seven-
ties, and to his brothers. He wanted them to be reconciled
to the *fait accompli* of his marriage, but all his efforts went
aground on their stubborn resistance. In the eyes of the
Meneghini family, Maria was an intruder, and a foreigner
to boot, who had succeeded in ensnaring a wealthy protec-
tor to promote her own ambitions.

Maria thus unwittingly became the cause of a serious
rift in a once closely knit family. Her concern over Battista's problems was aggravated by the occasional letters
from New York. The Callas parents, though far from being
as overwrought over the marriage as were the Meneghinis,
still questioned her wisdom in binding herself to a man
twice her age.

Fortunately, there was music to offer relief and com-
pensations, also to bring new challenges and stimulations
for further conquest. Maria was re-engaged by the Rome
Opera for a series of Isoldes. But even before that, she had
added another important theater of the world to her list of
conquests, the San Carlo of Naples, on the opening night
of the season, December 22, 1949.

It was an event surrounded by the uncommon excitement that was soon to turn into a pattern for "Callas openings." The choice of the opera was, in itself, exciting— Verdi's early, powerful biblical opera, *Nabucco,* seldom mounted even in Italy. Gino Bechi, Italy's then reigning baritone, sang the title role. Vittorio Gui conducted. With her flaming characterization of the Babylonian ruler's vengeful, venomous daughter Abigaille, Maria Callas added another memorable portrait to her growing gallery of unique operatic women.

Nabucco, of course, contains the stirring chorus "Va, pensiero," replete with patriotic reminders of Italy's revolutionary struggles for independence. With the war still far from forgotten and the Trieste controversy a vital political issue, Verdi's soaring melody filled Italian hearts once again with the patriotic fire that had stirred the audience of the first *Nabucco* in 1842.

The 1949/1950 season established Maria Meneghini Callas as one of the most sought-after sopranos in Italy. In Rome she sang, in addition to Isolde, Aida and Norma. It was her Norma, again, which caused the most fervent comments. The veteran Giacomo Lauri-Volpi, that most literate among operatic tenors, was in the audience on February 26, 1950. We can read his impressions in his book *A viso aperto:*

"Norma is divine! I enjoyed it at the Opera to the very roots of my soul. Those who are perplexed by the thought that it was first interpreted by Malibran should have heard Maria Callas to understand that Bellini was right in assigning the part to a powerful voice. Voice, style, bearing, force of concentration and that vital pulsation of the spirit—all these rise to an uncommon height in this artist . . . . In the final act, Norma's imploring voice came to me as art's purest joy."

The Naples and Rome engagements should have been

enough for that season, but Callas also managed to repeat her successful Norma in Venice. She followed this by appearing in Bologna in a role she had not sung since Athens, Floria Tosca. There was also a performance of *Aida* at Brescia, undertaken against Serafin's advice, who rightfully thought that Maria was carrying an unnecessarily punishing schedule of commitments.

In the midst of all this activity an offer appeared that could not have been turned down under any circumstances. It came from La Scala, the only major Italian theater not yet open to her, whose management had found in 1947 that her accomplishments were not quite up to La Scala standards. The invitation was to sing *Aida* on April 12th, coinciding with the opening of the Milan Fair. She was to replace the ailing Renata Tebaldi.

The press was waiting for the Meneghinis when they arrived in Milan. No sooner had they moved into their hotel, than Maria was asked by the reporters about her impressions on the eve of such an important occasion in her life, about her relationship with La Scala, about future plans. She was remarkably unrestrained in her answers. By then her Italian had become not only completely natural and free-flowing but had also assimilated her husband's Veronese dialect. Her thoughts gushed forth in an uninhibited, temperamental stream:

"What a life, moving in and out of hotels, living out of trunks . . . . Some people say they envy me for my trips around the world. Some trips, from one stage to another . . . . The public? What about the public? If I sing well they applaud, if they don't like me, they whistle. It's the same everywhere . . . . They say my voice is uneven. Well, let them say what they want. I sing the way I sing . . . . La Scala? Magnificent theater . . . . Yes I am thrilled, of course I am thrilled. Great theater. But I am near-sighted, you see.

For me all theaters are alike. If I am excited? La Scala is La Scala, but I am near-sighted; *ecco tutto*."

And so she went on, sometimes detained momentarily by Meneghini's gentle interjections, then rolling along un-interruptedly—and quite disarmingly.

At La Scala, and at Italy's major opera houses in general, the season's first performance of *any* opera is a momentous event and is celebrated as such. The box-office scale goes up, formal attire is mandatory in the orchestra and in the boxes, and an atmosphere similar to the actual opening of the season descends over the theater. This seasonal first performance is called a *prima*.

The 1950 La Scala *prima* of *Aida* was a brilliant affair. With President Einaudi, ministers, and foreign dignitaries in the buzzing, bejeweled audience, even the near-sighted soprano could not write off the occasion as being merely routine. The imposing cast, under Franco Capuana's direction, included Fedora Barbieri, Mario del Monaco, Raffaele de Falchi, and Cesare Siepi. Maria gave a very creditable performance but, interestingly enough, she drew more remarks about her passionate, realistic acting than about her singing.

Press comments the following day were indifferent. Battista Meneghini, who had taken it for granted that Maria would immediately be engaged as a regular member of La Scala, looked in vain for an encouraging sign. Antonio Ghiringhelli, the icy and enigmatic superintendent, was even more aloof than usual.

As no further word was forthcoming, Maria sang the second *Aida* for which she had been contracted and departed for Naples, where she appeared in the same role, this time under Serafin's direction, with Stignani, Picchi, and Siepi in the cast. "Potente e originale interpretazione," was the critical verdict.

In May, 1950, her first Cetra recordings were released

in Italy. They were subsequently exported to the United
States, where opera enthusiasts who had been reading
about the exploits of the American-born soprano could,
for the first time, judge her art on direct evidence. Like
most high-priced imported records, these first examples of
the Callas vocal art could hardly have been expected to hit
the general public with a sensational impact. They did,
however, impress many a connoisseur and they also caught
the artistic and merchandising fancy of Dario Soria, head
of Cetra's American branch.

The soprano herself crossed the Atlantic during the
same month, bound for an engagement in Mexico. Business
reasons compelled Meneghini to stay behind. But this time
their separation was not to last very long. Maria traveled
by air and interrupted her journey only for a short visit
with her parents in New York.

George Callas was waiting for his daughter at the
airport. His wife was undergoing treatment for an eye
infection at a hospital. The two were feuding as always.
Maria immediately went to see her mother and cheered her
up by inviting her to Mexico as soon as her condition
permitted.

There were a few hours before plane departure time.
New York was hot and humid, and Maria felt no desire
whatever for sightseeing. She invited her good friend and
colleague, the mezzo-soprano Giulietta Simionato, who was
traveling with her, to her parents' apartment on West
157th Street to spend these few hours relaxing.

Parched with thirst, Simionato attacked the refriger-
ator as soon as they entered the apartment and seized what
she thought to be a bottle of carbonated beverage. She took
a deep draught—and a moment later doubled up in excru-
ciating pain. The bottle, as Maria's frantic telephone call
to her father disclosed, contained insecticide.

With Maria's administration of first aid, following her

pharmacist-father's expert telephone instructions, and a
quick dash to a neighboring hospital, disaster was averted.
But the two friends were still half-shivering from exhaustion and the after-effects of the unscheduled crisis when
they emplaned toward Mexico City late that night.

Evangelia followed shortly afterwards. She had not
heard Maria sing since the far-away days of Athens. Her
daughter was now not only one of the undisputed stars of
the season but also the embodiment of success, enjoying
riches, fame, and adulation. Applause, compliments,
flowers everywhere they went! Maria was celebrated like
a queen, and Evangelia Callas adored being the queen
mother.

Maria sang two of her familiar parts in Mexico City
that summer of 1950, Norma and Aida. She also added an
important new role to her repertoire, Leonora in Verdi's
Il Trovatore. Her good friend Giulietta Simionato appeared with her in all three operas, as did another, and even
older friend, the basso Nicola Moscona. Metropolitan tenor
Kurt Baum sang all three tenor parts. It was his first artistic collaboration with Callas, and a rather stormy one.
After one violent backstage argument, Baum made it
known point blank that he would do everything in his
power to prevent her engagement at the Metropolitan.

Unconcerned about backstage rows, press and public
acclaimed Maria's "tones of miraculous beauty" with
fervent unanimity. "After hearing her 'Casta Diva,' "
wrote Salomon Kahan in *Musical America,* "no one could
doubt her importance in the realm of opera." In *Aida,* the
same critic found her "fascinating from beginning to
end." Tullio Serafin would have been proud of his protegée.

The Mexican season lasted only two weeks. Maria left
Mexico City by plane to rejoin her husband, who was wait

ing for her in Spain. Before leaving for Europe, she pre
sented her mother with a valuable fur coat and gave her one
thousand dollars as a parting gift. Then, after an affec
tionate good-bye, Maria flew back to Europe.

Evangelia, after a short rest in Mexico, returned to
New York. After the excitements of the season, the ova
tions and festivities which she had enjoyed to the limit,
Maria's sudden departure and her own return to New
York's drab routine disheartened her. But neither mother
nor daughter knew that this would be their last meeting for
a long, long time.

Back in Verona, Maria could finally take a well-earned
rest of three weeks. She spent the days visiting friends,
shopping, and decorating the apartment, which grew more
and more inviting and luxurious. Evenings she played the
piano for her delighted husband and allowed Chopin and
Rachmaninoff to assume temporarily the place in her
affections normally reserved for Verdi and Bellini. Other
evenings they would simply sit and talk. Battista listened
to his wife's Mexican reminiscences with eager interest
and pride. He assured her that the next time she undertook
a transoceanic trip there would be no separation.

Maria resumed her operatic career in the fall of 1950
in an interesting and certainly different role.

A group of enterprising young intellectuals were preparing a two-week season of rarely heard operas in Rome's
Teatro Eliseo, and planned to open the series with Rossini's seldom-played comic opera *Il Turco in Italia*. Maria
was cast in the role of the minx Fiorilla.

She had never sung in a comic opera before. In the
past she had been entombed alive as Aida, burned on the
pyre as Norma; she had stabbed herself as Gioconda and
leaped to her death as Tosca. Here was an opportunity to
impersonate a woman neither grief-torn nor woebegone,

but full of temperament and vivacity. Maria was excited by this new challenge.

Learning new roles had always been one of the most stimulating aspects of her work as a singer. Creating an impersonation for an entirely new audience, a portrayal of her own creation, without any remembered historical precedents, aroused her excitement immeasurably. She was also impressed by the artistic freedom and zeal of the producers, a group that included Luchino Visconti—a descendant of Milan's leading aristocratic families, with several art patrons and a former superintendent of La Scala among his forbears—as one of its artistic advisers.

Visconti had by then established himself as one of Italy's outstanding stage and motion picture directors. An enthusiastic opera lover, he had many original ideas about the way opera ought to be staged for modern audiences. He had first seen Callas during the Rome Opera performances of Parsifal in 1949 and had instantly realized her unusual dramatic potential.

The rehearsals of the Rossini opera established a close friendship between two dedicated artists with similar and sympathetic views. Both Visconti and Callas approach opera from a dramatic point of view. Both believe in the closest integration of singing and acting, in credible, purposeful movements and gestures—in short, realism of the highest possible degree.

For all his experience on the stage, Visconti was relatively new to the world of opera, and the *rapport* he established with Callas far exceeded both his expectations and his image of an operatic diva. For her part, Maria's intuition immediately detected Visconti's genius and she willingly followed his numerous suggestions. In her work with this brilliant director, she found another vital link in the formation of her art, a source of stage wisdom that was to

assume an ever-increasing role in her transformation from
a vocal phenomenon into a great singing actress.

Il Turco was presented on October 19, 1950, with a cast
that included Cesare Valletti, Mariano Stabile, and Sesto
Bruscantini. The Eliseo is a rather modest theater, and the
production was far from lavish. But the singers were good,
and the audience responded heartily to the vivacious com-
edy and to Rossini's bubbling music. There was no question
about the star of the evening.

"Maria Callas . . . sang with the utmost ease in what
one imagines was the style of sopranos at the time this work
was composed. . . . The solo voices were splendid, but it
required Maria Callas's superb musical flair to keep the
others together in the concerted numbers." (T. de Bene-
ducci in *Opera)*

After the pleasant Rossini episode, the artistic career
of Maria Callas continued its steady upward climb. By
then, she was known everywhere as an artist who could sing
everything. Thus, no one was startled when, a short four
weeks after delighting the Rome audience in the *leggiera*
role of a comic opera she returned to Rome to sing Kundry
in Wagner's *Parsifal* on a radio broadcast conducted by
Vittorio Gui.

During the last months of 1950 she learned a new role,
Elisabetta di Valois in Verdi's *Don Carlo*. She was scheduled to appear in this opera in both Naples and Rome, but
ill health forced her to leave the rehearsals. Jaundice, which
had occasionally plagued her in the years past, necessitated
complete rest this time.

At Meneghini's insistence, Maria canceled the *Don
Carlo* series and retired to Verona to recuperate. It was of
little use to brood over the cancellations and the interruption of her career. Maria had to bow to the inevitable. She
celebrated a quiet Christmas in the intimacy of her home,

but Battista needed all his persuasive powers to keep his wife in reasonably good spirits.

Maria's absence from the musical scene lasted six weeks and carried her into 1951, the Verdi year.

Italians, of course, need no excuse to stage the operas of Giuseppe Verdi. However, musical Italy seized upon the fiftieth anniversary of his death as a particular opportunity to pay special homage to the idolized composer. 1951 brought Verdi festivals all over the land and with them a wholesale dusting-off and new stagings of some of the Master's long-absent and half-forgotten works.

For Maria Callas, the Verdi year began at the Teatro Communale of Florence. Here she was to sing her first *Traviata* on January 15th. It was a part for which she had prepared with enormous concentration under Serafin's guidance.

The rehearsals were unusually stormy. Maria was feeling weak from the after-effects of her illness, and she was quite irritable. Her irritability brought on her first real quarrel with Serafin, who had reproached her, among other things, for not acting with the dignity and aloofness becoming a prima donna.

But, when the final curtain rang down on *Traviata,* smiles were shining on all faces, and the widest of all belonged to Tullio Serafin. The critics complimented Francesco Albanese and Enzo Mascherini, the Germonts fils and père. They praised Maria for her expert coloratura in Act I with as much enthusiasm as they applauded the pathos and sensitivity of her tragic scenes in the final act. "Hers was a great accomplishment and surprised many," remembered Serafin in 1960.

More Verdi was to follow. On January 27th, the actual day of the composer's anniversary, Maria sang her first

Italian *Il Trovatore*. This time the city was Naples. The conductor was again Serafin. Again, tempers flared high at the rehearsals, but this time Maria was not involved.

Tullio Serafin and stage director Gioacchino Forzano, two septuagenarians of long experience and short temper, disagreed so violently about scenic deployment and lighting on the first day of rehearsal that all singers and musicians were left flabbergasted. But the following day, the elderly combatants posed willingly for the photographers, arm in arm, in the vestibule of San Carlo, while the marble bust of Verdi beningnly smiled down upon them.

It so happened that Forzano and Serafin walked away with most of the critical encomiums after the *prima* of *Il Trovatore*. The cast, which included the redoubtable Giacomo Lauri-Volpi in the title role, Cloe Elmo as the Azucena, and Paolo Silveri as the Count di Luna, was treated rather coolly. Lauri-Volpi, never one to run away from a fight, addressed an open letter to the Naples press, protesting what he termed a "dreadful indifference" to vocal art. He was particularly disturbed by the lack of appreciation for Callas's magnificent singing, which he attributed to local intrigue and chauvinism.

From Naples, Maria went to Palermo, where she opened the spring season in *Norma*. Here she received an urgent call from Antonio Ghiringhelli of La Scala to come to Milan and take over *Aida* from the indisposed Tebaldi. It was the first sign of life from the august theater in almost a year, and Callas was not impressed. A year ago, she thought, they had asked her to help out La Scala under identical circumstances for the same opera. It was all right to do it once, but she was not going to become La Scala's emergency relief. No, she told Ghiringhelli, if La Scala wants Callas she is ready, but only as an artist in the front

rank. She was perfectly capable of creating her own interpretations, but not at all interested in taking over parts
already portrayed by other artists in the same season.

Maria did go to Milan in the spring of 1951, but La
Scala had nothing to do with her visit. Arturo Toscanini
was there, and he was looking for the right singer to interpret Lady Macbeth in a production of the Verdi opera he
was planning for New York. His old friend, Vincenzo
Tommasini, the noted composer, suggested Maria Callas
to the Maestro. Toscanini's daughter Wally made the
introductions and arranged for the audition.

Verdi never conceived the role of Lady Macbeth for
the conventional soprano voice. "I would like Lady not to
sing," reads the composer's famous letter to librettist
Cammarano. " I would like her voice to be harsh, choked,
dark. . . . There are pieces which must not even be sung but
acted and declaimed, with a covered dark voice."

In Maria Callas, Toscanini, Giuseppe Verdi's spiritual
heir and artistic custodian, would have undoubtedly found
the ideal artist for Lady Macbeth. But the projected
Macbeth never materialized. Whether this was due to the
Maestro's failing health or to other reasons is not clear.
New York and the world of recorded music was deprived
of a memorable event, and Maria Callas of what could have
been one of the outstanding landmarks of her artistic life.

However, the Verdi year was still in full flower, and
the Maggio Musicale Fiorentino was still ahead. The Verdi
opera chosen for Florence that year was *I Vespri Siciliani,*
a rarely performed and uneven work for the stage, but a
tremendously effective vocal display when the right kind
of singers are available. With the exception of an unim-
pressive tenor, the Maggio Musicale had an uncommonly
inspired cast that year with Maria Callas, Enzo Mascherini, and Boris Christoff. The conductor was Erich Klei-

ber, an early champion of this neglected Verdi score, who was making his operatic "debut" in Italy on that occasion.

Vocally and dramatically, the Callas performance was superb. "There was an assurance and tragic bravura about her singing which was frequently thrilling. The smouldering fury of the aria 'Il vostro fato' was extraordinarily vivid," commented one observer. The greatest moment came at the end of Act IV, when she concluded her solo with a long chromatic scale in which every note stood out in pearl-like clarity.

Many singers pay only casual attention to scale passages, regarding them merely as a not-too-direct means of getting from one note to another. But when these carefully planned note-progressions are given their due, and when the composer's design emerges in its original inspiration, the effect can be striking and revelatory. This is what Callas accomplished at the Maggio Musicale of 1951, and this is how she has succeeded in influencing audiences since then to embrace one half-forgotten opera after another as if they were established box-office attractions.

Maria sang four performances of *I Vespri Siciliani,* always to clamorous applause, but her greatest victory was won off-stage. Antonio Ghiringhelli, the suave superintendent of La Scala, presented himself, contract in hand, ready to meet Maria Callas on her own terms. Ghiringhelli bowed to the undeniable fact that La Scala needed Callas.

In her Scala contract, Maria was offered not only three leading roles, but also the honor of opening the 1951/1952 season in the very same opera of her Florence triumph, Verdi's *I Vespri Siciliani.* Her appearances were required for thirty evenings during that initial season, at the considerable sum of 300,000 lire ($480) per appearance.

This was "it." A singer can go no higher in Italy. The vague dreams and whispered hopes of Athens in 1945; the

frustrations of New York in 1946; the halting beginnings
of Verona in 1947; the spiraling climb through Venice,
Rome, Naples, and Florence; all the episodes and all the
struggles suddenly fell into place. They had all proven to
be part of a pattern, purposeful and inevitable, pointing
toward the goal, La Scala.

Maria signed the coveted contract and then went on to
sing her second opera in Florence, compared to which
I Vespri Siciliani was a familiar warhorse. It was Haydn's
Orfeo ed Euridice, a 1791 creation, but practically unknown
in Italy and almost everywhere else.

Howard Taubman, music critic of the New York
Times, was in the audience at the second and final performance of the Haydn opera on June 10, 1951. The following
day his report appeared under the heading NEW YORKER
EXCELS:

"Maria Meneghini Callas, a New York girl of Greek
parentage, who has done well in Verdi's *Sicilian Vespers*
here, proved that she could manage the classic florid style
with assurance. She has full control of voice in soft singing,
and she did coloratura passages with delicacy and
accuracy."

The name of Maria Callas was, by then, known to
American opera lovers who followed musical developments
abroad. Her handful of Cetra recordings had also attracted
attention, for they highlighted her unusual versatility,
always a good subject for conversation among the connoisseurs. The artistic stature of Callas had already reached
remarkable heights as the summer of 1951 approached.

However, Maria Callas's personal life was not going
along as smoothly as was her professional life. Her peace
of mind was continually disturbed by family troubles. In
the fall of 1950, Evangelia Callas had decided, with dramatic suddenness, to leave New York for another visit with
her older daughter, Jackie, in Greece. She did so without

discussing the matter with her husband, a circumstance which brought their already precarious relationship to a complete break.

There followed a stream of bitter letters from Mama Callas to Maria. At first, they were full of recriminations against George Callas. Later, as Evangelia began to be concerned about her financial security, there came reminders of what a dutiful daughter should do to ease her mother's burden. Finally, failing to strike a properly sympathetic echo, her letters grew more and more reproachful and demanding, with unmistakable and unkind references to the "millionaire" Meneghini.

All this, and most particularly the attacks on her husband, were bitter pills for Maria to swallow. She tried desperately to prevent bickerings from casting a shadow on her otherwise happy and peaceful married life. Her work, as always, was the best medicine. Another summer season beckoned in Latin America. This year, Maria was to sing in Brazil as well as in Mexico. This time, however, she would be traveling with her husband.

The flight to Mexico City was their first transatlantic trip together. Battista was gradually withdrawing from his industrial interests and was assuming his new role as a manager-guardian-adviser-secretary-bodyguard. As always, he was a devoted, attentive, and fanatically loyal husband.

In Mexico, they were joined by George Callas. Now, at Maria's invitation, it was his turn to shine in his daughter's glory. This was the first time he saw her perform on stage. His doubts and disbelief about artistic careers became a thing of the past. To make one's first contact with opera by witnessing a Callas performance would be fascinating in any case; for the father it was an overpowering experience and, undoubtedly, the proudest moment of his somber life.

Maria was the darling of the Mexican press and public.

"The season reached its climax with the Callas appearances," said one reviewer. She sang Aida opposite Mario
del Monaco, and Violetta opposite Cesare Valletti. In the
latter role, which she sang in Mexico for the first time, she
was praised "for sweeping dramatic power and vocal
beauty." Oliviero de Fabritiis conducted both operas. Old
friend Tullio Serafin was on his own Latin American tour
in Buenos Aires.

After the pleasant Mexican sojourn, Maria headed for
her first season in Brazil. It began most inauspiciously.
São Paulo was the first stop, with a brief operatic season
scheduled during which she was to repeat her Mexican
roles of Aida and Violetta. Poor health—swellings all over
her legs,—forced her to cancel the Aida performances. In
the role of Violetta, she alternated with her good friend
Renata Tebaldi.

The longer and more important season in Rio de
Janeiro, which assembled an extraordinary array of
Italy's leading singers, opened in late August with Giordano's *Fedora*. Elena Nicolai and the sixty-one-year-old
tenor idol Beniamino Gigli sang the principal roles.

Maria's health was restored in time for her appearance on September 12th in a role she had made particularly her own, Norma. The ovation that evening, and when
she repeated the opera four nights later, compensated her
for the disappointing São Paulo episode. Her press could
not have been better. Enrico Nogueira Franca wrote in the
Correio de Manhã:

"Callas is a great singer, an extraordinary figure on
the operatic scene. Her art encompasses all degrees of
dramatic passion, from the subtle purity and lyric phrasing
of her 'Casta Diva' to the impetuosity and magnificent
ardor of the second act...." Neither press nor public were
easy to please. For their favors, the "new" soprano had

to contend with Elisabetta Barbato, a great popular favorite in Rio, and Renata Tebaldi.

Renata, on the rebound from a singularly unsuccessful
La Traviata at La Scala, was having an extraordinary
Brazilian summer. She had made her debut in Rio a week
before Maria in the very role of her Milan fiasco, Violetta.
Here, her performance of this role was received with a
tremendous ovation. But success failed to alter her over-
sensitive mood.

Both prima donnas shared a tense, irritable state of
mind, further provoked by the fiercely competitive atmosphere. Anyone familiar with the effects of these
environmental pressures on operatic personalities could
understand the severe trial to which their friendship was
subjected under such circumstances.

The first crisis came at a benefit concert at which, as
Maria Callas remembers it, each participating artist had
agreed to sing only one operatic selection. Maria sang her
scheduled number, "Sempre libera" from *Traviata,* took
her bows, and withdrew. When Renata's turn came, however, the applause after her "Ave Maria" (*Otello*)
electrified her into giving not one but two encores.

After the first shock of consternation, Maria reasoned
that her colleague had evidently been seized by an impulse
beyond control. Tebaldi's recollection of the same event,
however, is different. The encores were, in her opinion, her
tribute to the audience for its applause; a gesture in which
artists may or may not indulge. If it was Maria's decision
not to give an encore under similar circumstances, that was
entirely her affair. But there had been no previous understanding between the artists, emphasized Renata, with
respect to encores.

One thing was certain: whoever was to benefit from
that benefit concert, it was clearly not Maria Callas or

Renata Tebaldi. The relationship between them grew cool
and tense after that evening. A few nights later, the two
sopranos were having dinner together with friends. The
temperature was high. As the evening wore on, tempers
rose higher. What had started out as an amiable after-
dinner discussion in company would have erupted into a
heated argument had it not been for the calming intervention of Meneghini and other colleagues.

On the evening of September 24th, Maria sang her first
Tosca in Rio, with Gianni Poggi and Paolo Silveri in the
cast, Antonino Votto conducting. Immediately after taking
her final curtain calls, she was called into the office of
director Barreto Pinto and informed that, because of what
he termed the adverse audience reaction, she would be
relieved of all further performances. In plain words, her
services were no longer required.

Maria was thunderstruck. No artist could take such
humiliation lightly. But she regained her composure soon
enough to remind Pinto of his contractual obligations.
Appearing or not, she insisted on being paid for her performances. Apart from another *Tosca* there were still two
nonsubscription *Traviatas* to be done.

"All right," Barretto Pinto relented, "sing the two
Traviatas. Chances are that no one will want to see you."

He couldn't have been more wrong. Both *Traviatas*—
on September 28th and 30th—were sellouts. As an opera
director, Pinto should have been gratified, but by then his
relationship with the outspoken prima donna had flared
into open animosity.

"I should not even pay you considering the kind of
success you had," he sneered as Maria came to his office
for the financial settlement. Whereupon Maria, blind with
fury, seized the first heavy object on Pinto's desk that came
into her hand. Fortunately, some bystander, the thoughtful

Meneghini, perhaps, prevented any bloodshed. The ink-
stand, or whatever object it was, did not fly, but the incident, with more violent details added, became an oft-quoted
component of the Callas legend.

To make Maria's humiliation complete, her replacement at the next performance of *Tosca* turned out to be
none other Renata Tebaldi. And, judging by appearances,
it all seemed to Maria, in those distracted, emotion-charged
moments, like a prearranged scheme between Tebaldi and
Pinto to get her out of the way. This, inevitably, brought
the onetime friendship of the two sopranos to an end.

Returning to Italy, in their separate ways, their
thoughts turned to the new season at La Scala that was
dawning for both of them. They would be members of the
same company and, to the absolute delight of the press,
the gossip-mongers, and that vociferous breed of opera-
lovers who thrive on the personality cult, bitter rivals.

On their way to Europe, Maria and Battista Meneghini
stopped briefly at New York's Idlewild Airport to change
planes. They were met there by Dario Soria, head of
Cetra's New York branch. By then, reports of Maria's
glowing success in Mexico had reached Soria by way of
Antonio Caraza Campos, manager of the Mexico City
Opera, who, in complete contrast with his Rio counterpart,
was a virtual one-man cheering section for Maria Callas.
Conscious of Maria's spreading worldwide fame, Soria
did his best to talk her into a long-term contract with Cetra.

Maria was all business. Money, however, was not part
of the discussion.

"What operas will be recorded?"

"Who will conduct them?"

"Will the cast be carefully chosen or just thrown
together by using whoever is available?"

The more Soria listened, the more impressed he

became. After Maria's artistic qualms had been stilled, the travelers departed for Europe, leaving a new friend behind.

Soria followed them to Italy soon thereafter, and the contract with Cetra became a reality. It called for three complete operas, to be recorded during 1952.

The wounds of the humiliating Rio episode did not heal quickly. But with all the challenges of the future, there was little time to brood over the past. La Scala and the city of Milan, with its unparalleled opera consciousness and its one million vociferant and violent opera critics lay waiting.

1951, the Verdi year, was nearing its end, and a new operatic season was about to begin. In the midst of the many Verdi festivals, comparatively little attention was given to the fact that the year also commemorated the 150th anniversary of Bellini's birth. But it was duly remembered by the composer's birthplace, the Sicilian city of Catania. The doors of Catania's Teatro Bellini opened on the composer's birthday with a gala performance of *Norma*. Flanked by Giulietta Simionato, Gino Penno, and Boris Christoff, Maria Callas—now recognized as the most authoritative contemporary interpreter of Bellini's tragic heroine—responded to the Sicilian ovations on the night of November 3, 1951. It was just five weeks before the day of St. Ambrose, the traditional opening of the La Scala season.

CHAPTER 6

A Crucial Year

Turandot
Ecco . . . è ora
della prova . . .

P U C C I N I — T U R A N D O T

Milan is Italy's industrial center. Its importance to the nation's economic well-being is enormous, a truism its proud citizens seldom fail to emphasize. The rest of Italy agrees, but not without a certain condescension, for Milan's artistic and cultural significance, in contrast to its industrial standing, is rather negligible by Italian standards. Apart from its monumental Gothic Cathedral on the square, and Leonardo's fading *Last Supper,* the city's artistic contribution pales before the riches of Rome, Florence, and Venice. In fact, were it not for La Scala, tourists would find it remarkably easy to overlook Italy's largest city in their itinerary.

But, there *is* La Scala, a lyric theater like no other on earth, a swirling focus of artistic and social activity, a perennial topic of conversation, and a source of immense and consoling civic pride. In its almost two hundred years of history, La Scala has introduced many of the world's greatest operatic masterpieces. Its stage is the coveted goal of all singers, its history—past, present, and future—the history of opera.

La Scala has always been known for its lavish productions. It was founded by a group of aristocrats who, year after year, covered the theater's deficit with becoming princely generosity. La Scala was never expected to pay its way, nor was it ever reduced to the charity-beholden insecurity of New York's Metropolitan. Today it is assured of a huge government grant, about a million dollars every year, and the city's powerful industrialists, who inherited the civic duties of the founding dukes and princes, see to it that La Scala gets what it needs.

Antonio Ghiringhelli, the present Superintendent, who assumed his position in 1946, is a member of this powerful group. He devotes all his time to the task and accepts no remuneration, a combination of virtues that should, theoretically, have a deflating effect on critics of his regime, but, in fact, has nothing of the kind.

Opening nights at La Scala, which take place every year on St. Ambrose Day (December 7th), are like opening nights in other great opera houses, only more so. The theater is a forest of carnations, the audience is dressed to the teeth and bejeweled to blind the eye. But unlike its similarly ostentatious counterpart at the Metropolitan, La Scala's opening-night audience takes its opera seriously and voices its endorsement and disapproval with traditional Mediterranean demonstrativeness.

Milanese prefer spectacular productions for these

opening nights. Verdi's *I Vespri Siciliani,* the opera chosen
to initiate the 1951/1952 season, fitted the bill perfectly.
It had been staged with memorable success in Florence
during the summer. Now, Italy's foremost opera house
was determined to do it even better.

Ghiringhelli wisely retained the nucleus of the Florence cast: Maria Callas, the baritone Enzo Mascherini,
and the bass Boris Christoff. He added a new tenor, the
American Eugene Conley, to bolster its only weak flank.
The staging was entrusted to the Metropolitan Opera's
Herbert Graf. Victor de Sabata, La Scala's artistic
director and senior conductor, led the orchestra. *I Vespri
Siciliani* may not be a great opera, but it can be a spectacular production, and La Scala was determined to stage it in
a manner that would bring the Verdi year to a glorious end.

Throughout the rehearsals, Maria impressed everyone
with her dedication and businesslike seriousness. She
moved about with complete familiarity among the seasoned
La Scala veterans, undismayed by the momentousness of
the occasion, calm and sure of herself. In her conversations
with Eugene Conley, she would occasionally remember her
frustrating experience with the Metropolitan with a
decided chip on her shoulder. But she was far more interested in the task at hand and determined to make her debut
successful.

In the part of Elena, she was able to show off both her
dazzling coloratura agility and her formidable range. She
gave a demonstration of the prodigious vocalism opera-
goers often read about in faded annals, but seldom
experience in real life.

The morning after opening night, the Milanese critics
reached for some of their choicest superlatives. The
Corriere della Sera hailed "the miraculous throat of Maria
Meneghini Callas ... the prodigious extension of her tones,

their phosphorescent beauty and her technical agility which is more than rare, it is unique.'' It was, to put it very modestly, an auspicious beginning.

There followed a series of appearances in Bellini's *Norma,* a role which was by then regarded as a Callas specialty. Franco Ghione conducted the *prima* on January 16th, and there were eight performances during the ensuing four weeks. (La Scala policy dictates that an opera be removed from the season's repertoire generally within a month after the *prima*). Maria's partners were Ebe Stignani as Adalgisa and Gino Penno and Nicola Rossi-Lemeni in the principal male roles.

Milan's monthly opera magazine, *La Scala,* called her performance ''vibrant, incisive and occasionally brilliant.'' More enthusiastic was the American conductor Newell Jenkins, who noted in his report for *Musical America* that ''she electrified the audience by her very presence even before singing a note.'' Eight curtain calls testified to the degree of public acceptance.

On April 2nd, Maria appeared in the role of Constanze in Mozart's *Abduction from the Seraglio.* Remarkably enough, that was the first time this enchanting Mozart opera (a work dating back to 1782) had been given at La Scala. Italy's Mozart productions seldom appeal to Mozartian purists. La Scala's *Abduction* that year was no exception. However, it received a hearty response from the Milanese, largely due to the expert comic characterization of Salvatore Baccaloni in the role of the harem-keeper, Osmin.

For Maria, the occasion was less significant. The opera gave her dazzling opportunities for technical display, and she conquered the fiendishly difficult role of Constanze with spectacular ease, but this role could not be called one of her spectacular triumphs. To this day, Maria

Callas has not added another Mozartian role to her repertoire. It was evident from the outset that she did not find
Mozart operas particularly congenial.

With the end of the *Abduction* series in late April,
Maria Callas completed her first season as a member of
La Scala. Evidently she was there to stay. She had not
taken the city by storm, nor had she established her absolute primacy during that initial season. After all, Renata
Tebaldi was a powerful favorite (she sang in Boito's
Mefistofele and Verdi's *Falstaff* during 1951/1952), and
Margherita Carosio, Rosanna Carteri, and Clara Petrella
were other sopranos very much in evidence, to say nothing
of the artist whose spectacular portrayals in *Don Carlo,
Norma,* and *Cavalleria Rusticana* had perhaps overshad-
owed all others, the matronly but still magnificent
mezzo-soprano, Ebe Stignani.

However, there was no doubt in any observer's mind
that in Maria Callas La Scala had gained an artist of
powerfully individual talents who had lived up to her
advance notices, and who would have to be seriously
reckoned with in the theater's future plans. It was equally
evident that her artistry was not the kind to please
everyone.

She conquered, to be sure, but her conquests were not,
as a rule, followed by unconditional surrender. Operatic
connoisseurs who regard sensuous tone quality and even-
ness throughout the registers an absolutely indispensable
factor could point, with a good deal of justification, to
Maria's vocal shortcomings. At the same time, her rare
technical command, her ability to act with the voice, and
her uncanny dramatic instinct increased the size of her
following with each performance. For this growing group
of partisans, Callas meant a discovery of a new concept of
vocal beauty, one achieved by augmenting nature's not

overgenerous gift with the added dimensions of insight and expressiveness.

Without a doubt, Milan was to be Maria's future artistic headquarters. With this prospect in mind, Maria and her husband set up a permanent apartment in the Grand Hotel, a landmark of some significance as it had long ago served as a home away from home for Giuseppe Verdi. In fact, it was there that the great composer died on January 27, 1901. Because of Maria's nonstop schedule, however, the Meneghinis enjoyed very little of the Grand's comforts during the spring of 1952.

A return visit to Florence, the scene of her memorable 1951 triumph, was to follow within days after the end of Maria's Milan commitments.

Tullio Serafin, the old mentor whose influence over the Callas career continued, despite the fact that the artist was getting more offers and invitations than she could possibly fulfill, had been re-engaged as the musical director of the Maggio Musicale. This, of course, not only guaranteed the return of Callas, it inevitably signaled another spectacular rediscovery of buried musical treasures.

The Festival opened on April 26th with the first performance since 1817 of Rossini's *Armida*. The entire 1952 season, in fact, was dedicated to Rossini, a special favorite in Florence, where his remains are buried in the city's famous Santa Croce Church, the Westminster Abbey of Italy.

Some operas are unaccountably neglected, but the reasons for *Armida's* obscurity are not far to seek. In this fiendishly conceived bravura piece, Rossini defied all conventions, saturating the score with technical hazards seemingly directed *against* the performers. (Rossini composed so many operas in his prolific prime that he could easily gamble on leaving one or two permanently on the shelf.)

Not content with writing nearly unmanageably florid parts for the singers, Rossini saw to it that his orchestra also had its collective hands full. He contrived a difficult duet for the French horns, another one for clarinets; he inserted a lengthy cello solo; and he wrote a big, tricky violin obbligato part to keep the concertmaster busy. To compound the absurdity, he confronted his soprano star with no less than five tenors and wrote an elaborate ballet to keep things on the stage from getting too static!

Rising to the challenge, the Festival management invited Leonide Massine to do the choreography and gave Maria Callas five tenors from the front rank to vocalize against. For Maria, the impossible part, with its tessitura ranging from the lowest chest notes to dizzying heights, turned out to be par for the course: she learned it in five days. Technically, it was full of formidable hazards. Because the part required practically nothing of her dramatically, she could concentrate her considerable energies on the dazzling vocal fireworks. She conquered them masterfully. Rossini would have enjoyed her performance immensely, not only because of her technical wizardry but also because of her undeviating respect for the printed page.

"We could not hope for a better revival," wrote Giorgio Vigolo in *Il Mondo* after the opening. ". . . high praise is due Maria Callas for singing with such agility a part that must have been most difficult, even in 1817."

The same critic was beside himself with admiration a week later when Maria appeared on the stage of the Rome Opera in the first of several stagings of Bellini's *I Puritani*, opposite Lauri-Volpi, Silveri, and Neri, Santini conducting.

"A great personal triumph for Maria Callas. Shuttling between Florence and Rome she went from Armida's witchcraft to Elvira's passion to exhibit not only agility,

range, and the *four voices that sing in her throat,* but also
a full and vibrant interpretation such as we have never
heard from her."

Milan, Florence, Rome—Maria's achievements were
wrought by an unrelenting schedule of work, work, and
more work. For her, there could be no time for rest, no
relaxing private life, no diversions. Battista, of course, was
always by her side, watchful, considerate, and immensely
helpful. He was assuming more and more the role of an
efficient business manager. In his deceptively jovial manner, he was always vigorous and demanding in matters
concerning Maria's interests.

Somehow, despite her heavy schedule during these
months of spring, 1952, Maria managed to add two important new roles to her repertoire—Gilda in Verdi's *Rigoletto*
and the title role of Donizetti's *Lucia di Lammermoor.*
Both represented a further invasion of what had been considered coloratura territory. She had another Mexican
commitment coming up for the summer and planned to
try her Gilda and Lucia there before exposing these interpretations to Italy's far more demanding audience.

The pace Maria Callas had set for herself continued
unabated. Three weeks after the *Armida-Puritani* series
in Florence and Rome, she and Battista arrived in Mexico
City. This was her third consecutive summer season in that
capital, and it promised to be the most ambitious yet
undertaken—nine operas in as many weeks.

The season, built quite obviously around the talents
of Maria Callas and Giuseppe di Stefano, opened on May
29th with *I Puritani.* Subsequently, Maria appeared in
Traviata, Tosca, and the two operas new to her repertoire,
Rigoletto and *Lucia di Lammermoor.*

Mexico was, and still is, a focal point of ardent Callas
fans. One eloquent critic acclaimed her during that season

as "the diva of the century, a phenomenon to be compared with the aurora borealis." Hearing, for the first time perhaps, a full dramatic voice executing Lucia's florid music with stunning agility, the audience went wild and rewarded her with a twenty-minute ovation after the Mad Scene. Her Gilda, however, and indeed the entire performance of *Rigoletto,* was somewhat disappointing.

The reviews which summed up the season were eulogistic, but not without some dissenting voices. The unevenness of registers and occasional shrillness at the extreme top did not go unnoticed by the more discriminating critical element. But these observations seemed trifling when weighed against her stunning exhibition of musicianship and versatility.

After the Mexican season, commitments in Italy compelled Maria and her husband to return to the continent immediately. New York was not a scheduled stop. As things turned out, it was all for the good, for a family reunion in New York at that time would hardly have brought relief from tension, or a change of pace from the exigencies of a busy career. On the contrary, it would have led to added strain and complications.

Maria's mother had returned to New York toward the end of 1951 to initiate separation proceedings against George Callas. While their daughter was making musical headlines in Milan, Rome, and Florence, the Thirty Years War of the parents' married life was approaching its predictable end with a blissful absence of publicity. While Maria sang in Mexico, Evangelia Callas obtained a temporary judgment assuring her of a weekly alimony. Shortly thereafter she returned to Greece.

It was then that Mother Callas decided to do something about the future of her elder daughter, Jackie. Maria's sister had been living quietly in Athens, giving piano lessons and an occasional concert now and then. Evangelia had always maintained that, in her own way, Jackie was as talented as her younger sister, and deplored the way her gifts remained undiscovered by the world of music.

The contrast between Jackie's humdrum life and the spectacular career of Maria, whom Evangelia's romanticized imagination envisioned as being bathed in adulation and luxurious living, prompted the mother to action. She wrote to Maria and asked her for steady financial support for herself—the weekly allowance fixed by the New York court had not been forthcoming—as well as for outright sponsorship of Jackie's career.

Maria's reply hit the Athens home like a bolt of lightning. Jackie's career, she felt, was not her responsibility. As for Mama Evangelia, she was healthy and young enough to earn a livelihood. A few bitter exchanges followed between mother and daughter. Then the letters stopped altogether. For the time being, however, these crises were restricted to their rightful place, the inner circle of the Callas and Meneghini families.

The bitter correspondence, the mutual recriminations, the reawakened memories of a joyless childhood, mixed with inevitable guilt feelings caused by the abrupt break with her mother left their inescapable mark on Maria. She was in a completely rundown state when she and Battista returned to Verona in mid-July.

"Artists are human beings of flesh and bones, like you and me," cries Leoncavallo's clown in his *Prologue*. But what can an artist do with her emotional problems if she is determined not to be deterred from her way to the top? "We live by our songs and sing to whoever wants to hear them," is the way Gioconda describes her way of life in

Ponchielli's opera. Operatically speaking, this all adds up to the old saying, "the show must go on."

There was no rest for Maria, no time to retire for a few weeks, or even a few days, to let the wounds of her unhappy family battle heal. The Verona summer opera season was about to start. Of course, its main attraction was to be Callas.

La Gioconda was the opera chosen to open the 1952 season. Maria sang the title role haunted by the recurring memories of her Italian debut in the same opera, in the same surroundings, five years before. Laura, her rival on the stage, was again impersonated by the same artist, Elena Nicolai. This time, however, in place of the good-humored, volatile Serafin, La Scala's somber, scholarly Antonino Votto conducted. Other things had changed, too.

In contrast to the meager fee of her first Italian contract, Maria now received the regal sum of 500,000 lire for each of the six performances. She was now a major figure in Italian operatic life, and a particular favorite in her "home town" of Verona. She was welcomed back enthusiastically by the Arena's huge audience on opening night. Because of her depressed state of mind, these affectionate signs of popularity could not have been more welcome.

Interestingly, and as if to emphasize the changes that passing time had wrought, one critic found that Callas did not seem as much at home in the part of La Gioconda as in her *usual* roles. He failed to indicate what the *usual* roles were, but he must have meant the *Norma–Puritani–Armida* repertoire. In other words, the roles in which she had no competition.

While the Verona season was in progress (Maria also sang *Traviata*) a vital change took place in her career as a recording artist. Although at that moment she was still under contract to the Cetra firm, and committed to record three complete operas for them, Maria decided that, upon fulfilling these obligations, she would cast her lot with Great Britain's huge Electric & Musical Industries Ltd. (E.M.I.). The exclusive recording contract was signed on July 21, 1952, in the Meneghini home, where Walter Legge, director of E.M.I., had come to conclude negotiations which had been pending for several months.

There was a powerful reason behind Maria's switch of allegiance. The British firm had just completed a long-term contract with the management of La Scala under which future E.M.I. operatic recordings would be released bearing the official La Scala emblem. To Maria and Battista, the tremendous prestige and material advantages of the connection were obvious, and Maria's ever-present artistic reservations took comfort in the assurance that La Scala's outstanding conductors and singers would be her future recording associates.

Elisabeth Schwarzkopf, the brilliant German soprano and herself one of the most prominent names in E.M.I.'s roster of artists, is Mrs. Walter Legge in private life. Although primarily known today as a Mozart and Richard Strauss specialist and an outstanding song recitalist, she is actually a versatile operatic soprano with a huge repertoire that includes many Italian parts. Violetta was one of these parts—until that summer of 1952. After seeing Callas's Verona performance, Schwarzkopf never again returned to the role. "What is the sense in doing a part that another contemporary artist can do to perfection," is the way she explained her decision. The two artists are great friends today and, excelling in completely different repertoires, are likely to remain so.

During September, 1952, Maria completed two operatic recordings for Cetra in Turin, *La Gioconda* and *La Traviata.* The projected third opera never materialized under the Cetra aegis. When she resumed her recording activities six months later, she did so under E.M.I. auspices. Her association with the English firm, and later with its vigorous American affiliate, Angel Records, has continued blissfully to the present, to the enormous artistic and material benefit of both parties.

All in all, the fall of 1952 brought exciting new changes. Maria knew that recordings were the key to international fame, and her new contract assured her that this phase of her career was in the best of hands. She was spreading her wings, and not just via records. Another vital new adventure was ahead on her projected road to worldwide stardom, a trip to London. She was to make her debut at Covent Garden singing the title role of *Norma* during a five-performance tour of La Scala.

The English capital's opera-lovers seldom get to see Italian opera Scala-style. Their anticipation of the 1952 visit was raised to a feverish pitch. To conduct *Norma,* La Scala sent Vittorio Gui, an old favorite in England. The principal singers were Ebe Stignani, another admired favorite of Covent Garden, Mirto Picchi, the ascending tenor, and, in the title role, Maria Callas. Excitement was further heightened by the fact that *Norma* had not been heard in London since Rosa Ponselle had sung it there in 1930.

The name of Maria Callas was well known in London. The young prima donna's meteoric rise, her unbelievable feats of versatility, the tremendous range of her voice, her miraculous technique—all these were talked about, as were the more controversial aspects of her gifts. In London, too, she had legions of admirers and a considerable body of detractors. Between them, they filled Covent Garden for every one of the five evenings. Hundreds had to be turned away.

The London trip was an event of great significance for Maria. This was her first appearance in a major European theater outside of Italy. It was the first time she would display her art to the Anglo-Saxon breed of music critics, whose artistic outlook is frequently at odds with the more passionate, more unpredictable, but generally easier-to-please Italian brand of the species. When Maria and Meneghini arrived by plane on a foggy October day, they both realized the importance of the occasion. Covent Garden was, after all, one of the world's operatic centers, with a history emblazoned by immortal names.

Some of *Norma's* most effective and poignant moments are the duets between the Druid priestess Norma and her confidante and secret rival Adalgisa. There were spectators in that Covent Garden audience on November 8, 1952, to whom Maria Callas and Ebe Stignani appeared reminiscent of two massive columns in the Druid temple. But there was a heavenly blend in their voices, and Londoners rejoiced in being treated to their kind of exquisite vocalism.

Callas dazzled all critics with her technique, gathered some compliments on her restrained but expressive gestures and her ability to act with her voice, and drew the by-now-expected reservations on the occasional unevenness of her tones. Desmond Shawe-Taylor, one of the most influential London critics, called her "... if as yet an imperfect vocalist, the most interesting new singer heard in London for many years." There were more than a dozen curtain calls after the performance, leaving little doubt as to the overwhelming popular opinion.

Artistically, the London sojourn was a resounding

success. But the inexorable pace of the year's activities, the accumulating tension, the rewarding but relentless routine of travels, rehearsals, performances were visibly undermining Maria's health. In those days, she suffered from fainting spells and, frequently, carsickness. She was, more than ever, conscious of her weight and her appearance. The English newspapers were quite outspoken on the subject, and some of their comments made a deep impression. And, underneath it all, there was the continued pressure of family problems weighing on her mind.

The Meneghinis returned to Italy in mid-November. There were only a few weeks before the opening of La Scala's 1952/1953 season. Maria had no new roles to learn for Milan that year, but she immersed herself in restudying the roles assigned her—Lady Macbeth, La Gioconda, and Leonora—with renewed concentration, searching for new dramatic insights, subtler accentuations of vocal details. After the London journey, her attention turned, with ever-increasing consciousness, to enhancing her appearance on the stage and to selecting the costumes which would contribute most effectively to the impact of her portrayals.

Maria had met Madame Biki, one of Milan's leading fashion designers, at a dinner party given by Wally Castelbarco-Toscanini earlier in the summer. During the ensuing months, Biki, the granddaughter of Giacomo Puccini, became one of her closest friends. That fall, she was entrusted with the creation of Maria's new costumes. Thereafter, she designed all her dresses and contributed expert fashion counsel which was to become particularly important in the succeeding years.

In those last months of 1952, Maria made a decision that was to have far-reaching consequences on both her professional and personal life. She became determined to remove what she believed to be one of the main causes of her poor health and the only remaining deterrent to a truly great career as a singing-actress. Encouraged by her devoted husband, and confiding her secret only to a handful of intimate friends, Maria Callas began a rigorous and systematic reducing plan.

Battista Meneghini had, by this time, sold all his interest in the family business and had reinvested his fortune in real estate. Managing the business affairs of a sought-after diva had become a full-time occupation. Concert managers all over the world would have, of course, frantically vied for the privilege. But Maria would have none of them. She remembered all too clearly the early days of her career, the many fruitless auditions, the rejections, the casual and patronizing comments, the complete lack of interest. Now times had changed. All Italy wanted her, and the offers were so numerous and so lucrative that she could only consider the most important ones.

With demand far exceeding supply, the very act of "managing" had conveniently become reduced to discussions between husband and wife over the breakfast or dinner table. It was an ideal arrangement. "Now they need me, but no manager will have me, ever," Maria once exclaimed. Nor would they share, she could have added, in the managerial cut of ten or twenty per cent.

Actually, Maria *did* have a manager by virtue of that hastily signed contract in the long bygone days of 1947. Maria knew that Edward Bagarozy, empowered by that contract as her sole agent, and entitled to ten per cent of her earnings, would not long remain in the background. Ten per cent of her income was a substantial enough amount to bring the matter to a showdown sooner or later, Maria thought. But whatever she had achieved was the result of her own talent, hard work, and determination. Certainly, she could never have risen so high without her husband's protection and guidance, or without Serafin's encouragement and connections. But no *manager* had had anything to do with her career, and none would reap the rewards! Nothing had come to Maria Callas without a struggle, and she was not disposed to give up any part of her achievement idly standing by!

On December 4th, Maria Callas reached her twenty-ninth birthday. One half of her life had been spent in relentless pursuit of a career. Of all those years, none had been packed with more crises, decisions, triumphs, and turbulence than the crucial year of 1952. But she had never hoped to attain her goals without a struggle. Her star was rising —Maria was ready for greater glory, and she was ready to pay the necessary price of fame.

CHAPTER 7

Queen of La Scala

Lady Macbeth
O voluttà del soglio!
O scettro, alfin sei mio!
VERDI — MACBETH

The day of St. Ambrose had dawned again, and Maria Callas had the honor of opening La Scala for the second year in a row. For the 1952/1953 season Antonio Ghiringhelli had come up with an experiment designed to divide the Scala "kingdom" between its two queens. Queen Maria was to rule over the first half of the season, in new productions of Verdi's *Macbeth* and *Il Trovatore,* and Ponchielli's *La Gioconda.* Then, as Maria would depart to fulfill her obligations in Rome and elsewhere, Queen Renata would take over in Puccini's *Tosca* and Cilea's *Adriana Lecouvreur* during April and May. This, he hoped, would keep the rabid partisans in line. That music hath charms,

Ghiringhelli knew as well as the next man. But music alone would not soothe the savage breast. Not in Milan, anyway.

After the triumphant opening night, Lady Macbeth, the role Maria had once hoped to sing under Toscanini's baton, was admitted into the gallery of the most striking Callas interpretations. The musical delineation of this role, in which Verdi faithfully mirrored the commanding and terrifying Shakespearean model, cannot be accomplished by singing alone. Although not yet the mistress of the histrionic art she was to become later, Maria already possessed the rare gift of being able to communicate an impressive range of human emotions by vocal means. She electrified the audience with the forcefulness and intensity of her performance, and earned seven curtain calls for her blood-curdling "Sleepwalking Scene."

The following day, there were glowing comments for everyone: Maria, Victor de Sabata, who conducted, Enzo Mascherini in the title role, Italo Tajo, and Gino Penno. One critic detected an "almost inhuman vocal quality" in Maria's portrayal, which is exactly what Giuseppe Verdi would have wanted of the macabre Lady.

Perhaps because it followed so soon after the sensational *Macbeth,* Maria's portrayal of Gioconda, in a series which began on December 26th, appeared rather conventional to the experts. Neither she nor Giuseppe di Stefano, in the part of Enzo, appeared in their best vocal form at the *prima.* Some observers detected signs of fatigue in her appearance and vocal condition, which was hardly surprising after the string of strenuous activities of the preceding months.

But, as the new year approached, it brought no slackening in tempo. Maria's career had reached a commanding position. Like all top artists at La Scala, she was not an exclusive property of Milan. She was in demand everywhere in Italy. The gaps left open by La Scala in Maria's calendar of engagements were quickly filled by invitations from Italy's other operatic centers. In both 1952 and 1953, peak years of activity, she amassed a total of fifty-three performances each.

The first days of January, 1953, found her again at the scene of her earliest triumphs, Venice. The Fenice was celebrating the one hundredth anniversary of *La Traviata's* world premiere, one of the memorable and almost inexplicable failures in operatic history.

"*La Traviata* last night a fiasco," wrote Verdi tersely from Venice to a friend on March 7, 1853. "Is the fault mine or the singers? Time will tell." It did.

The anniversary gala took place on January 8, 1953, with the same cast that had collaborated a few months before in Cetra's recording: Maria Meneghini Callas in the title role, Francesco Albanese as Alfredo, and Ugo Savarese as his father. "A complete artist," was the terse but gratifying Venetian press verdict of Maria's performance.

When the identical cast repeated the Verdi opera in Rome shortly thereafter, the praise was not as unanimous. "La voce è troppo forte" (the voice is too strong!) was heard in the aisles as some operagoers with long memories recalled the touching characterization of Toti dal Monte in the thirties. Still, the house was full, the spectators at the *prima* argued, criticized—but came again to argue some more.

Before returning to La Scala, Maria sang her first *Lucia di Lammermoor* in Italy, on January 25th, at the Teatro Communale of Florence. The audience response was just as ecstatic as that in Mexico during the previous summer. "An immense triumph," recalled Giacomo Lauri-Volpi, the Edgardo of the evening. The veteran tenor, who by then had developed into one of the young diva's most outspoken admirers, remarked in print shortly thereafter:

"This young artist, with her ability to rouse the multitudes, may yet lead the lyric theater to a new golden age of singing."

Maria sang three Lucias in Florence. Following her engagement, this potent dramatic characterization was captured by E.M.I.'s microphones in the company of Giuseppe di Stefano and Tito Gobbi, with Tullio Serafin conducting from the pit of the Teatro Communale. It was the first in a series of complete operas uniting these artists, and one of the first major productions to speed the spectacular emergence of E.M.I.'s American branch, Angel Records, as an imposing force on the United States recording scene.

While comments about the Callas Lucia lingered in the musical headlines, Maria returned to Milan to fulfill her last obligation of the season with La Scala, the role of Leonora in Verdi's *Il Trovatore*. After the *prima* of February 19th, there were more superlatives. "A stupendous vocalism in perfect control, and strong dramatic skill," reported *Oggi*. The same critic was unimpressed by Gino Penno's Manrico but found Ebe Stignani's Azucena "nothing short of a vocal lesson to all." Antonino Votto conducted.

During March, while the season was still in progress, Maria completed her second operatic recording for E.M.I.-Angel, Bellini's *I Puritani*. Again, Giuseppe di Stefano was her tenor partner. Although Tullio Serafin was not connected with La Scala in an official capacity, it was he who conducted all the recorded "Callas operas." Times had changed. Now it was Maria's turn to select the conductors. Now she was in a position to reciprocate Serafin's unflagging faith in her during the years when she could count her supporters on two fingers.

Thus, with a recording that was to make something of a sensation on its appearance, and with repeated triumphs in what was to become one of her greatest roles (Leonora), ended Maria Meneghini Callas's second season at La Scala. In accordance with the prearranged plan, she departed in mid-season to make room for the arrival of the rival queen.

It had been a highly rewarding season. Her career had made powerful strides. Her popular following had increased tremendously, and her press could hardly have been better. Freshness of imagination, burning intensity, depth of characterization, rare musicianship—these were the qualities for which she was acclaimed, and which justified the frequency of the *ESAURITO* (SOLD OUT) sign at Callas performances.

But it had also been a stormy season, its pleasures tainted with some bitterness. If the number of her partisans had multiplied, so had, apparently, the opposing faction. The more successful she was, the more resentment she inspired in these circles. Persistent whistling and disturbances of an organized nature accompanied nearly every one of her performances. The genuine ovations were always more emphatic, and the unwelcome noises usually disappeared in the gathering cheers, but the hostile demonstrators would return a few evenings later with renewed determination. Renata Tebaldi was a great favorite, and her rabid devotees watched the rival's rise with resentful apprehension.

These noisome activities are not to be confused with the controlled and never destructive activity of La Scala's "official" claque, a group of experienced and dedicated morale-builders operating under the leadership of Ettore Parmeggiani, once a leading tenor.

The official claque dispenses its bolstering volleys

without partisanship; its allegiance remains with the theater and not with individuals. It pinpoints the moments in each opera where applause is encouraged, helps to make a tentative effort into something more substantial, and, in some cases—particularly with modern or unfamiliar operas—contributes its approbation unassisted by any spontaneous audience reaction. At such times, of course, the presence of the claque is invaluable.

Wildcat claqueurs are another matter. They are an international breed, unruly, violent, and essentially destructive. Uncritically idolatrous, they are insensitive and sometimes indifferent to opera as music. They often sacrifice the most sublime musical moments to their unwelcome exhibitionism. In Italy they have always been a kind of unholy tradition, resented but tolerated. In time, Maria Callas was to have her own demonstrators who rallied, uninvited and unencouraged, to counteract the efforts of the opposing band of blusterers who were dedicated, with a similar lack of encouragement, to uphold Tebaldi's banner.

In that spring of 1953, such annoyances left Maria completely unruffled. Things were going well, very well indeed. Apart from triumphing in the theater, she was winning one of the decisive battles of her life. The reducing cure—a combination of methodical dieting, electrical massages, and the ever-present psychological factors—was progressing famously. As her weight diminished her self-confidence seemed to grow in equal proportion, a phenomenon students of musical counterpoint would describe as "contrary motion."

Maria enjoyed her success, and she considered all signs of envy, jealousy, and intrigue only a reassuring proof of her exalted position. Happily driving about in a smart, light-green Alfa Romeo—Battista's gift delivered

by the salon of designer Pinin Farina—she was heard to
remark: "If an ordinary artist has a Cadillac, how can I
have a Cadillac, too?"

With her part of the Milan season over, Maria returned to fulfill her seasonal obligations at the Rome
Opera. If Romans harbored reservations about her Violetta earlier in the season, her Norma impressed all in the
way she imparted rare dramatic meaning to that stately
Bellinian figure. Accompanying her in the series of *Norma,*
which began on April 9th, were Fedora Barbieri, Franco
Corelli, the new tenor sensation, and Giulio Neri. The veteran maestro, Gabriele Santini, was the conductor.

Her Roman farewell that spring was in the role of
Lucia, the most widely acclaimed Callas portrayal of the
season. In Rome, one critic called it "the undisputed peak
of the entire season."

It was May again—time for the Maggio Fiorentino,
and time for another portrayal that would assure that
Maria Meneghini Callas would remain the talk of operatic
Italy. In 1951, it had been *I Vespri Siciliani,* which fas-
tened the seal on her La Scala contract. In 1952, it had been
Rossini's *Armida,* the museum piece she had brought to
life after its 135 years of slumber. The work earmarked for
the special Callas treatment of 1953 was Cherubini's
Medea.

This opera had a thoroughly undistinguished Italian
career in the years B.C. (before Callas). Today, due to her
powerful impersonation of this vengeful, tigerish figure of
mythology, the opera has been returned to currency and
draws full houses on two continents. Its title role, however,
is virtually "owned" by Callas. Few are the artists so ill-
advised as to undertake the risk of a Callas comparison in
this role.

Opera-goers who have seen the Callas Medea in Lon-

don or Dallas in recent years have had the benefit of the
artist's fully formed characterization, gained after living
with this extremely demanding part for several years. The
Florence audience of May, 1953, saw a portrayal mastered
after only eight days of study. How did she do? "She
sounded as if she had been born singing it" in the words
of one critic. Another (Robert Mann in *Musical America*)
remarked that "The oblivion that has shrouded this opera
for 150 years is explained by the fact that singers of Miss
Callas's artistry and intelligence are so very rare."

The presence of the Metropolitan Opera's General
Manager, Rudolf Bing, at the Maggio Musicale might have
suggested to some observers that history was about to repeat itself. Ghiringhelli of La Scala had visited Florence
to see Callas in 1951, and a contract had ensued. It was
quite obvious, too, that Bing's visit was not motivated by
the splendid treasures of Florence's Uffizi Gallery. He did
talk business with the Meneghinis, but no agreement was
reached. Maria was not ready to sing in New York on the
Metropolitan's terms.

Meneghini was later quoted by the press: "My wife
will not sing at the Metropolitan as long as Mr. Bing runs
it. It is their loss." It was a statement characterized more
by loyalty than by prophetic foresight, but it undoubtedly
reflected the atmosphere of their discussions. At the same
time, Meneghini was carrying out his function as Maria's
manager with astute effectiveness.

His philosophy was simple: Maria Callas was the
world's greatest operatic artist. No greater honor and no
better business investment could come to any opera house
than to obtain Maria's services. No one could expect to reap
the benefit of her art and immense attracting power without paying for it, and it was Meneghini's task to make them
pay for it. Already in 1947 he had known he was dealing

with vocal gold; now, and in the years to come, more and more opera directors and impresarios would come around to share his views.

Instead of New York, the road led right back to London for a gala summer season during the Coronation festivities. Aside from repeating her Norma, in which she had been so widely admired by Londoners, Maria sang in *Aida* (June 4th) and *Il Trovatore* (June 26th). Her accurate technical execution of *Trovatore's* trills, scales, and arpeggios, particularly in the last-act aria "D'amor sull'ali rosee," brought resounding critical raves and gave many spectators the sensation that they were hearing these thrice-familiar melodies for the first time in the manner in which the composer had meant them to be sung.

By contrast, Maria's own impressions of her second London sojourn were far less favorable. The productions were all poorly staged, particularly *Il Trovatore,* the sight of whose shopworn settings moved her to a scornful outburst at rehearsals. Nor was she happier with the standard of the performances. This time British singers had been added to the casts, thus causing a noticeable loss in authenticity and homogeneity.

But if Callas's opinion of that short London season was not fully satisfactory, she nevertheless left England with new laurels added to her already considerable reputation. She made many friends among the British artists, her popularity with audiences increased, her press was excellent.

When she returned to Italy, Maria was confronted with a series of recordings. Henceforth, the summer months were to become periods dedicated to recording activity in Milan under La Scala auspices. This July and August, the operas to be recorded were *Cavalleria Rusticana* and *Tosca,* both with Giuseppe di Stefano in the tenor leads. Tullio

Serafin conducted the Mascagni work. *Tosca* brought Victor de Sabata to one of his all-too-rare appearances before the microphones.

On various occasions, Callas has expressed the opinion that Tosca is *not* one of her favorite parts. Perhaps the unpleasant memories of the Athens and Rio de Janeiro Toscas are responsible for this surprising statement. Surprising, because her recorded Tosca is an inspired and overwhelming performance, held by many as perhaps her outstanding achievement for the phonograph.

After the recording sessions were over, Maria went immediately to Verona. She was scheduled to sing six performances there in August, including the gala *Aida* which celebrated the fortieth anniversary of the Verona summer festival.

That evening, however, the ovations centered on the conductor, Tullio Serafin. Oldtimers still remembered the opening night in 1913 when Serafin, directing the same opera, gave out a cry of "Viva Verdi" before beginning the Prelude. Now grey, dignified, but hardly less vigorous, he bowed to the prolonged applause, visibly moved.

With September came a period of rest, delicious, well-earned, much-needed rest. For the first time in many months, the Meneghinis could enjoy their beautiful Verona home, relax, reminisce, plot future conquests, and entertain their friends. Maria, a passionate cook and fond manipulator of kitchen gadgets, could finally devote some time to these hobbies. She enjoyed it all immensely, especially after the unceasing tension of the past ten months. But her attention soon turned to future challenges, for she knew that, by all indications, the months to come would not be any different.

In November, the rest period was over. Plans for the new season began to crystallize. The Rome Opera again wanted Maria's services. She was eager to return, but the schedule of the Roman engagements had to conform to La Scala's plans.

While opening the season in Trieste, singing *Norma* with an all-Scala cast of Franco Corelli, Elena Nicolai, and Boris Christoff, with Antonino Votto conducting, Maria received word of La Scala's plans for 1953/1954. Donizetti's *Lucia di Lammermoor,* Verdi's *Don Carlo,* and Gluck's *Alceste* were the operas chosen for her. All were to be new productions. In addition, Cherubini's *Medea,* the sensation of the *Maggio Fiorentino,* would also be incorporated into the Scala repertory. To conduct the Cherubini opera, Ghiringhelli engaged, to some Milanese consternation, the brilliant young American, Leonard Bernstein, already known for his symphonic achievements, but generally regarded as a stranger to opera.

For a young conductor to make an operatic debut at La Scala, of all places, was in itself a mighty challenge. To do so while restoring a nearly forgotten work from limbo before an exacting and chauvinistic audience added multiple burdens to the task. But, on top of all that, to be encumbered by having to conduct Maria Callas, who was beginning to acquire a somewhat forbidding reputation, seemed more, in the opinion of some of his advisers, than Bernstein had bargained for. Contrary to all expectations, however, maestro and diva formed a sympathetic and mutually responsive combination.

The honor of *opening* La Scala's 1953/1954 season went to Renata Tebaldi. The opera was *La Wally,* commemorating the sixtieth anniversary of the death of its composer Alfredo Catalani. In the proscenium box sat Arturo Toscanini, who had conducted the première of this opera at La Scala in 1892, and his daughter Wally, whose very name had been inspired by the opera's heroine. Tos-

canini was, as all Milan knew, Tebaldi's most prominent
champion. It was his endorsement that had brought
Renata, then a comparative unknown, to La Scala in 1946.

With Tebaldi on opening night, and committed later
to sing in *Otello, Tosca,* and *Eugene Onegin,* there was no
way of dividing the "queendom" according to the uneasy
but successful Ghiringhelli formula of the previous year.
Excitement among the habitués, claqueurs, and opera's
lunatic fringe was scorching. Sensing trouble ahead,
Emilio Radius, music critic of the Milanese weekly
L'Europeo, suggested that the rivals bury the hatchet and
have a great big public handshake for the greater glory of
the vocal art which, he felt, offered ample room for both
of them.

No press comments ever escape the eye of Maria
Meneghini Callas. On opening night there she was, resplendent, smiling radiantly, and applauding fervently,
showing, for all the world to see, that she was ready to
follow Signor Radius's good advice. Her presence drew
this optimistic comment from Bruno Slawitz, a critic of
Milan's *Musica e Dischi:* "The rivalry that divides the
public into admirers of a great voice (Tebaldians) and
admirers of technical mastery (Callasians) brings life to
the theater. Happily, rivalry goes hand in hand with chiv-
alry. All were gladdened to see Signora Meneghini Callas
in her box, cordially applauding Renata Tebaldi's
success."

All were not gladdened, however. There were many, in
fact, who regarded Callas's gesture as a calculated act of
defiance to unnerve her more sensitive colleague.

Tebaldi gave no sign of recognition on opening night
of Maria's obviously conciliatory move. Nor did she
appear at the theater the following night when Cherubini's
Medea was first given with Callas in the title role, opposite

Fedora Barbieri as Neris, Gino Penno as Jason, and Giuseppe Modesti as Creon. The feeling of rivalry only grew more intense with each day of the season.

Medea had made a lukewarm impression at La Scala when it was first given in 1909, and more than forty years later the critics were still reluctant with their encomiums. But it was clearly a triumphant evening for Leonard Bernstein and Maria Callas. Maria's noticeably more slender appearance enormously aided her in creating a striking characterization. With her flowing tresses, classic features, and eloquent gestures, she reminded many of the great tragediennes of the stage. There was a ten-minute standing ovation following the aria ''De' tuoi figli,'' and no end of curtain calls after the final act.

All of a sudden, the shrill noise of a whistle clashed with the hearty hurrahs and purring sounds of contentment. After a few more blasts of unwelcome interruption the perpetrator, a young girl, shrouded beyond recognition in a brown cape, was seen running out of the theater with an angry mob at her heels. Callas appeared at the stage entrance a few minutes later, surrounded by a legion of admirers. Happy but visibly exhausted, she begged them: ''If you really love me, you'll let me go home and get some rest.'' They finally did.

Medea, a role tailor-made for Callas, gave her some of her greatest moments in Milan. Fired by her characterization, Teodoro Celli declared in *Oggi* that in mastering the right style and right technique for the music of the *ottocento,* Callas, in fact, had discovered the secret of the great Maria Malibran.

Medea was repeated several times, to sold-out houses. It was the only part she sang in Milan during the remaining days of 1953. On December 16th, she returned to Rome to make her first seasonal appearance as Leonora in *Il Trovatore,* with Barbieri, Lauri-Volpi, and Silveri.

In Italy, many consider Lauri-Volpi the greatest Trovatore of his generation. He was then, at sixty, past his prime, but still able to generate enormous power. It was he, observed music critic Giorgio Vigolo, who set the tone of the performance, and not Gabriele Santini, the permissive conductor.

The stentorian tenor galvanized the cast into a volcanic melee, with flaming melodramatics and high notes held to the point of exhaustion. In the midst of all the fury the voice of Maria Callas rose "... in its admirable purity, like a radiant stem from a bloody battlefield covered with helmets, shields, and abandoned cannons," summed up the poetic Mr. Vigolo. Even more excitement attached to the repeat performance of the opera, when Barbieri fainted onstage and had to be replaced in the middle of the second act.

Coinciding with that Rome *prima* of *Il Trovatore,* the late Leonard Warren made his Italian debut at La Scala. The world outside operatic Italy had generally regarded Warren as the outstanding baritone in the Italian repertoire. But at La Scala, though he sang his most famous role, Rigoletto, his reception was unenthusiastic.

La Scala's management was under constant fire that year because of an alleged preference for foreign conductors and singers. Maria Callas was not involved in the attack. Although she retained her American passport and citizenship, she was married to an Italian and, to all appearances, identified herself completely with Italian life and viewpoints. The cold reception accorded to Warren, however, can be easily attributed to the peppery atmosphere, rather puzzling in the light of the cordiality with which Italian artists are welcomed year after year in London, New York, Chicago, Vienna, and all other operatic centers.

Maria spent Christmas, 1953, at her Verona home. A particularly joyful bit of holiday reading was provided by an article in the magazine *L'Europeo*. There her admirer Emilio Radius wrote: "If these were better times for music, Maria Callas would be the most famous woman in Europe." In Italy, certainly, she was just about the most famous woman already, except perhaps for Lollobrigida.

The opera-going public was still remembering her flaming Medea when the *prima* of La Scala's new production of *Lucia di Lammermoor,* on January 17, 1954, added more fuel to the smoldering memories.

La Scala in Delirium—A Rain of Red Carnations— Four Minutes of Applause for the Mad Scene In these headlines of the Milanese *La Notte* the story of the evening was told, so far as Callas was concerned.

The production itself was rather controversial. It was staged as well as conducted by the brilliant Herbert von Karajan, whose musical ideas were frequently at odds with Italian traditions, and whose stagecraft was not calculated to please everybody. It was, at any rate, not an auspicious year for "foreigners." Still, in the opinion of some, this was the greatest *Lucia* in La Scala history.

Callas displayed a depth of characterization never before associated with Walter Scott's hapless heroine. Coloratura embellishments seemed neither distracting nor extraneous; they became meaningful elements in the musical and dramatic design. A dozen curtain calls were her reward after Act II, and at the conclusion of the "Mad Scene," in which the vocal pyrotechnics and Maria's superior dramatic conception received further enhancement from Karajan's inventive lighting, pandemonium took

over. To make the evening's vocal glories complete, the
entire cast—Giuseppe di Stefano, Rolando Panerai, and
Giuseppe Modesti—was in superb form.

Two new productions followed during the spring of
1954 without quite attaining the level of the *Medea–Lucia*
peak. Gluck's *Alceste,* presented on April 4th under the
baton of Carlo Maria Giulini, was another in the series of
lavish mythological excavations. The title role was admirably suited to the Callas range and artistry, to her classic
features, striking hair-style, and statuesque appearance.
But it was not an opera to ignite the Italian temperament.

More exciting was the season's final production,
Verdi's *Don Carlo,* in which Maria was surrounded by the
splendid trio of Ebe Stignani as Eboli, Nicola Rossi-
Lemeni as King Philip, and Paolo Silveri as Posa, as well
as a rather undistinguished new tenor, Mario Ortica, in the
title role. She had learned the part of Queen Elisabeth in
1950, but this was her first actual appearance in the opera.
Although there were some reservations about a certain lack
of tenderness in her characterization, she was, in voice and
bearing, every inch the queen. It was rather fitting that she
ended the season on such a regal note.

The 1953/1954 season brought glory to many La Scala
artists—Tebaldi's star never shone brighter—but almost
everyone conceded that Maria Meneghini Callas had been
its dominating personality. She was the most glamorous,
the most talked about, the most flamboyantly idolized, and
most spectacularly attacked operatic figure of the day.
Loved or hated in person, praised or scorned in art, no
singer inspired so much discussion, nor exercised comparable power at the box office. At the end of that season no
one could talk of a divided kingdom. Maria Callas was the
Queen of La Scala. In keeping with her regal stature, her
remuneration at the end of the season rose to the regal

figure of 650,000 lire per performance (in excess of $1,000).
This was more than double her 1951 scale.

In contrast with this spectacular rise, there was a modest account meticulously kept up by husband and wife in the Meneghini home, a strange sequence of names and figures that showed a downward trend:

Gioconda	92
Aida	87
Norma	80
Medea	78
Lucia	75
Alceste	65
Don Carlo	64

In this progression lies, with telling conciseness, the history of what was perhaps Maria Callas's greatest victory. Between the *Gioconda* of December, 1952, and the *Don Carlo* of April, 1954, she succeeded in parting with 28 kilograms, nearly 62 pounds. She went from 202 pounds to 140 pounds. Before the admiring and astonished eyes of Giovanni Battista Meneghini, one-third of the woman he married in 1949 gradually but surely vanished into thin air. The matronly young girl of those early days in Verona achieved an almost unbelievable transformation into a trim, glamorous lady of fashion.

This was the Maria Callas who appeared at La Scala during May, immediately after the close of the season, to record Bellini's *Norma* for E.M.I.-Angel. With her was, of course, the inseparable Battista and another constant companion, a two-year-old black poodle named ''Tea,'' whose noisy expressions of happiness played havoc with the nerves of Walter Legge and his engineering staff.

As if to emphasize the emergence of the new, glamorous Callas, Maria had been transformed into a blonde. She radiated self-confidence, contentment, and good humor. It was almost unthinkable to recognize in her a woman once haunted by fears and insecurities. Together with the excess weight, all traces of her feelings of inferiority had vanished Now that she had the figure for it, she became clothes-conscious for the first time in her life. By the spring of 1954 her wardrobe, too, was drawing admiring comments from the ever-attentive press. It was a transformation that would have brought far-reaching changes in any woman. To Maria Meneghini Callas, however, it meant even more.

An artist above all else, she knew that her stage appearance would now enhance the design of her character-izations. She would no longer have to stand still, like a Greek column equipped with two semaphores, for fear of avoiding actions and postures that make overweight sopranos, even those with glorious voices, appear ridicu-lous. She could portray a regal Tosca, a consumptive Violetta, a savage Medea, even a fragile Butterfly, with the maximum of credibility. The realization of artistic growth filled her with new ambitions.

To Martin Mayer, who interviewed her at the record-ing of *Norma* on behalf of the American magazine *High Fidelity* she exposed her new credo: "Every year I must be better than the year before. Otherwise I'd retire. I don't need the money. I work for Art."

There was only one missing link in her string of victories, America. In her native land she was still known only through phonograph records. The time was ripe for a triumphant return. Maria Callas, whom experience had taught the wisdom of waiting for the *right* moment and the *right* opportunity, knew when to act.

Ettore Verna, a Milanese agent, had approached her in January with an offer on behalf of the budding Lyric Opera of Chicago. It was an attractive offer in many ways. In fact, her demands met with such an enthusiastic and determined spirit of compliance on the part of the Chicago managers that Maria promptly gave her consent to open the Chicago season on November 1, 1954.

In February, Carol Fox, President of the Chicago Lyric Opera, came to Verona to crown a European talent safari by paying her respects to the prize catch. In the course of a harmonious meeting with the Meneghinis, the last formalities of the contract were completed. Maria found it an interesting change to discuss business and technical matters with a young woman of her own age (once an aspiring singer), and a woman who, like Callas herself, was an energetic living negation of the term "weaker sex."

It was only proper that Chicago, the city that had come so close to launching the Callas career in 1947, should be the scene of her belated American debut. It was only right that the Metropolitan Opera, which had first ignored her, then failed to make an impressive enough effort to prove its interest, should be bypassed.

And it was only logical that she chose Chicago, for the management of the young opera company not only agreed to her choice of repertory and other artistic requirements but also accepted her terms, calling for six performances for a reported total of $12,000 and two-way travel expenses for husband Battista and herself.

During the brief "lull" that followed the recording sessions of *Norma,* Maria learned two new roles, Nedda in Leoncavallo's *I Pagliacci* and Marguerite in Boito's *Mefistofele.* Nedda was prepared for the recording of the opera, with Giuseppe di Stefano and Tito Gobbi, Serafin conducting, which followed shortly in June. By then Maria's recorded operas enjoyed so much worldwide demand that E.M.I. would undertake no recordings at La Scala without her. If the role was not in her repertoire, she would see to it that it would be. It was as simple as that.

Boito's *Mefistofele* was given that July in Verona with
a double cast. Nicola Rossi-Lemeni and Giulio Neri interpreted the title role; Giuseppe di Stefano and Ferruccio
Tagliavini appeared in the part of Faust. Maria sang in
three performances of the opera, alternating with Magda
Olivero. Her Marguerite was of "true Goethean inspiration, as Boito had envisioned it, the innocent maiden
haunted by tragic destiny," in the words of Teodoro Celli.

After the Verona commitments, Maria returned to
Milan to resume her recording activities. During August
and September, she completed the tragic *La Forza del
Destino* and the comic *Il Turco in Italia.* In the former,
which was conducted by Tullio Serafin, she sang opposite
Richard Tucker for the first time since their joint Italian
debut in the 1947 Verona season. In the latter, she was
reunited with conductor Gianandrea Gavazzeni and practically the entire cast which was responsible for the 1950
Rome revival of Rossini's charming *opera buffa.*

The exacting schedule of the recordings over, there
remained only a brief lull before her voyage to America.
Just enough time for shopping trips, consultations with
Madame Biki, with her hair dresser, and with a host of
other travel preparations. Maria was coming back to the
land of her birth, and she was coming back in style.

CHAPTER 8

Mad Scenes in Chicago

Aida
Ritorna vincitor!
VERDI — AIDA

The Lyric Theater of Chicago, which returned the glittering aura of grand opera to the Windy City after a period of more than twenty lean years, was a miracle brought about by two youthful and daring impresarios, Carol Fox and Lawrence V. Kelly. Both were socially prominent and blessed with the necessary contacts; both combined an idealistic love for opera with the down-to-earth realism of the business world. They were endowed with the gift of persistence and blissfully lacked the kind of experience imparted by age which, by revealing all the forbidding risks of their plan, probably would have deterred them from its realization.

In the time-honored tradition of operatic impresarios,

Fox and Kelly lacked the necessary funds. But they right-fully appraised the city's civic pride and knew that the potential patronage was there, though restrained by a great deal of reluctance and a decided unwillingness to support mediocrity.

They knew that if Chicago was to have opera it would have to be worthy of the city's glorious operatic past, symbolized by the memories of Mary Garden, Cleofonte Campanini, Lina Cavalieri, and Rosa Raisa. They also knew that the patrons would not be stirred by promises alone. (The stillborn efforts of the United States Opera Company of 1947 had not been forgotten.) To offer proof, Fox and Kelly decided to risk everything on one dramatic gesture.

Having gained access to more than ten million dollars worth of sets and costumes accumulated by the city's pre-vious resident companies, the Lyric Theater presented its "calling card" by pulling out of its hat a brilliant perform-ance of Mozart's *Don Giovanni* on February 4, 1954. It was led by the company's young musical director Nicola Rescigno, a gifted Italo-American protegé of the great Chicago favorite Giorgio Polacco, and boasted of a first-rate cast consisting of Nicola Rossi-Lemeni in the title role, Eleanor Steber, Leopold Simoneau, and Bidú Sayão.

That this hastily produced venture, built on friend-ship, promises, and hopes, exposed certain weaknesses in some of its complex elements was immaterial. The primary purpose was achieved: Chicago was shown that the new company had the courage, the skill, and the artists to present opera on the grand scale.

With considerable press support, Fox and Kelly succeeded in assuring the financial backing required for one season at least. Public interest in the venture steadily mounted after the auspicious *Don Giovanni*. Their an-

nouncement that Maria Meneghini Callas would make her
long-awaited American debut as a member of the Lyric
Theater came at the best possible moment to lend a powerful assist to ticket sales and contributions.

During 1953, E.M.I. had launched its American affiliate, Angel Records, and named as its President Dario
Soria, who as head of Cetra's American branch had built
a handful of imported single records into a million-dollar
enterprise by knowledgeable concentration on the field of
complete operatic recordings. In the United States, the rise
of Angel Records and the rise of Maria Callas were
synonymous—the Callas albums of *Lucia, I Puritani,* and
Tosca were the new company's top sellers. With a flamboyant but tasteful advertising campaign, directed by
Dario Soria's equally gifted wife Dorle, the image of
Maria Callas was thoughtfully and firmly implanted in the
American operatic consciousness as ''The Queen of
Opera,'' ''La Divina,'' and similar glamorous sobriquets
which called attention to her unique gifts by invoking the
kind of regal stature opera-lovers the world over like to
associate with prima donnas.

With the enthusiastic efforts of the Fox–Kelly team
and the seasoned experience of the Sorias, the combined
debut of the Chicago Lyric and Maria Meneghini Callas
was trumpeted into news of national significance. Ticket
orders came from all over the United States, even Alaska.
The national magazines were present with a bevy of photographers, and the leading New York and California
dailies sent their first-string critics to cover the event.

The press was present in depth when the plane bearing
Maria Callas and her husband landed at the Chicago airport on a gray October morning. Maria thanked them for
their presence and introduced her husband with a few
charming, well-chosen words. She was tired but patient,

Callas in the role of Elena in Verdi's *I Vespri Siciliani* at her La Scala debut on December 7, 1951. (Photo by Erio Piccagliani.)

Callas's first appearance at London's Covent Garden occurred on November 8, 1952. She sang Norma. The great mezzo Ebe Stignani was Adalgisa in the Bellini opera. (Photo by Roger Wood.)

On December 7, 1952, Maria Callas opened the season of La Scala in Verdi's *Macbeth*. (Photo by Wide World.)

One of Maria's outstanding Milanese triumphs was achieved in the title role of Donizetti's *Lucia di Lammermoor* in January, 1954. Herbert von Karajan staged as well as conducted that memorable production. (Courtesy of *Opera News*.)

THE GREAT TRANSFORMATION. Maria Callas as seen in 1950, at the time of her first Milan appearance, and in 1957, as the most coveted prima donna in the world. (Left, photo by Pix, Inc.; right, courtesy of Angel Records.)

Nicola Rossi-Lemeni and Maria Callas in the Chicago Lyric Opera's production of *Norma*, in which Maria made her unforgettable American debut on November 1, 1954. (Courtesy of Lyric Opera of Chicago.)

The affair of the process servers, which brought Callas's second Chicago season to a stormy end on November 17, 1955. (Photo by Wide World.)

Spontini's *La Vestale* opened La Scala's 1954/1955 season. This historic picture showing Arturo Toscanini, Victor de Sabata, Antonino Votto, and Maria Callas was taken during rehearsals. (Photo by Erio Piccagliani.)

Callas and Luchino Visconti. *La Vestale* was Visconti's first La Scala production. (Photo by Erio Piccagliani.)

Maria Callas at her Metropolitan debut. Here she takes one of her many curtain calls, flanked by Cesare Siepi and Mario del Monaco, on October 29, 1956. The opera: Bellini's *Norma*. (Photo by Paul Seligman.)

Maria Callas and Rudolf Bing on February 6, 1958, when Maria began her second season at the Metropolitan in the title role of Verdi's *La Traviata*. (Photo by European.)

Maria Callas left La Scala after a feud with Superintendent Ghiringhelli. Here she is surrounded by a throng of admirers after her last performance of Bellini's *Il Pirata* on May 31, 1958. (Photo by Publifoto–Black Star.)

serious, almost solemn, and the very opposite of the tempestuous diva for whom the reporters had been waiting in readiness, pencils poised.

Her new associates, however, lost no time in discovering what made her tick. En route to the Ambassador Hotel with Lawrence Kelly, she fired one question after another at him about how the preparations were progressing, about the ticket sales, the whereabouts of other artists, the schedule of rehearsals. She met Nicola Rescigno that same evening, and the questions continued just as relentlessly about staging, tempi, musical approach to one scene or another. In a way, Maria subjected the young conductor to an examination. She had definite ideas about the music and its interpretation and, after having sung under Serafin, De Sabata, Votto, Von Karajan, and Bernstein, she wanted to be assured that her performances would be in good directorial hands.

During the week that followed, Maria amazed everyone by the range and unflagging zeal of her interests. She was full of helpful suggestions and eager to hear the opinion of others. This was no self-centered diva, but one of the hardest-working members of the "team," who listened attentively when her colleagues rehearsed and worked patiently and painstakingly with the chorus. To achieve the proper tonal balance, she sang the taxing "Casta Diva" nine times during rehearsals of *Norma*. While it was sometimes exhausting to watch her in action, she was, herself, untiring. In the words of Lawrence Kelly, "she lived opera twenty-four hours a day."

On the evening of November 1, 1954, Chicago's venerable Opera House nearly erupted with fierce local pride. In the resplendent audience of some 3,500, opera-goers fondly recognized Edith Mason, Eva Turner, Giovanni Martinelli, Rosa Raisa, and Giorgio Polacco, reminders of the city's bygone operatic glory. Grand opera had returned to Chicago after too long an absence. The big question was: Will it stay around this time or will it again follow the heartbreaking fate of former failures?

The answer could be read on 3,500 faces as they streamed out of the theater three hours later. Seasoned veterans, society matrons, and starry-eyed novices melted into a homogeneous body of beaming, gesticulating contentment. Callas was on everyone's lips, but her colleagues —Giulietta Simionato, Mirto Picchi, and Nicola Rossi-Lemeni—were all hailed extravagantly, as was Nicola Rescigno and the excellent orchestra recruited mostly from members of the Chicago Symphony. There were only heroes connected with the stunning success of that opening *Norma.*

That night, producers and patrons, stars and choristers celebrated their triumph with pomp and style at the Angel Ball, organized, with the publicity-wise assistance of the Sorias, for the benefit of the Illinois Opera Guild.

Chicago's proud musical press made the swelling hearts beat even faster the following morning. Each critic tried to outdo the other in glorifying the company. "Once more," announced the Chicago *Sun-Times,* "this city has raised an operatic voice which deserves to be heard around the world."

As for Callas, she exceeded all expectations. "For my money," wrote Claudia Cassidy of the Chicago *Tribune,* "she was not only up to specifications, she surpassed them. ... Her duet with Giulietta Simionato was something to tell your grandchildren about. ... Her voice is more beautiful in color, more even through the range, than it used to be. Her range is formidable, and her technique is dazzling. She sang the 'Casta Diva' in a kind of a mystic dream, like a goddess of the moon briefly descended. ..."

During the opening week the delirium continued with a stylish *La Bohème,* in which Rosanna Carteri and Giacinto Prandelli conquered the audience, and with a spirited *Barber of Seville* boasting of Giulietta Simionato, Tito Gobbi (in his American debut), and Rossi-Lemeni. Maria repeated her triumphant Norma before a sold-out house on November 5th. When she was sighted in the audience of *La Bohème* the following evening, she was greeted with a thunderous ovation.

Whether on stage or off, she conquered everywhere. Her relations with the press were superb—not a dissenting or carping note throughout the entire season. She remembered faces and dropped names with the astuteness of a campaigning politician. Interviews were cheerfully granted, and many an impassive or downright cool observer was completely disarmed by her display of unaffected naturalness and candor. There was not a press agent in sight, a phenomenon remarkable in itself in this age of controllable popularity. Maria was her own tireless manager and promoter, and she did her job superbly.

Battista Meneghini was somewhat out of his element. He could not speak English and thus had to relinquish some of his usual activities—liason with management and press, in particular—during the Chicago stay. He did so, however, with the greatest of calm, for the management of the Chicago Lyric yielded to every wish cheerfully and immediately. In turn, Maria was full of praise for her new associates, with an occasional side dig at the Metropolitan:

"Several times Rudolf Bing has contacted me. But we cannot agree on repertoires. There are other things, too, and not only money. . . . I enjoy being treated as a woman and an artist. . . ."

In her press interviews she was remarkably plain-spoken. "Of course I am well paid. Why shouldn't I be? We ask our fee, and whoever is crazy enough to give it to us will give it to us," she replied to one question about her salary. To another query about her alleged fights with colleagues she had a brief reply: "Colleagues? I love them all!"

Her spectacular loss of weight came in for a round of questioning. Some of her interviewers even expressed concern about its possible effect on her singing. Maria set their minds at ease. "Weight has nothing to do with the voice. I don't have to eat like a horse to sing." To those who pressed for more specific details on her reducing cure she gave patient and charmingly uninformative answers. "I had a tapeworm, and I no longer have it," was her simple explanation of the phenomenon to Claudia Cassidy. On this point, Meneghini offered his own theories: "Fatness can be caused by a glandular disturbance. In her case, the disturbance ceased. Since then, she is gay—a different person."

The serenity of the Chicago atmosphere was threatened by storm clouds on November 4th when Henry Kalchheim, Chicago attorney, brought suit against Maria Meneghini Callas on behalf of E. Richard Bagarozy, claiming that his client had spent $85,000 on Callas's behalf. The suit cited the 1947 contract which granted Bagarozy power as the artist's sole representative. It also alleged that Callas refused to pay the prescribed percentage and that she "wrongfully attempted to sever the contract." The amount named in the suit was $300,000, and warrants of attachment were filed on Angel Records.

Maria promptly issued a denial of the Bagarozy claim, declaring that the 1947 contract was obtained under duress and that Bagarozy had done absolutely nothing to promote her career. A deposition hearing was ordered for November 8th, at which Maria failed to appear. But she retained a Chicago firm to represent her in what was to turn into three years of continuous legal maneuvers, with moves and countermoves on two continents. For the time being, however, there were no further disturbances of a legal or any other nature to cast a shadow on Chicago's 1954 love affair with Maria Callas.

Her conquest was not built on glamour alone. Other aspects of her career also seized the public fancy. Here was another American girl who had made good by her own talent and determination, another career launched and perfected abroad in the face of indifference at home, another poor girl attaining high status—in short, a good American success story.

It *was* a good story, much too good to be overlooked by the press. The presence of Maria's father, George Callas, solemn, proud, and somewhat overwhelmed by the dazzle and excitement, served to underline the "homecoming" aspect that appealed to one segment of the popular mind. The news about Maria's setting up her own housekeeping at the Ambassador Hotel, cooking Battista's favorite dishes on the evenings the Chicago Lyric did not require her services, and her frequent shopping excursions to the supermarkets took care of another. Who can resist a diva who is as handy with the gas range as she is with the funeral pyre?

On November 8th, the day Maria failed to appear in court, she went on stage as Violetta, a role she repeated on the 12th. By then the uncritical ecstasy of the opening week had subsided into more level-headed observations that allowed at least some division of opinion. Maria's tense and passionate approach to this Verdi heroine was too highly individual to be received anywhere with unanimous praise.

The *Traviata* performances also exposed the fact that the Chicago Lyric was far from being a smoothly oiled mechanism, which no one had expected it to be in the first place. True, it had Maria Callas, Leopold Simoneau, and Tito Gobbi in the principal roles—a cast of unquestioned magnitude. But the essential and often unsung core of singing character actors in the minor roles was hardly adequate to the task. What artists like the Metropolitan's Alessio de Paolis, George Cehanovsky, or Thelma Votipka can contribute to an evening's performance is evident only when they, or artists of their caliber, are *not* available to fill the same parts. Among the critics who were not fully convinced by Maria's characterization of Violetta was James Hinton, in whose view, as published by *Opera,* "the idea of Miss Callas mounting a pyre whose construction and lighting she had herself ordered is quite believable. But belief in the idea of Miss Callas lying poor and neglected in a furnished room is too much to ask of any audience."

All reservations disappeared, however, when the diva sang her first *Lucia di Lammermoor* on November 15th, opposite Giuseppe di Stefano and the giant-voiced baritone Gian-Giacomo Guelfi. "An innocent bystander wandering into last night's *Lucia* in the Civic Opera House might have thought Donizetti had scored the Mad Scene for the audience," observed Claudia Cassidy. What happened was that Callas was stopped right in the middle of her scene for an unprecedented two-minute ovation. Then she was allowed to finish the great aria only to be greeted by a much longer and even wilder jubilation. "No previous interpreter of Donizetti's score imbued the Mad Scene with so much heart-gripping poignance," wrote Felix Borowski in the Chicago *Sun-Times,* thereby paraphrasing the emphatic impressions previously voiced by critics in Mexico, Florence, Rome, and Milan.

Two evenings later, *Lucia* was repeated as the closing performance of the Lyric's 1954 season. Maria had twenty-two curtain calls and an ovation that lasted seventeen minutes. The audience found it difficult to let her go. Indeed, it was difficult to contemplate a full year without opera in Chicago. The consoling thought in everyone's mind was that the Lyric would be back in 1955, and so would Callas.

The Lyric's first season *was* an enormous success. Box-office take amounted to nearly $218,000, only $40,000 short of the possible maximum. The reported deficit was $13,958.42, a mere pittance as operatic deficits go, and it was promptly covered by the newly established Lyric Guild. The dream of Carol Fox and Lawrence Kelly, with the valuable assistance of Nicola Rescigno, who had conducted all performances, had turned into vigorous reality. The trio was already full of plans for the 1955 season and wanted, first of all, to secure the services of the Lyric's most valuable property, Maria Meneghini Callas.

But the Callas–Meneghini team did not operate that way. Clear heads above all, was their motto, and let no emotions and sentiments influence vital business decisions. The operatic season throughout the world was only beginning then—St. Ambrose Day was three weeks away—and La Scala was waiting. There were other commitments, other invitations. All had to be taken up and considered at the proper time. For the moment, good-bye kisses and a fond promise was all Maria could offer to her devoted Chicago associates. A contract? We shall see. With that, and with renewed expressions of affection for the Chicago public, Maria and her all-too-obviously happy (at the prospect of returning home) husband flew off to Italy.

Milan was astir with excitement about the activities of La Scala. One look at the printed program convinced any citizen that, in splendor, variety, scope, and daring, the 1954/1955 season would be nothing short of fabulous.

Another look was enough to reveal that the chauvinistic
agitations of the preceding season had had no effect
whatever on Ghiringhelli.

Of the twenty-one productions scheduled, no less than
eighteen were entirely new. (This fact alone would make
a Metropolitan habitué turn green with envy!) There was
to be a Wagner series with guest artists from the top of
the Bayreuth roster, the European première of Menotti's
The Saint of Bleecker Street, the La Scala première of
Gershwin's *Porgy and Bess.* Herbert von Karajan was
back, and so was Leonard Bernstein. Luchino Visconti,
one of the most coveted stage and motion picture directors,
was listed among the members of the directing staff. And,
the most sensational news of all, Arturo Toscanini, for the
first time in a quarter of a century, appeared at the head
of La Scala's conductors. The Maestro was to conduct
Verdi's *Falstaff* to inaugurate *La Piccola Scala,* the newly
built intimate theater adjacent to the main building (a plan
which, unfortunately, failed to materialize due to Toscanini's retirement that year).

Spontini's *La Vestale,* an opera absent from La
Scala's boards since 1929, was chosen to launch the new
season in style. Luchino Visconti was charged with the
responsibility of revitalizing the work for the exigencies
of the modern theater. To make the director's task somewhat easier, he was given a production budget of about
$140,000, an unprecedented amount, the disclosure of which
left the Italian press somewhere halfway between pride and
horror. The title role of *La Vestale* was one of five parts
Maria Callas was to assume that season. Renata Tebaldi
was scheduled to appear in only one opera (*La Forza del
Destino*)—this was the beginning of the end of their
Milanese rivalry.

The rehearsals of *La Vestale* were enlivened by

Toscanini's presence. The Maestro's relationship with Musical Director Victor de Sabata had been extremely cool for the past two decades. Now they were seen huddled together, discussing the finer points of the production with Antonino Votto, the conductor, and Luchino Visconti. Every move Toscanini made was big news in Milan, and his renewed interest in the theater's activities, as well as his reconciliation with De Sabata, received wide attention.

When Maria entered the theater for the first time after her Chicago triumph, svelte, blonde, and bubbling, she was delighted to see Toscanini. The Maestro was also in high spirits. His greeting came right to the point:

"What have you done with all that weight? How did you make yourself so pretty?"

"I've left all that weight to the other singers, Maestro," replied Maria.

When opening night came, everyone agreed that in point of lavishness *La Vestale* was an excellent choice to complement the luxury, pomp, and excitement of Milan on St. Ambrose Day. At the same time, many observers found the opera hopelessly outdated with its stilted libretto, noble but somewhat monotonous melodic lines, and absence of drama. It was a "minor league" *Norma,* worth re-examining on occasion but hardly strong enough to sustain itself in the repertoire.

However, the production was highly praised. Visconti had been working against heavy odds, production budget notwithstanding, and his staging displayed some anachronistic touches, but on the whole it pleased the press. Maria Callas shone again in a great tragic part, tailor-made for her stunning appearance and mastery of stagecraft. She was supported by Ebe Stignani, still the accomplished mistress of bel canto, Franco Corelli, already recognized among the leading Italian tenors, Nicola Rossi-Lemeni, the statuesque interpreter of High Priests, and Enzo Sordello, a promising new baritone.

Toscanini and De Sabata applauded with the rest of the audience from the proscenium box. At the end of the second act, when Maria came forward and was greeted by a downpour of carnations, she presented one, with a graceful bow, to Toscanini. The gesture, a superbly inspired combination of affection and primadonnaship, was greeted with a deafening applause and cries of "Viva Toscanini!" whereupon the Maestro retired to the sheltered rear portion of the box. The incident made front-page news the following day.

The season's next "Callas opera" should have been Verdi's *Il Trovatore,* but at the request of tenor Mario del Monaco, Giordano's *Andrea Chénier* was hastily substituted. Maria learned the part of Maddalena in five days, which seemed like old times. She did not resent this unscheduled crisis, but she did resent the fact that rumors were circulating blaming *her* for the substitution. If her partisans were steadily increasing, so were her antagonists who, in Maria's own words, "wanted her blood!"

Milan's restless natives, the hostile claque, made a particularly distasteful showing at the *prima* of *Andrea Chénier* on January 2, 1955. They chose the soprano's greatest moment, the third-act aria " La mamma morta," for a noisy demonstration. The incident bruised the evening's artistic pleasure but detracted very little from the over-all interpretation which, in the words of critic Emilio Radius, ". . . would have left the good Giordano open-mouthed with admiration." The composer's widow was on hand to congratulate the prima donna after the performance.

After the series of *Andrea Chénier,* Maria went to Rome to bring her celebrated interpretation of Cherubini's

Medea to the stage of the Rome Opera. La Scala's spectacular production by Margherita Wallman was transferred to Rome in its technical entirety. There were changes in the cast, however. Although Fedora Barbieri repeated her Milan interpretation of Neris, there was a new Jason, Francesco Albanese, and a new Creon, Boris Christoff. Gabriele Santini was the conductor.

It was a stormy Roman holiday. Renata Tebaldi had opened the Rome season six weeks earlier, and the local ranks of the *Tebaldiani* were keeping their powder dry for the rival.

Maria, ever the perfectionist, insisted on the maximum number of full dress rehearsals, which her colleagues considered unduly tiring and excessive. But Maria's wishes prevailed, a fact which only increased resentment. At the *prima,* on January 20th, noisy demonstrations by rival claques sporadically kept attention from centering on the stage. To add fuel to the backstage fires, Boris Christoff had a violent disagreement with Maria Callas. It ended by the basso's bodily blocking Maria's attempt to make a solo bow.

At the more subdued repeat performances, more attention could be given to musical values. Again, *Medea* was hailed as a great scenic triumph. By this time Maria's theatrical mastery, partly under Visconti's influence and partly due to her own intuitive gifts, had reached full flower. Her stage movements, for instance, were a science in themselves; her gestures, her magnetic oval eyes, her billowing cloak, her leopard-like sweep along the elaborate staircase—all were parts of a dramatic design subtly controlled and calculated.

"It was a fiery, shrieking, demoniacal, truly stupendous characterization," commented Giorgio Vigolo. "It is no wonder that she has had so much success in creating sorceresses (Kundry, Armida, Medea). There is something strangely magical in her voice, a kind of vocal alchemy...."

At that time, however, the *real* Maria Callas was very far from being a sorceress. Back home, completely exhausted from the harrowing Rome episode, and troubled by a painful and annoying boil on the back of her neck, she was forced to retire to her apartment at Milan's Grand Hotel for a prolonged stay. Her next La Scala production, Bellini's *La Sonnambula,* originally scheduled for February 17th, had to be postponed two weeks.

The days of calling the Grand Hotel her home were numbered. Meneghini was already supervising the final touches on their new town house on Via Michelangelo Buonarroti, a four-story building, more a palazzo than a house, all glass, metal, and red marble, with Renaissance paintings, antique decorations, and luxurious furniture. Meneghini was no longer tied to his paternal Verona by business interests. Milan, the home of La Scala and Italy's operatic capital, had become their home.

While Maria was obeying her doctor's orders, resting her nerves and treating the pain on her neck—amidst frequent visits to her piano to practice La Sonnambula, her newly acquired role—Lawrence Kelly arrived, deeply concerned about the approaching Chicago season, for which Callas was an absolute must. Maria was cordial, full of fond reminiscences about the Chicago days, but still not ready to talk business. She did have one suggestion to make, however, and a rather startling one:

"You should sign up Renata Tebaldi. Then your audience will have the opportunity to compare us, and your season will be even more successful."

But without Callas, thought Kelly, there might not be a season. So as soon as the diva was feeling better and began circulating, he followed her doggedly in the hope of landing the coveted contract. They would meet at the swank Biffi Scala restaurant while Maria went over scenic details with Visconti and musical ones with Leonard Bernstein, conductor of the Bellini opera. The Chicago repertoire was discussed again, the casts, and the terms. Kelly agreed to all requests. Finally, several days later, when they ran out of points to discuss, she signed the contract.

By that time, however, the document had incorporated several unusual clauses. The management of the Chicago Lyric had taken on the responsibility of keeping an eye on Bagarozy's legal maneuvers, to protect Callas and her husband against legal proceedings and any harassments during the season. The document had only the reluctant blessing of the Meneghini attorneys. They would have preferred it if Maria had abstained from the journey altogether.

In early March, *La Sonnambula* was finally mounted. It was another winning entry of the Callas-Visconti combination. In the elegant, somewhat mannered, pastoral atmosphere Visconti conjured up for Bellini's gentle opera, Callas moved with the grace and agility of a ballerina. She sang the final bravura air "Ah! non giunge" with all the lights turned on—another inspired Visconti touch.

Turning back to a coloratura part after a swing through the big dramatic roles of *La Vestale, Medea,* and *Andrea Chénier* left no noticeable strain on Maria's vocal equipment. But, as one of the critics aptly pointed out, she was ". . . not a *leggiera* in the ordinary sense. She goes about refining and ennobling her strange, mysterious, and sometimes even unyielding voice from one act to another, by degrees, until she reaches the heights of Paradise." Great compliments were also paid to the admirable rapport beween Callas and conductor Leonard Bernstein. The latter, though less ideally suited to Bellini's gentle lyricism

than to the stormy drama of the previous season's *Medea,*
nevertheless made a favorable impression with the critics.

During April, La Scala's audience was finally allowed
the rare pleasure of enjoying both Maria and Renata under
the same ornate roof. Maria appeared in Franco Zeffirelli's
effervescent production of Rossini's *Il Turco in Italia,*
which Milan had not seen since the composer was a young
man back in 1814. The well-oiled precision of the ensemble
—once again composed of the veterans of the opera's 1950
rediscovery and its subsequent recorded interpreters—was
a delight to watch. Callas, Rossi-Lemeni, and the old master Mariano Stabile sang with gusto and acted in the grand
manner of the *commedia dell'arte.*

Renata Tebaldi, who had made her Metropolitan
Opera debut on January 31st, returned to La Scala on
April 21st as a sumptuous-voiced Leonora in Verdi's *La
Forza del Destino.* She came, saw, conquered—and departed. Without fanfare, without any press announcements (at that time), she decided to remove herself from
the arena. Neither her rabid partisans nor her detractors
had foreseen just how firm she would remain in her decision. La Scala was not to see her again until December 9,
1959. In the spring of 1955, however, even such sage observers as critic Emilio Radius dismissed the rivalry as an
artificial phenomenon. "Let us be thankful," he wrote,
"that we have two such great sopranos. Would that we had
two similar rivals among the baritones!"

Maria was giving little thought to rivalry in those
days. She was getting ready for the season's most eagerly
awaited event, a completely new and adventurous production of Verdi's *La Traviata* under Visconti's direction,
with Giuseppe di Stefano and Ettore Bastianini as her
partners.

Visconti approached the Verdi opera from a highly

original viewpoint. Reducing the superficial glitter of conventional productions, he highlighted the story's tragic undertones. Even more significantly, he advanced the action some forty years into the gaslit atmosphere of Paris in the late 1880's. Violetta thus was fashioned into an operatic cousin of Zola's *Nana,* surrounded by countless touches of Zola-esque realism.

To Maria Callas, the part represented a tremendous challenge. She had sung Violetta many times before, frequently to clamorous ovations. Still, she knew that the absolute, unreserved success of her Norma or her Medea had never been hers in this elusive role. She also knew that when Renata had sung the role in 1951 she, too, had failed to please the public. In 1955 Maria had no contemporary rivals as Violetta, but she still had to contend with the long-lingering memories of Toti dal Monte and Claudia Muzio.

She went about perfecting her interpretation in every painstaking detail. Nuances of movements, gestures, facial expressions were rehearsed endlessly, to the equally fastidious Visconti's untiring delight. Witnessing their rapt concentration on countless time-consuming minutiae, and growing visibly more and more tired of it all with each passing day, was Giuseppe di Stefano. An operatic artist, he would openly say, has one principal duty, to sing. Acting is important, but it can be carried to the extreme, to the point of interfering with the beauty of the singing. The impatient tenor made no effort to hide his resentment over what he plainly considered exaggerations.

The *prima,* on May 19th, aroused some critics to an outcry of consternation against Luchino Visconti's innovations which, in the opinion of Teodoro Celli, "disfigured and defiled" the Verdi opera. There were two instances in particular which provoked the critic's ire. One occurred at

the end of the first act, when Violetta sat on a table and
threw away her shoes before attacking the brilliant aria
"Sempre libera." The other, and even more controversial,
innovation took place in the final scene where Violetta was
made to collapse and expire with her hat and coat on, ready
to leave the house. It was decidedly not Visconti's day.
Some critics, evidently annoyed that the star system had
already extended to stage directors as well, voiced their
dislike even at the obtrusive way Visconti's name appeared
on the posters.

But for Maria Callas, the evening was an almost
unanimous triumph. "This aristocrat of the dramatic and
vocal art," wrote the critic of *24 Ore,* "was able to return
the opera its aura of fervor, its atmosphere of throbbing
anguish of which the director was determined to rob the
performance." Maria's pathetic, death-haunted portrayal,
admirably supported by a seemingly limitless range of
vocal shadings and accents, caused many to recall Garbo's
Camille. Here and there some voiced certain reservations;
but there were always reservations, they were nothing new.
There were also audible expressions of disapproval by the
open antagonists for whom she could never do right. Yet,
somehow, even violent antagonism would not keep them
from missing a Callas opening.

After a string of ensemble curtain calls, conductor
Carlo Maria Giulini suggested that Maria take a solo bow.
Thunderous ovation greeted her. As she retired behind
the curtain to rejoin her colleagues, her Alfredo, Giuseppe
di Stefano, was nowhere to be found. While Maria had been
taking her solo curtain call, he had stalked back, fuming,
to his dressing room. He dressed quickly and, without a
word, left the theater, left the production, and, as it turned
out, left the city. In *La Traviata's* subsequent showings,
his role was taken by Giacinto Prandelli.

The night *La Traviata* was given for the third time,

the soprano's great moment in the first act, the bravura aria "Sempre libera," was interrupted by a noisy demonstration calculated to occur at an exposed vocal passage and ruin the entire effect. It all worked according to plan. Maria's singing was brought to a perplexing halt. The audience gasped. An ominous silence hung over the auditorium. But a moment later Maria composed herself and, regaining her strength from the sudden shock, completed the aria. The curtain fell.

This was no time for diplomacy. Maria insisted on a solo curtain call. She wanted to defy her enemies, to face the reaction of the entire public, to witness a display of their true feelings. As always, the persistent whistles and catcalls disappeared in the gales of fiery homage and admiration. In the face of that vivifying reaction, the artist's cold and contemptuous expression soon reverted to smiles of gratitude, appreciation, and renewed confidence.

So ended Maria's busiest, most taxing and most tumultuous season at La Scala. If she was the Queen, as the press asserted, the crown was more often than not a heavy burden. Nearly every performance brought audible and often violent demonstrations of hostility. Resentment followed her every step within the walls of La Scala.

Opera singers thrive on adulation and glorification, and nearly every famous colleague felt that an excessively large share of public attention had been monopolized by Maria Callas. It was she who always appeared in the press, it was she who could, in the popular view, make or break a performance. Everything she did, her stubborn self-righteousness at rehearsals, her perfectionist exaggerations, her independent mind versus the management, the homage that followed her everywhere, the way she held court at the elegant Biffi Scala restaurant surrounded by socialites, snobs, and sycophants, led inevitably to resentment.

Nor was Maria's attitude calculated to calm the atmosphere. Defiance and unwillingness to retreat from real or even imagined hostility were her characteristic traits. Formal, courteous, but aloof in her relationship with fellow artists, she made no effort to seek the cloak of modesty to conceal her pride. Toward the management, she acted in full awareness of her value, secure in the knowledge that her art was in demand everywhere in the world. Art was all important, she would often say, but if she could not serve Art in her own way, at her own terms, she could always retire from opera. At times when momentary tensions and pressures might have forced a temporary weakening, the steady reassurance and encouragement of Battista Meneghini quickly infused her with renewed strength.

Maria knew her worth to La Scala, knew that her presence meant excitement, unflagging interest, and sold-out houses, and saw no reason to be retiring about it. She would even appear in Ghiringhelli's proscenium box on occasion, a privilege not usually granted to artists, as if to underline her Queen-like status, to applaud her colleagues on the stage. To some it was a sight to provoke cold fury.

This controversial situation was hotly debated in musical and extra-musical circles. During the summer of 1955, it elicited an editorial in the magazine *La Scala* which gave proof that the artist was not inaccurate in appraising her own significance to the theater.

"No doubt Callas has many enemies. First of all, her colleagues who are convinced that to be a native Italian and endowed by nature with a lovely voice is all that is needed. They are only concerned with the emission of notes and with singing in the manner of fifty years ago, without ever straying their eyes from the conductor's baton. These people, who are organically incapable of sacrifice and effort, who owe nothing to study and all to nature and accident, accuse Maria Callas of aggressiveness because, as a result of much sacrifice and effort, she is vocally and physically able to sing and interpret everything. Then there are some critics, people whose taste was formed in our own times. They hate traditional opera, and detest the artist who is capable of attracting the attention of this generation to the beauties of *Norma, Lucia,* or *La Traviata.* Shall we say that the clamorous recognition and her own striking personality will rise above the attacks? Is this a consolation for Callas? One thing is certain: the price to pay for separation from the herd is high."

To commemorate the end of another great season, and in special recognition of Maria's triumph in *La Traviata,* Ghiringhelli presented her with an exquisitely wrought silver mirror. In the summer months that followed, Maria busied herself with decorating her beautiful new home on the Via Buonarroti. Ghiringhelli's gift was given a prominent place among the many treasures she and Battista had collected.

Pictures soon began to circulate in the magazines showing the sumptuous interiors of the Meneghini residence—everything about La Callas was news. "La Divina," "Voce di Angelo," the papers would call her, sometimes facetiously, sometimes scornfully, sometimes in dead earnest. They reported on her shopping trips through the fashionable stores in Milan. They followed her on the daily strolls down the Via Monte Napoleone with fashion magazines tucked under her arm, gazing intently at the inviting windows through rimless glasses.

There was no traveling about Italy that season. Rome did not see her after the stormy January series of *Medea.* On the horizon loomed her first appearance in Germany. After that, Chicago. . . .

As usual, summer brought with it the inevitable and important recording obligations. Callas had spent July

learning a new role, Madama Butterfly, for the coming
Chicago appearances; she sang it for the first time before
the recording microphones in early August. Herbert von
Karajan conducted in his capacity as official La Scala
conductor. Then the podium was taken over by the familiar
jovial figure of Tullio Serafin, under whose baton *Aida* and
Rigoletto were added to the swelling list of Maria's recorded operas. In the latter, the Duke of Mantua was
sung by temperamental Giuseppe di Stefano, now in a
simmered-down, post-season mood.

In August, Elvira de Hidalgo, who had been teaching
at the Conservatory of Ankara, Turkey, for the last several
years, came to Milan for her vacation. Teacher and former
pupil had a fond reunion reliving old memories. Much had
happened in the intervening years, but Maria had lost none
of her affection and gratitude toward the artist and friend
who had been so vital in the formation of her own career.
In a way, they had never been far apart. Correspondence
had never stopped between them; De Hidalgo was always
informed first-hand about Maria's plans, engagements,
impressions, and, sometimes, problems. Another link was
Luis de Hidalgo, Elvira's brother, a resident of Milan, and
one of Maria's close friends.

On September 24th, a sterling contingent of La Scala
singers arrived at the West Berlin airport for a two-eve-
ning guest appearance at the City Opera. The event was
incorporated into the "Berlin Festival Weeks." Interest
was unprecedented. Hundreds of enthusiasts spent the
night in front of the theater, waiting for the box office to
open, with the result that both performances were sold out
immediately. Berliners were reminded of La Scala's unforgettable 1929 visit, when Arturo Toscanini had still
been at the helm.

For the Berlin journey, La Scala had assembled a first-

line cast of principal singers: Maria Meneghini Callas,
Giuseppe di Stefano, Rolando Panerai, Nicola Zaccaria.
The conductor? Herbert von Karajan, the musical Pooh-
Bah, now in his capacity as musical director of the Berlin
Philharmonic. The opera to be performed on the two eve-
nings was Donizetti's *Lucia di Lammermoor,* the joint
Callas–Karajan triumph at La Scala in 1954.

On both evenings, September 29th and October 2nd,
the Berliners were completely overwhelmed. "Maria Meneghini Callas made it clear in this interpretation what
song and art can be," wrote *Der Tagesspiegel.* "This was
no mere virtuosity but an all-encompassing characterization which turns the voice into an instrument of unlimited
expressivity. . . . One does not know what to single out in
her characterization, it was *complete,* with her incompa-
rable magic, her portrayal, her pale beauty."

Desmond Shawe-Taylor, the visiting English critic,
commented revealingly in *Opera* on another aspect of the
Callas art:

"Her performance did not end with the Mad Scene;
through ten minutes of solo curtain calls she remained with
consummate art half within the stage character, with her
air of wondering simplicity, her flawless miming of un-
worthiness, her subtle variation in the tempo of successive
appearances and in the depth of successive curtseys, and
her elaborate byplay with the roses which fell from the gallery—one of which, with such a gesture and such capital
aim, she flung to the delighted flautist! An artist to her
finger-tips!"

While La Scala was touring Berlin, Chicago returned
to the throes of operatic fever. According to all indications,
the new season would leave even the miraculous two weeks

of 1954 far behind. This time, five weeks of opera were programmed, all with mouth-watering casts. Fox and Kelly had Maria Callas for opening night, and Renata Tebaldi for the night to follow. To keep them company, Giuseppe di Stefano, Tito Gobbi, Jussi Bjoerling, Ebe Stignani, Nicola Rossi-Lemeni! To share the directorial responsibilities with Rescigno, no less eminent a figure than Tullio Serafin!

So La Divina returned to the buzzing excitement of Chicago, the city which, to quote her own words "gave her its heart." She was more glamorous than ever, resplendent in Madame Biki's newest creations and, as was inevitably noted by the sharper eyes, a number of Dior originals. There were also sizable additions in her jewelry, a testimony to Meneghini's devotion and generosity. Battista was, of course, at her side, energetic and attentive at all times, but still resenting the unavoidable English language.

By then there were familiar faces to greet, many friends everywhere, admirers without number, and open manifestations of adulation. The inner circle gathered at the small apartment hotel the Meneghinis elected for the occasion, but Maria and Battista attended all the necessary social functions and never missed an opportunity to compliment the opera management, to further the interests of the Lyric, and to say the kind and diplomatic things that assure the best possible public relations.

Maria's press in Chicago was undivided in its devotion. The height attained by the city's collective ardor can be illustrated by a brief excerpt from a column by Roger Dettmer, music critic of the Chicago *American*:

"The Town, we all know, has been Callas-crazy for more than a year, and none has been more demented than I. In the proper role and in good voice, I adore the woman; I am a slave in her spell."

It may be counted among Maria Callas's most remarkable attainments that she was able to inspire music critics —and not only in Chicago—to such fervent effusions.

The program of the first two weeks of that season bears reproduction:

October 31/November 2	*I Puritani:* Callas, Di Stefano, Rossi-Lemeni
November 1/4	*Aida:* Tebaldi, Varnay, Antonioli, Gobbi
November 5/8	*Il Trovatore:* Callas, Stignani, Bjoerling, Bastianini
November 7/9	*La Bohème:* Tebaldi, Di Stefano, Gobbi
November 11/14	*Madama Butterfly:* Callas, Di Stefano, Weede
November 15	*Faust:* Carteri, Bjoerling, Rossi-Lemeni

The audience that jammed the Opera House on opening night was so primed, remarked one of the critics, that "... anything short of a disaster was almost bound to be a triumph." From the moment Callas stepped out on stage in the beginning of the second scene, and was greeted with an ovation that stopped the performance for minutes, the evening remained true to expectations.

The following day, the critics were unanimous in Maria's praise—with the usual observations about moments of strain and unsteadiness—but took a rather dim view of *I Puritani's* ineffective drama. Bellini's opera had not been seen in Chicago in anyone's memory prior to that evening, and even the exceptional singers failed to swell measurably the ranks of its devotees. All hands agreed, on the other hand, that the new season of the Lyric was off to another glittering start.

Renata Tebaldi came and triumphed the following evening. Maria was in the audience, applauded politely,

and made complimentary remarks about her rival throughout the evening. During the two weeks of their stay, the
two prima donnas shared the same dressing room, shared
the warmest ovations in the evening and the highest acco-
lades in the daily press, enjoyed the homage of an equally
large and equally demonstrative throng of fans—and managed to avoid each other completely. In a press interview,
Renata disclaimed all rumors of animosity and refused to
concede the existence of a rivalry between them.

What Bellini's low-keyed tragedy failed to accomplish
on opening night, Verdi's torrid *Il Trovatore* most emphatically succeeded in doing on November 5th. The audience
that evening was reminiscent of the most frenzied moments
of the previous season. Verdi's blood-stirring music received its most exciting performance in America in many
a year. Ebe Stignani, a rare visitor in America and never a
member of the Metropolitan, sang an unforgettable
Azucena. Jussi Bjoerling was a Manrico beyond vocal comparison. As Leonora, Callas gave an "exquisitely Spanish" color to the role and revealed unsuspected dramatic
subtleties in her characterization. Her singing, particularly in the last act, was "breathtakingly beautiful." In the
words of Jussi Bjoerling—whose career, regrettably, did
not again cross that of Callas—"her Leonora was perfection. I have heard the role sung often, but never was there
a better one than hers."

Il Trovatore was repeated on November 8th. That
afternoon, at 5:30 p.m., shortly before going on stage,
Maria Meneghini Callas and the Metropolitan Opera
finally came to terms. To Maria's terms. The momentous
agreement was signed at a dinner table, with Maria sitting
between Jussi Bjoerling and Rudolf Bing. The latter implanted a courtly kiss on Maria's hand to seal the agreement, which went over so impressively that he had to repeat

it several times for the benefit of the onrushing photographers. The big story, of course, hit the late editions of the evening papers immediately.

Although the exact terms were never revealed, it was a foregone conclusion that the Metropolitan's long-standing top limit of $1,000 for a performance was consigned to history with the signing of that contract. It was a great triumph for Maria Callas—the scene was reminiscent of Appomattox, though Robert Lee Bing looked much too pleased in his state of "vanquishment." It took little to discover that there was only one loser in the turn of events —Chicago. The announcement was made immediately that Maria would open the Metropolitan's season on October 29, 1956. Because of the conflict of dates she would, therefore, be prevented from returning to Chicago for another season. Maria made no immediate comments on that issue. To an inquiring reporter, who was anxious to learn the terms of the newly signed Metropolitan contract, she volunteered her opinion that "no fee is high enough" for singing *Norma*.

The season continued. *Madama Butterfly* was mounted on November 11th with the staging by Hizi Koyke, an authentic and expert Butterfly of the previous generation, whose directing touches contributed to Maria's interesting portrayal. It was the first time she sang the role on any stage.

Like most artists, Callas found it an almost insuperable challenge to bridge the gap between the dramatic characterization of a fifteen-year-old and the sensuous, passionate music Puccini wrote for this fragile heroine. Unlike many artists who do not even try to convey the illusion of childishness through dramatic and vocal means —physical endowments make this a formidable if not impossible task for most sopranos—Callas was determined

to accomplish just that. The amount of thought and preparation that went into her portrayal was astonishing.

Completely immersed in the part of this graceful and
delicate figure, she performed in the words of one critic
(Irving Sablosky of the Chicago *Daily News*) "as if she
were a fully trained member of the Kabuki Theater. After
the crucial first act she handled Butterfly's transformation
into a woman matured in despair and suffering with penetrating insight. Her characterization grew increasing powerful as the opera moved inexorably toward its heartbreaking climax." But even with all her superior efforts,
the role remained the least convincing of the six characterizations undertaken in Chicago. In the light of her success, this conclusion simply enhances the glory of the other
five.

After the second *Madama Butterfly* on November
14th, Maria's contractual obligation had been fulfilled. But
Chicago was in no mood to let her go. She consented to
appear once again in the Puccini opera on November 17th.
Lines began to form immediately after the announcement
was made, and the house was completely sold out in a
matter of hours.

On the evening of November 17th, Chicago's Callas
fever reached its zenith. The applause after the first and
second acts seemed never-ending. When the final curtain
rang down the diva was called back repeatedly, and she had
another opportunity to confirm the oft-voiced observation
that even curtain calls can become artistic performances at
times. Finally, visibly exhausted and tear-streaked with
emotion, she waved her final fond good-bye, left the stage—
and ran headlong into a platoon of process-servers who had
swarmed into the privacy of her dressing room like the
furies out of Hades, waiting in ambush for their prey.

These faithful and constitutionally insensitive servants of Justice, acting in the methodical manner of their profession, treated La Divina with about as much consideration as she would have expected from the sansculottes of the French Revolution in *Andrea Chénier's* final act. While Maria stood transfixed with speechless bewilderment, one of them met his triumphant moment of truth—bodily contact with the subject in the manner required by law—by forcing the summons into Maria's kimono.

With this, Maria found her voice. But if it was the voice of an angel, it resounded with the terror of the final judgment. Out of the costume of the fragile Cio Cio San came the shrieking, near-hysterical fury of Medea in a streak of venomous epithets. The room was filled with photographers, and in that instant she was captured, for posterity, eyes aflame, face distorted with uncontrollable fury, kimono flying, and finger pointing with an outraged gesture toward the bewildered figure of Marshal Stanley Pringle, servant of law and order, who had probably left his home that day in the belief that he was carrying out a routine assignment.

Carol Fox and Lawrence Kelly stood by dumbfounded as they heard the operatic idol exclaim "Chicago will be sorry for this!" The outraged Meneghini was consoling his wife, with one arm protectively around her shoulder, the other shaking menacingly to the accompaniment of fuming and fanciful Italian imprecations. The situation was tragic and grotesque at the same time. The sustained glory of hard work and inspired effort was nullified by one moment's shocking turnabout.

How did it happen? During Maria's stay in Chicago the Lyric's managers had maintained the careful vigil required by Maria's contract. However, the excitement of her farewell performance, the festive and emotional occasion, had brought about a relaxation of caution. Edward

Bagarozy's legal representatives had waited for just such a moment. They found allies in certain disgruntled elements within the very organization of the Lyric who were upset about the prima donna's "abandoning" the city in favor of the Metropolitan. With the aid of this fifth column, the protective curtain was broken, and the trap was set.

Her temper spent, her diatribes dissolved into helpless sobbing, Maria Callas set secluded in her dressing room. In the city that had surrounded her with avowals of affection, where she had thought she had had only friends, she was betrayed and delivered to her enemies. The impersonal, unfeeling methods in the "due process of law" were transformed in her eyes into manifestations of black treason. There was no way to stop her tears. There was no way to gain her forgiveness, or even attention.

The press made the most of the incident. The Associated Press photo of the historic event adorned newspaper front pages from coast to coast. Talks about the oft-intimated Callas temperament sprang into prominence. Comments were made about her alleged childhood in the slums, which some imaginative chroniclers placed in Brooklyn, others in Manhattan's Hell's Kitchen. It was a shattering and ignoble end to a two-year love affair.

The following day, with nothing but bitterness in her heart, the unforgiving diva left the United States.

CHAPTER 9

At Last, the Metropolitan

Leonora
Sono giunta . . . grazie o Dio
VERDI — LA FORZA DEL DESTINO

No sooner had the dust finally settled on the tempestuous Chicago episode, than the Italian newspapers had another Callas headline. This one was more in a comic vein; and, had Maria been in a more light-hearted mood, she might even have found the new development somewhat entertaining. As things were, however, she could see no humor whatever in the advertisements circulated in the late fall of 1955 by Pastificio Pantanella, a Roman firm of spaghetti makers.

According to their flamboyant claim, Maria Callas's spectacular slimming-down had been caused by a steady diet of Pantanella's "psychological macaroni." To lend medical support to the allegation, an affidavit was incorporated in the advertisements by a certain Dr. Giovanni Cazzarolli. It was cautiously worded, but the implication was quite clear.

First, Maria issued a telegraphic demand to desist from the unauthorized use of her name. Then she filed suit. The resulting litigation, which was subsequently christened "the battle of spaghetti," lingered on for years. When last heard from, in August, 1959, Maria was awarded damages by the Rome Appeals Court, which upheld the decision of the lower bench.

Against this improbable background, Maria Meneghini Callas celebrated her thirty-second birthday and made her preparations for her fifth Milan season. On December 7th, she appeared in La Scala's gala opening-night showcase for the fourth time, an honor which was automatically hers, as Renata Tebaldi was no longer a member of the theater. Although by then opening nights were hardly a novelty to her, the aura of excitement was still there.

The theater celebrated St. Ambrose Day 1955 with becoming magnificence. President Gronchi was in the audience. Stunning gowns and sparkling diadems paraded against a background of floral designs especially created for La Scala by Balmain of Paris. The opening-night attraction was Bellini's *Norma.*

Observers detected a slight vocal strain in Maria's performance, but dramatically, her Norma was impeccable, ranging from melting femininity to imperious power. "Watching her perform is hard on Maria Callas's adversaries," noted critic Emilio Radius (a consistent nonadversary), "for while she does have moments that fortify one's opposition, they are usually followed by impressions which compel admiration against one's wishes for this greatest and most unusual artist of the century!"

The disturbing demonstrators, "hissing snakes," Maria called them, were back as expected. Apart from the usual noise, their activity this time was also responsible for spreading the rumor that Maria, determined to take a solo bow, had prevented Mario del Monaco from joining her by a well-aimed kick in the shin. This contributed another fictitious entry to the blossoming Callas lore.

On the other hand, to call the Callas–Del Monaco relationship during these *Norma* performances idyllic would also be grossly misleading. The storm clouds had already begun to gather during rehearsals when the tenor served notice on Ghiringhelli that he would not consent to solo curtain calls *for any artist*. (Del Monaco was a veteran of several seasons at the Metropolitan and, evidently, sympathized with Bing's "American plan.")

Thus, ensemble curtain calls were strictly observed on opening night and thereafter, in a rather cool atmosphere. At one of the repeat performances, in early January, there must have been an unusual number of fervent Del Monaco admirers present, judging by an unprecedentedly enthusiastic ovation during the first act. The ever-watchful, ever-faithful Meneghini grew immediately suspicious. During the intermission, he complained to Ettore Parmeggiani, the official claque chief, suggesting that the claque had perhaps overstepped the boundaries of nonpartisanship.

Parmeggiani indignantly refuted the charge, and sought Del Monaco's support. The tenor, boiling with rage, took after Meneghini.

"You and your wife don't own La Scala, you know!" he thundered at the top of his Otello voice. "The audience applauds whoever deserves applause."

Words followed and the fracas ended by Meneghini's walking away while Del Monaco was still storming at him.

During the remainder of that evening, the joint cur-

tain calls were even more strained than usual. Maria and
Mario faced the audience with their hands linked in de-
ceptive comradeship, while alternately smiling through
clenched teeth and arguing incessantly as the curtain rose
and fell. When the performance was over, the arguments
grew even more intensified, each artist calling the other a
poor colleague. At one of the tenor's particularly sharp-
tongued remarks, Maria came close to lunging at him when
Meneghini finally managed to spirit her away.

This flareup, like other similar crises among opera's
high-strung personalities, did not have a lasting effect on
the relationship of these two artists. Reminiscing about the
incident a year later in an Italian magazine, Del Monaco
commented: "Much has been said about the clamorous
clash between us that took place in January, 1956. On the
other hand, no one talks about other aspects of our artistic
coexistence in various parts of the globe, which denote
sincere mutual respect. One has to look at both sides of the
coin."

On January 18, 1956, Visconti's controversial production of *La Traviata* was returned to La Scala's repertoire
as a holdover from the previous season. Once more Ettore
Bastianini sang the elder Germont, while Gianni Raimondi
assumed the part of Alfredo. The critics were again
divided. Some, including certain visiting foreign observers,
voiced rapt admiration, while Celli, unrelenting in his
opposition, went to the point of protesting against the
management's abandoning two earlier and still perfectly
serviceable production settings (left over from 1947 and
1951) for the Visconti escapade.

But whatever the critics may have thought of Visconti's innovations, *La Traviata* again proved to be the
most exciting and provocative production of the season,
with an extraordinary total of twenty performances. Judg-

ing by the enthusiasm of the audience—nearly all performances were sell-outs—Maria's intense and individual portrayal of Violetta was gaining rabid partisans with each
repetition. Her identification with the heroine seemed to
deepen with each performance, and the totality of her
characterization, equally rewarding in its dramatic and
musical aspects, was irresistible. Conservative critics were
delighted with the Callas solution to the thorny problem
of the final scene : she followed Visconti's direction up to a
point, then let the controversial hat drop to the floor un-
obtrusively at the crucial moment, allowing Violetta to
expire bare-headed, as sanctioned by tradition, and not in
the all-dressed-up-and-ready-to-go manner of Visconti's
innovation.

One of the twenty *Traviatas* of that season will be long
remembered. The final curtain had fallen and Maria came
to take her bows before the cheering, applauding audience.
Bouquets were brought on, roses and carnations were
thrown before her feet—all this was warm and affectionate, but in no way unusual. Suddenly, a bunch of radishes
and carrots fell on the stage, pitched from the gallery. The
audience gasped in astonishment, recognizing the insult
several seconds before it became apparent to the near-
sighted recipient. Finally, Maria disgustedly kicked the
bunch to a remote corner of the stage, and left. Meneghini,
at his customary post in the wings, was livid with rage. He
would not let Maria go on with her career, he swore, if it
meant one indignity upon another. After all, she did not
need La Scala, and she did not need money. . . .

For several days, the incident kept Milan buzzing. The
vegetables in question were out of season, noted some fastidious observers. Numerous wild theories circulated about
the mysterious perpetrators. That intramural intrigues
had played a part in the episode was doubted by hardly

anyone, least of all by Maria Callas. At least this made it easier for her to get over the bitter taste of the vegetable tribute.

The second half of La Scala's season was to bring excitements of a vastly different kind for Maria. Following Norma and Violetta, her most famous characterizations, she was to add two major roles to her repertoire and, in characteristic fashion, two that were poles apart: Rosina in Rossini's *The Barber of Seville,* and the title role in Giordano's *Fedora.* A parallel undertaking of this sort is probably unmatched in the annals of opera.

Unless undertaken by a coloratura mezzo, the rare type of voice for which Rossini had conceived the part, Rosina is generally interpreted by coloratura sopranos with voices suitable in range and technique to such roles as *Rigoletto's* Gilda and *La Sonnambula's* Amina. Fedora, on the other hand, requires the voice of a dramatic soprano capable of handling such parts as Tosca and Maddalena of *Andrea Chénier.* In point of dramatic character, the two roles are no less divergent. Rosina is a youthful schemer, carefree, capricious, and virginal. Fedora is glamorous, passionate, intense in her love and hate, an ominous *femme fatale.* Rosina is the embodiment of the late eighteenth century's stylized delicacy; Fedora a full-blooded creation of the late nineteenth century's stormy *verismo.* The contrast was forbidding in its challenge, but meeting such challenges head-on was precisely what has made Callas the operatic personality she is.

The Rossini opera was staged first, on February 16, 1956. It did not please the critics, who deplored the heavy directorial hand, which substituted vulgarity for true Rossinian lightheartedness. Nor was Maria's interpretation received with unanimous praise. The part lay very gratefully in her range, displaying both the agility of her upper register and the richness of her lower tones. What disturbed the experts—and later some listeners of Maria's recorded portrayal of the role—was that Maria had failed to emerge as a convincing ingenue. With her powerful personality, the magnetic qualities of her acting, and a voice that impresses even in moments when it fails to please, she made the amorous by-play with gentle-voiced tenor Luigi Alva a rather lopsided affair. Even more significantly, she shifted the emphasis from Tito Gobbi's endearing, graceful but not overly dynamic Figaro—the central point of plot interest—to her own doings. Librettist and composer may have conceived Figaro as the motor behind the opera's fast-moving action. But, as Teodoro Celli observed, alongside the high-powered Diesel of Callas, Gobbi seemed more like a modest "scooter."

Maria's highly individual Rosina was recorded a year later with the almost identical cast of La Scala's 1956 production. After leaving this audible replica for posterity, she has evidenced no further interest in the role.

Between these two Scala productions during the spring of 1956, the paths of opera's two reigning queens converged on Naples. After completing her second Metropolitan season, Renata Tebaldi had come to participate in a memorable revival of Rossini's *William Tell* under Tullio Serafin's baton. The opera was returned to the repertoire of San Carlo after an absence of twenty-six years. Renata was in excellent form and the production, first introduced on March 21st, turned out to be the top sensation of the Naples season. Maria's appearance as Lucia on April 8th was the first in five years at San Carlo. She was not in her best voice, but had a warm reception nevertheless. Their schedules worked out so that there was no contact between the two leading sopranos.

Tebaldi went on to a series of engagements in Rome

and thence to inaugurate the Maggio Musicale Fiorentino in Verdi's *La Traviata*. A group of Callas fanatics there caused such a noisy demonstration against her that Renata came close to a nervous breakdown. Apparently, whether the rivals were present in the same theater or not, the battle of the claques raged on.

From Naples, Maria returned to Milan to prepare for her final Scala series of the season in Giordano's *Fedora*. In transplanting this Sardou melodrama to the operatic stage in 1898, Giordano established an outpost in modernism with his plot of political intrigues, Russian emigrés, nihilists, a "contemporary" setting, and a straightforward approach to the state of unwedded bliss. But by 1956, the shock appeal had gone out of *Fedora,* the erstwhile trailblazer had turned into a faded period piece unredeemed by Giordano's rather inferior score, with its long stretches of functionality and only sporadic sparks of inspiration.

However, La Scala spared no effort to make its production a memorable success. The opera was staged with lavish elegance and was excitingly conducted by Gianandrea Gavazzeni, a widely hailed recent addition to the theater's staff of conductors. Callas, gorgeously costumed and oozing worldliness and mystery, squeezed every bit of melodrama out of Giordano's music. Her suicide and lengthy dying scene in the last act magnetized the audience and left an impression that lingered in the minds of operagoers for several seasons thereafter.

With *Fedora*, La Scala's official 1955/1956 season had ended. Another ensemble tour, however, was scheduled immediately, following the example of the successful Berlin visit of the previous year. This time the destination was Vienna.

A critic once said of Maria Callas that she had a shelf full of voices, each earmarked for different occasions. In

June, 1956, it was time to shelve the soaring fullness and melodramatic urgency of the "Fedora voice" and pull out her "Lucia voice"—a voice of agility, poignancy, and measured passion. Maria was to make her first appearance, as the Bride of Lammermoor, before the knowing, discriminating, and opera-obsessed Viennese public.

Vienna's majestic Staatsoper, severely damaged during the war, was celebrating the first season after its reconstruction. June has traditionally been a festive month in Vienna, marked by the presence of some of the world's leading artists. This June, the visit of La Scala and its celebrated star, Maria Meneghini Callas, formed a logical high point of the "Festwochen" at a time when the Staatsoper once more occupied the central position in Vienna's cultural life. The prime mover behind the scenes was again Herbert von Karajan, by then bearer of the spurious though well-merited title of *Generalmusikdirektor* of Europe.

Back in 1929, when he was still a nameless student of music, another La Scala troupe had visited Vienna to present *Lucia di Lammermoor*. Karajan traveled a hundred miles, partly on foot, to see Arturo Toscanini conduct the Donizetti opera with Toti dal Monte in the title role. Ever since his memorable Scala production of 1954, Karajan's mind had been set on bringing *his Lucia* before the Viennese public, together with Maria Callas, with whom this production was inseparably linked. The Vienna Festival Weeks of June, 1956, fulfilled the conductor's ambition.

When the Meneghinis checked into Vienna's famous Hotel Sacher, around the corner from the Staatsoper, Maria discovered to her dismay that her favorite good-luck piece, a miniature oil painting of the Madonna, was missing. It was Meneghini's gift to her on the occasion of her Verona debut in 1947, and an intimate companion ever since. A phone call to Milan allayed her anxiety. A faithful friend retrieved the amulet, rushed to a plane—and she, the Madonna, and Callas were reunited in time before the performance.

On the evening of June 12, 1956, Maria Meneghini Callas bewitched Vienna's hard-to-please connoisseurs. As a sign of ensemble triumph, the famous Sextet was repeated. Maria's performance of the Mad Scene, the crucial test, with its overpowering intensity unparalleled even in the longest reaches of Viennese memory, prompted an ovation that lasted almost twenty minutes. Theodor Körner, President of the Austrian Republic, applauded with the rest, and received the visitors during one of the intermissions. When it was all over, all traffic was stopped between the Staatsoper and the Hotel Sacher. Extra police troops had to be called in to disperse the crowds and to allow Maria to leave the theater.

A curtain call, shared between Maria and Herbert von Karajan, with the exclusion of Di Stefano, provoked, with some justification, the tenor's anger. The resulting tension somewhat disturbed the serenity of an otherwise joyful occasion. But not too much. Maria and Meneghini went on, after the performance, to rejoin a group of friends and admirers, and spent a carefree, typically Viennese night in a café, with wine, merriment, and songs, till the early hours of dawn.

If the audience was charmed, so were the critics. "Her technique seems to be a part of nature," wrote the *Bild Telegraf,* "what voice, what art, what intensity!" The *Neues Österreich* went into specifics:

"This extraordinary singer is a phenomenon . . . her technique is stupendous, her phrasing exemplary . . . the clarity and brilliance of her *fioriture* nearly unreal. In the high register, the voice occasionally becomes hard as glass, similar to the tones of a flute, and the Mad Scene resembled a duet of flutes—a very natural effect.''

London, Berlin, Vienna—the world's operatic capitals conquered one after another. Maria's fame had preceded her on every occasion, the public had come to see if she was real, the critics had come disposed to praise or bury with complete equanimity, but the verdict was always favorable. The Callas art which traveled around the world via the phonograph was not a myth—its real-life counterpart was just as impressive and immeasurably more magnetic.

She had reached the zenith of her career. The world of opera was at her feet. Theaters and managers everywhere competed for the artistic and financial gratifications invariably assured by Callas engagements. This was Maria's tenth year in Italy. In 1956, her fee was twenty-five times what it had been in 1947. The figures contained in the following table eloquently testify to the steady progress involved in this amazing accomplishment.

Year	*Maximum fee received per performance* (1,000 lire = $1.60)
1947	40,000
1948	50,000
1949	100,000
1950	200,000
1951	300,000
1952	400,000
1953	500,000
1954	650,000
1955	700,000
1956	1,000,000

After Vienna, an entire month awaited the Meneghinis with no commitments in sight. Maria could have accepted engagements at any of the summer festivals, but the days of overtaxing herself with far-flung engagements were a thing of the past. Heavy recording activity beckoned for August and September, the Metropolitan Opera was waiting in October, La Scala again in December. . . . No, the month of July had to be devoted to a gradual unwinding from tension, with time for rest and for a carefree vacation at Ischia, visiting the beaches and night spots, away from opera, away from critics, claques, and curtain calls. For a few weeks, even the press could hardly find their traces. Then the Meneghinis appeared in mid-August, in Venice, with Maria as guest of honor at the XVII Annual Motion Picture Festival.

While Maria was resting, the sleepless forces of publicity were planning future campaigns. Her long-awaited Metropolitan debut was still two months away, but Maria had already learned that she would be gracing the cover of the *Time* magazine issue coinciding with her New York opening. While Maria was soaking in the Lido's sunshine, *Time's* researchers began their distribution of questionnaires to friends and foes, and their interviews with people in and out of music on two continents. The well-known artist, Henry Koerner, visiting his native Austria, received an urgent commission to paint Maria's portrait for that recognized symbol of international status, the *Time* cover.

Koerner caught his first glimpse of the diva as she sat, wearing dark glasses, under a canvas tent at the Lido on a hot Friday afternoon. She was not available for business discussions, but Meneghini was responsive. After disposing of the amenities, with a nearby Italian count as an interpreter, the understanding was quickly reached for the sittings to begin the following week, and the artist was invited for the following Sunday to the Meneghini home in Milan to discuss the exact time and place for the sittings.

Maria, who was playing cards "like a princess with her merry playmates," flashed a winning smile from under her dark glasses and held out her hand. "See you Sunday in Milano, Mr. Koerner."

That Sunday afternoon, at 3:30 P.M., the artist took a closer look at his subject: "She looked forbidding, like a New York career girl; black dress, dark-rimmed glasses. A very, very important man was to arrive at the same time with an important contract. I was a nuisance. . . ." Despite the seemingly discouraging start, however, Maria agreed to formal sittings, one hour each day for a week, beginning the following day.

But it turned out differently. During that week Maria was recording at La Scala, and Koerner made his appearance at the great house each evening to watch her at work, to study her moods and expressions, which he found most intense whenever she listened to playbacks of her own voice.

"On a hot summer midnight in La Scala," remembers Koerner, "Maria Callas sat, her head lowered, intensely listening to her voice from the speaker. Di Stefano, in black and white, stood aloof, somewhat bored, outside in the corridor. The engineers and musicians, sweating and endlessly patient, were waiting for Callas's final approval. Callas, oblivious of her surroundings, her face transfigured with bliss, her wide lips spread open over her large teeth, repeated silently the tender phrases of Mimi: '. . . ma quando vien lo sgelo, il primo sol e mio. . . .' 'Fulfilling herself, and her ego, through perfection, love poured out toward you, caressing, overwhelming you.'

" 'This is my Maria; nobody sings like her,' Meneghini had said shortly before when he watched from the loge as she was singing; and afterwards, with a little drink and a little crying, he would wait for her, like a sad bird, in the corner bar. Then the happy, hungry singers were coming down and devoured everything in sight."

The sittings did not always go smoothly. In the hushed atmosphere of the Meneghini home artist and model faced each other, one with a demanding singlemindedness of purpose, the other exhausted from the nightly work of recordings, from lack of sufficient sleep, from the unnatural silence and concentration of posing. Two days before the completion of the portrait, Koerner had the unmistakable feeling that he was getting on Maria's nerves. "I hated her, yet enjoyed painting her beautiful face, and I paid her back by making her pose even harder. The impasse amounted to something like being thrown out, and only Meneghini's kind words softened the blow." But then, ten days after the initial sitting, the portrait was finished. Maria, pleased with the results, asked forgiveness for her irritation and bade Koerner good-bye in a charming, delightful mood, utterly relieved.

While the *Time* portrait was being created, two complete operatic recordings emerged from La Scala: Puccini's *La Bohème* and Verdi's *Il Trovatore*. Maria had learned the role of Mimi expressly for the recording; she is yet to sing the part on stage. In early September, the sessions continued with Verdi's *Un Ballo in Maschera*. Giuseppe di Stefano sang the principal tenor roles in all three operas. Herbert von Karajan conducted *Il Trovatore*, Antonino Votto the other two. *This* was unusual. Where was Tullio Serafin, the trusted friend and constant and indispensable conductor of Callas operas?

Unbelievable though it may have seemed to those who followed Maria Callas's astonishing career, the venerable Maestro, one of the mighty pillars which had supported that career, at that precise moment was living in a state of

banishment from the diva's favor, and appeared to be
rather crushed by the totally unexpected turn of events.

Earlier that year, E.M.I. had also recorded Verdi's *La
Traviata,* one of Maria's most memorable recent successes.
She had very much wanted to perpetuate her Violetta on
discs, but there was the obstacle of a legal technicality:
having recorded the same opera for Cetra in 1952 she was
contract-bound not to duplicate the role for five years.
Apparently, E.M.I. needed a *La Traviata* for its growing
catalogue. So it was decided not to wait for the time when
Maria would be free to participate. Antonietta Stella, a
soprano star of growing stature, was assigned the role—
opposite Giuseppe di Stefano and Tito Gobbi—and the
recording was carried out under Serafin's direction.

These developments filled Maria with fury and frustration. The role in question was one of her favorites, more
than that, one of her most important artistic achievements.
Being prevented from recording it by conditions that had
nothing to do with art enraged her to a point where her
soundness of judgment was affected. She could hardly
expect sympathetic solidarity from her colleagues, but she
branded Serafin's participation in the venture as an act
of disloyalty. As a result, the old maestro's name is missing from Callas's entire recorded output for the year 1956.

October came, and operatic New York was stirring
with anticipation of the coming Metropolitan season.
Callas was, of course, the main attraction. Opera enthusiasts need little provocation to discuss artists in words
seething with fever and fire, particularly when partisanship is involved. This time, however, the restless ranks of
opera's faithful following were vastly expanded to include
thousands who care little about opera, who may never read
the musical pages, and whose thirst for knowledge finds
adequate satisfaction in headlines, exposés, and gossip

columns. For this faction of readers, the name "Maria Callas" conjured up pictures of celebrity and notoriety— two terms which need not be synonymous, yet are so in an alarming number of cases.

Among the closer, but still very sizable, ranks of opera aficionados, the approaching season signified the resurgence of the prima donna wars. Renata Tebaldi and Maria Callas, the erstwhile rival queens of La Scala, would be meeting again! All indications pointed to violent partisan clashes that would do honor to the bygone days of their Milanese rivalry. In New York, to make the situation even more provocative, there was another queen to be reckoned with, the longtime favorite, Zinka Milanov, who had her own substantial and fervent following.

Ever since he assumed the reins of the Metropolitan in 1950, General Manager Rudolf Bing had advocated the abandonment of the star system and an emphasis on ensemble spirit. But October, 1956, was no time to promulgate such vigorous theories. The star system may be rampant with artistic pitfalls. But it decidedly stimulates interest in opera, and it can have a positively glorious effect on the box office!

As details about the coming season's program schedule began to circulate, Rudolf Bing's handling of the prima donna problem emerged in all its circumspection and diplomacy. His careful logistics averted a head-on collision between Maria and Renata, through arranging for Tebaldi's engagement to begin after Callas's departure. The coveted plum of opening-night glory would be Maria's, but she would get no new productions. Tebaldi, on the other hand, would appear in Tyrone Guthrie's brand-new staging of *La Traviata,* and Zinka Milanov would be rewarded with the spectacular revival of Verdi's *Ernani.*

All through these days of anticipatory agitation, cash

registers jingled merrily. The Metropolitan's nine thousand subscribers, who had first call on opening-night tickets, snapped them up immediately, in spite of the exorbitant prices. (Removing opening nights from the regular series and setting up a separate ticket scale for them, in keeping with their spectacle character, was a wise and remunerative Bing innovation established back in 1950.) Tickets for this particular opening became the hottest thing on Broadway, and the scarce few that managed to trickle into black-market channels sold for as high as $125.

On October 13th, the long-awaited diva landed at New York's Idlewild Airport. Her entourage consisted of husband Battista, a girl secretary, and a precious new acquisition, a miniature poodle named Toy. Two other girls, acting as secretary and maid but in reality close friends, had arrived several days earlier to form the advance guard, charged with setting up hotel accommodations and establishing the imposing Meneghini ménage. Waiting for Maria at the airport was her father, George Callas, Dario Soria, and representatives of the Metropolitan, including an attorney, to be present in the event of legal complications.

The landing was smooth—not a process server in sight. But there was a great deal of legal activity behind the scenes. Bagarozy had filed suit in New York's Supreme Court coinciding with Maria's arrival, with warrants of attachment served on the Metropolitan Opera and Angel Records. The amount named in the suit was the same already cited in Chicago, $300,000. As a result of backstage understanding between the lawyers representing the two sides, the embarrassment of process servers was avoided by Maria's consent to receive a summons at her hotel apartment the following day. Now she was liable for court action in both Chicago and New York.

To all onlookers, Maria appeared unruffled. "I am

fully confident in American justice," she declared to the press. "I do not care about attempts to frighten me through writs of attachments and other means. I am simply awaiting the final ruling of an American judge who will say the last word in this boring affair."

If her appearance radiated utter calm, it failed to reflect her true feelings. Her first days at the Hotel Sulgrave on Park Avenue were spent in virtual seclusion. Bagarozy's attorney came and presented the summons on the morning of the 15th. But the annoyance of legal entanglements was not the only issue that weighed on her mind. The impending opening night was, after all, her New York debut. Here she was, at last, in the city where she was born and where she had not appeared in public since that far-away graduation exercise in 1937. Now the Metropolitan was waiting. Enrico Caruso once said that it may be all right for other singers to give 100 per cent of their talent— the public here would expect *more* from a Caruso.

The same public would also expect *more* from a Callas! Maria was aware of the tremendous anticipation that awaited her debut. She was fully aware of the enormous publicity surrounding her person, publicity which attached to her everywhere she went with never—well, hardly ever—a conscious effort on her part. A great deal of that publicity was hostile, *that* she also knew. There would be many in that opening-night audience who would rejoice in a fiasco. She was only human. The Queen of La Scala, the toast of Covent Garden, the idol of Chicago had the jitters.

But this was her secret. When she appeared at her first Met rehearsal on October 19th, she was the embodiment of calm, methodical assurance. Promptly at the scheduled hour of 2 p.m. she made her entrance, with her inseparable

Titta, and the apparently no less inseparable Toy. While Meneghini assumed his usual position in the orchestra, Maria surveyed the stage intently, walked about in every direction, thinking about her lines and pacing out her stage action. Then she deposited Toy and went to work, poised, polite, and all attention. She was again Maria Callas, the nearsighted soprano to whom all the world's theaters were alike, including, to all appearances, the Metropolitan.

When it comes to appraising the quality of the productions in which she participates, however, Maria Callas is anything but nearsighted. And here came her first major disappointment. Although the *Norma* settings, dating from 1953, were not old by Metropolitan standards, they were a far cry from the splendors of La Scala. The scenery was shabby in spots, the costumes appeared worn and contrasted sharply with her own specially designed attire. Furthermore, as she was to learn in the succeeding days, rehearsals, under the Metropolitan's time-conscious, budget-conscious, labor union-conscious atmosphere, fell far short of her perfectionist standards. She was intensely unhappy about it all, but wisely avoided all public demonstration of displeasure, apart from protesting murmurs to her friends and intimates. She was reassured, on the other hand, by the presence of colleagues in the cast with whom she had shared many a challenging experience in the past: Fedora Barbieri was the Adalgisa, Mario del Monaco the Pollione, and Cesare Siepi the Oroveso. By an interesting coincidence, the same three artists had been her partners at her "unofficial" Scala debut in 1950.

Throughout these trying days, Rudolf Bing was a steadying influence. "He was helpful and kind without being gushing" is the way Maria remembers it. With his courtesy, seriousness, and devotion to artistic principles—

qualities he shared with the new star—the relationship between Maria and the General Manager started off most auspiciously.

Two days before the season's opening, all America's newsstands displayed Henry Koerner's portrait of Maria Callas. *Time* magazine was out, with a four-page cover story to coincide with the national interest generated by the Callas debut. The story was exhaustive, far-reaching, revealing, and, as far as Maria's inner peace was concerned, totally devastating.

It introduced Maria rather accurately, as "a diva more widely hated by her colleagues and more widely acclaimed by her public than any other living singer." After a concise appraisal of Maria's technical prowess, the built-in dramatic qualities of her voice, and her stage mastery, the article proceeded to portray her "human" side. It painted a picture of "ruthless ferocity" by using a shrewd composite of facts, implications, and simplifications, liberally larded with *Time's* familiar statements in quotation marks, attributed to nameless informants.

Maria was pictured as a ruthless demon versus her colleagues. Her Roman backstage feud with Boris Christoff was exposed, and tenor Giuseppe di Stefano was quoted as having exclaimed, "I'm never going to sing opera with her again, and that's final." (Actually, he recorded Puccini's *Manon Lescaut* with Callas seven months later, and opened La Scala's 1957/1958 season with her shortly thereafter.) Renata Tebaldi was described as "Callas's first victim," and characterized by this summation: "She's got no backbone. She's not like Callas." The quote was not credited to anyone in particular, but the impression was created that it might have come from Callas. "The day will come," said another one of *Time's* nameless but omniscient spokesmen, "when Maria will sing by herself."

Naturally, the flareup between Maria and old Maestro Tullio Serafin was also publicized, with the ominous added note that Serafin "is finding that other singers are now mysteriously unable to sing under him." This was utterly without foundation. Maria had a complete reconciliation with her old friend in early 1957, at the instigation of Meneghini and other intermediaries, and nothing has disturbed their affectionate relationship since. But this later turn of events evoked no press comments whatever.

Just for the record, Tullio Serafin has become, contrary to the *Time*-implied boycott, the most sought-after operatic conductor of the world during the Callas years. His invitations year after year far exceed the number of engagements he can confidently undertake, having reached his eighty-first year on December 8, 1959. And as far as recordings are concerned, after that troublesome *Traviata,* he returned to record Maria Callas as well as her rivals— Antonietta Stella (*Linda di Chamounix* and *Tosca*), Renata Tebaldi (*La Bohème*), Victoria de los Angeles (*La Traviata*), and Rosanna Carteri (*L'elisir d'amore*).

But the article's most damaging parts were the paragraphs revealing the then as yet unpublished details surrounding the friction between mother and daughter. *Time's* researchers had interviewed Evangelia Callas in Athens and obtained the alleged excerpt from Maria's last letter which, according to her mother, had brought about the final break. In this letter, quoted *Time,* Maria had replied to her mother's 1951 request for financial aid: "Don't come to us with your troubles. I had to work for my money, and you are young enough to work, too. If you can't make enough money to live on, you can jump out of the window or drown yourself."

Since 1956, Evangelia Callas has released for publication several versions of that letter. According to a recent variant, the recipient was not herself but sister Jackie. Maria, on the other hand, has steadfastly refused to discuss the letter for publication. Privately, she has denied categorically the existence of any letter similar to the violent wording the *Time* quotation had attributed to her.

The real truth may never be known, as indeed the entire matter should have never been exposed for the benefit of anyone but the members of the Callas family. No newspaper or magazine reporter can be expected to withhold a similar scoop from his readers. But few are the mothers who would turn to the global press for solace, no matter how deep the wound. Be that as it may, in the eyes of millions of readers, Maria Callas was branded as a grave offender against the sacred institution of motherhood—on the eve of her Metropolitan debut. Callas the operatic artist was not affected by that article. But the public image of the temperamental prima donna, as reflected in the minds of a vast readership whose interest in music is casual or nonexistent, was dealt a damaging blow.

At the dress rehearsals of *Norma,* Marlene Dietrich, an enthusiastic Callas admirer, joined her in her dressing room to offer a reassuring handshake and a thermos full of hot broth. She was welcomed like an angel from heaven. Maria badly needed strength, and she needed friends even more. She was fighting off a cold and complained of a bad throat. Altogether, she was tense, jittery, feeling like a lamb about to be slaughtered.

October 29, 1956. "Never have so many Americans tried to pay so much money to hear an opera"—anounced The New York *Times.* The box-office take was $75,510—an all-time high for the theater—and everyone agreed that it could have been doubled, space permitting. It was estimated that the Metropolitan had actually lost another

$50,000 worth of business between mail-order refunds and by turning away hopeful would-be purchasers. *Norma* had never been a box-office opera in New York. Heaven knows, the box office, even at the official rates ($35 for orchestra seats), offered no bargains. It must have been Callas.

Inside, the atmosphere, framed by the old heavy red decor of the Metropolitan, seemed several degrees chillier than usual. Maria was greeted by cool applause upon her entrance, while her fellow artists Barbieri and Del Monaco received explosive volleys at theirs. Maria sang her "Casta Diva" cautiously and not in her best voice. She was applauded with nowhere near the vehemence that greeted Zinka Milanov a few minutes later, as she sailed down the aisle in the grand manner during the intermission. The standees, New York's answer to La Scala's noisemakers, seemed to be stirring for trouble.

But with the second act, the tide turned. Vocal imperfections began to fade into insignificance before the gathering momentum of a "Callas performance," intense, moving, and credible. Her Norma was a solemn, passionate, poignant figure and, above all, a suffering, believable woman, particularly affecting in the moments of her final self-sacrifice. With the inborn intuition of a natural actress, Maria sensed the changing pulse of the audience and drew added strength from it. When the curtain fell on the final act, she knew she had won the great battle against forbidding odds.

Now it was New York's turn to watch the unfolding art of the Callas Curtain Call. She was called out sixteen times, each appearance a study in stage-wise, disciplined graciousness. At one time she gathered up a bouquet from the many that had been presented by admirers, and with a disarming smile presented one rose to Mario del Monaco, another to Cesare Siepi. The next time before the curtain,

both partners gallantly withdrew and left Maria alone to
face the roaring applause of the Golden Horseshoe, in
defiance of Bing's stern dictum against solo bows. Maria,
her face transfigured, was on the verge of tears.

The morning after brought the reviews. New York
offered little of Chicago's uncritical intoxication. The New
York *Herald Tribune's* Paul Henry Lang paid tribute to
Maria's "commanding dramatic personality," but emphasized her vocal limitations and the veiled quality of
her middle register. "It is a puzzling voice," wrote
Howard Taubman of The New York *Times,* "occasionally
it gives the impression of having been formed out of sheer
will power rather than natural endowments." No less
aware of vocal imperfections, Irving Kolodin in *Saturday
Review* nevertheless acknowledged in Maria's performance "more than fine singing: a dramatic portraiture of
which the operatic stage has all too little." The same
thoughts were couched in a more down-to-earth style by
Time magazine's summation a few days later: "No doubt,
other great operatic sopranos can coax out of their ample,
placid figures tones that esthetes call more beautiful.
Callas's voice and stage presence add up to more than
beauty—namely the kind of passionate dedication, the
kind of excitement that invariably mark a champ."

"Now that this is over," Maria told her friends as she
was emerging from the ardent embraces of Meneghini and
the eager reception line of her throng of admirers, "I can
relax and get down to work." On the night of her triumphant debut, however, relaxation was not in the cards. A
glittering party gathered at the Ambassador Hotel in the
diva's honor, arranged by Angel Records. Present were
the ambassadors of Greece and Italy, representatives of
the press, Rudolf Bing and other Metropolitan dignitaries,
the opening-night principals and Fausto Cleva, conductor

of the occasion, Gladys Swarthout and Giovanni Martinelli, the Met's Adalgisa and Pollione of yesteryear. Count-
ess Wally Castelbarco-Toscanini represented La Scala.
Seated at the central table was that glamorous dispenser
of fortifying broth, Marlene Dietrich. She had to retire
early, having applauded her friend in the theater so violently as to cause blood blisters on her delicate hand.

Maria entered regally, on the arm of her beaming
Titta, and trailed by a private detective eyeing more than
a million dollars worth of borrowed jewelry from Harry
Winston, Inc.—an adequate representation of her own
Milan possessions. Amid toasts, gaiety, and bubbling
spirits, the party lasted into the small hours. Maria Callas
had arrived in her native city.

CHAPTER 10

Stormy Weather

Gioconda
Illuminata a festa splende
Venezia nel lontano.

PONCHIELLI—LA GIOCONDA

On November 9th, following her third Metropolitan performance, Maria Callas gave a press conference in her suite on the tenth floor of the Hotel Sulgrave. She was relaxed, soft-spoken, astutely diplomatic—the inquiring reporters got the expert Chicago treatment. They were charmed by her informality and by her speech, which, except for an occasional quaint turn of phrase and some random Italian intrusions, still retained many colloquial Americanisms. Despite her prolonged absence from her native land, and her complete assumption of Italian as her natural tongue, she still counted in English, Maria confided to the reporters.

"What about that famous temperament?" one inquired.

"Nonsense. It's all rumors spread by malicious colleagues."

"How about your press in New York?"

"The critics were just fine. If everything were flattery, wouldn't it be monotonous? No, the critics were fair, and the audience magnificent."

In the theater, the same atmosphere of amiability prevailed. Maria sang six *Normas* (one in Philadelphia) in November, always to sold-out houses. There was a cast change for the last two performances: Kurt Baum assumed the role of Pollione and Nicola Moscona was Oroveso, her two partners in the Mexican season of 1950. Baum, who at that time had vowed to prevent Maria's Metropolitan engagement, was now affable, courteous. Their feud, like many others growing out of the heated atmosphere that surrounds the making of opera, was forgotten.

Not so easily forgotten, however, was *Time's* controversial cover story. It had reached Renata Tebaldi in Chicago, where as unchallenged star she had opened the season that fall. Seething with fury at the sight of the alleged Callas reference to her absentee backbone, Renata dashed off an indignant letter to *Time's* editors, against the advice of her manager and close friends. The portion of the letter that the magazine published in its November 26, 1956, issue amounted to a declaration of war:

Sir:
I am truly astonished at the statements made by my colleague Signora Maria Meneghini Callas regarding me. The signora admits to being a woman of character and says that I have no backbone. I reply: I have one great thing that she has not—a heart.
That I actually trembled when I knew she was present at a per-

formance of mine is utterly ridiculous. It was not Signora Callas
who caused me to stay away from La Scala; I sang there before
she did, and consider myself a *Creatura della Scala*. I stayed
away of my own free will because an atmosphere not at all pleasant had been created there.

RENATA TEBALDI

Renata was not scheduled to begin her Metropolitan
engagement until the termination of Maria's. It was a pru-
dent and farsighted plan on Rudolf Bing's part to have
arranged the schedule in this manner.

Maria's second New York role was Tosca, which she
sang twice (November 15th and 19th) under Dimitri Mitropoulos's direction, with Giuseppe Campora and George
London in the cast.

"When I learned that I would sing Scarpia to Callas's
Tosca, I must admit I had a few forebodings," reminisced
George London in a magazine article shortly thereafter
(*High Fidelity*, March, 1957). "So much had been printed
about this 'stormy' star that I was prepared for almost
anything.

"The first rehearsal reassured me. Here was a
trouper, a fanatic worker, a stickler for detail. Remembering my first season at the *Met*, and the forlornness one can
feel, I crossed the stage before curtain time and, knocking
at Mme. Callas's dressing room, said a quick '*in bocca di
lupo*' (the Italian version of 'good luck'). She took my
hand in both of hers and seemed deeply moved. She later
told me that this insignificant courtesy had meant a great
deal to her."

Maria's Tosca was characterized by a carefully
planned dramatic design and firm control of vocal re-
sources. She had a few somewhat tentative moments in the
first act, but once these were over she played the part to
the hilt. Feminine, glamorous, utterly believable in appearance and action, she had the audience in the palm of

her hands after a beautifully controlled "Vissi d'arte."
Only her uncritical admirers failed to discover certain
vocal lapses in her performance, but, as it is usually the
case when Callas appears at her inspired best, these moments were dwarfed by the final, overwhelming impression.

On one Metropolitan patron, however, Maria Callas
made no impression whatever. Society columnist Elsa
Maxwell in the next day's New York *Journal American*
branded her "the devious diva," disapproved of her acting in the first act, did not like the way she sang "Vissi
d'arte," and objected to her dramatic exit at the end of
the second act. Maxwell's seemingly telescopic eye even
detected "a little bit of jealousy" in the way Tosca–Callas
had dispatched Scarpia–London to his well-merited doom.

It was also in the role of Tosca that Maria Callas made
her debut on a United States television broadcast (Sunday
night, November 25th, as part of the Ed Sullivan Show).
Again, she teamed up with George London in a super-
charged rendering of a scene from the second act. Two
accounts which appeared in the New York press describ-
ing the rehearsal for that broadcast make an interesting
contrast:

Dorothy Kilgallen's column in New York Journal American	*George London's own recollection in* High Fidelity
. . . Maria Callas almost caused her vis-a-vis, George London, to flip his talented lid. The tempestuous primadonna at one point stopped in the middle of an aria to accuse London of pushing a chair out of line, and in the death scene she stopped the music to cry out: "There's too much feet in my way."	. . . Again, she was the most cooperative colleague. At one point, during dress rehearsal, I fell too close to the desk and she couldn't pass to cross the stage. . . . Callas laughingly stopped and announced to the director: "There just are too many legs around here." We all had a good laugh. . .

Truth, as the saying goes, is stranger than fiction. But for sheer effectiveness in a news story, nothing can beat the judicious mixture of both.

The show of temperament for which the press had been impatiently waiting could have manifested itself at the rehearsals of *Lucia di Lammermoor,* the third and final opera of this, Maria's initial New York engagement. The venerable sets of the Donizetti opera had been decorating the Metropolitan's stage since 1942 and, like most operatic properties, wore their age most ungracefully. Remembering the gorgeous Milan and Naples productions in which she had participated, Maria shuddered, particularly at the sight of the "monstrous well that covers half of the stage and looks no more romantic than an oil tank."

But the rehearsals went off without a hitch, and so did the opera's first performance, on December 3rd, which acquainted New Yorkers with an entirely different conception of Lucia from any experienced in recent memory. Those in the audience expecting virtuoso vocal display, and remembering Lily Pons in her prime, came away somewhat disappointed. Callas, with all her agility and flexibility throughout a wide vocal span, displayed a darker tonal quality and a lack of abandon and acrobatic ease in the uppermost register. But for many others, the opera began to make dramatic sense for the first time, and the Mad Scene emerged as a gripping, tragic turn of fate, rather than a contrived piece of stage business.

New York's critics were unanimous in their praise of Callas's dramatic art, but rather sharply divided in assessing her vocal contribution. The strongest opinion, again, came from part-time music critic Elsa Maxwell:

"I confess the great Callas's acting in the Mad Scene left me completely unmoved. But I think she sang the aria in the first act beautifully. I was intrigued by the red wig she wore through the first two acts but in the Mad Scene she came on a platinum blonde. Why this change of color? What did it mean to this egocentric extrovert?"

The evening following the season's first *Lucia,* Maria Callas celebrated her thirty-third birthday at an intimate party given in the home of Dario and Dorle Soria. Elsa Maxwell's bristling comments were discussed. Maria was rather puzzled by them; the Sorias, on the other hand, were amused by it all. They told Maria that Maxwell and Renata Tebaldi had been close friends for years. They also assured her that a little running feud, with no one seriously hurt, was good publicity, with beneficial effects on record sales.

The Angel recordings of Maria's three Metropolitan operas—*Norma, Tosca,* and *Lucia di Lammermoor*—were selling in mounting quantities. Callas was a controversial artist, the Sorias contended. Wherever she went, publicity followed. When so much publicity surrounds a public figure, *all* of it cannot be favorable. . . .

December 7th. It was St. Ambrose Day in faraway Milan, and La Scala opened with Verdi's *Aida,* featuring Antonietta Stella and Giuseppe di Stefano in the cast. In New York it was just an ordinary December evening. But two nights later, following Maria Callas's second New York *Lucia,* the city had a Callas crisis, as the afternoon papers heralded the news: MET BARITONE FIRED!

According to the story, the young baritone, Enzo Sordello, who had sung Ashton in the first two *Lucias,* was fired by Rudolf Bing on Maria's insistence. His alleged crime: holding on to a high G at the end of the second-act duet past Maria's point of endurance, and thus vocally upstaging her. In complete opposition to the press, the Metropolitan issued an immediate denial. According to Bing's statement, Sordello had been uncooperative and insubordinate. Thus, actually his dismissal had come about as a result of persistent clashes with conductor Fausto Cleva.

Of the two stories, the press liked the first one better. For a few days, Sordello found himself surrounded by the kind of public interest that had theretofore eluded his artistic efforts. The foreign press was quick to seize upon the latest Callas "scandal." According to the French magazine *Jours de France,* Sordello received a kick in the shins for the "upstaging." A German book, published in 1959, even invented a sequel to the incident, according to which Maria reported sick and refused to go on until Sordello was dismissed.

In reality, she returned to sing two more *Lucias,* on December 14th and 19th, after canceling the performance on the 11th due to a throat condition. On the evening of the 19th, which was her last appearance at the Metropolitan that season, the part of Edgardo was sung by Richard Tucker. Frank Valentino took over the part of the villainous Ashton.

Between her last two New York appearances, Maria gave her first concert in the United States, on December 17th, at the Italian embassy in Washington, D. C. The audience was composed of two hundred invited guests of the capital's elite, including Presidential Adviser Sherman Adams and his wife and two Justices of the Supreme Court. Maria appeared without remuneration—the event represented a joint tribute to her own native land and to that of her husband.

The glittering audience was completely charmed, and Paul Hume, the able Washington music critic with something of a reputation for *not* eulogizing operatic sopranos, joined the ranks of the spellbound Callasites: "Neither newspapers nor magazines have yet conveyed any impres-

sion of the genuine, friendly manner of this, the most discussed soprano. . . . Callas can be discussed only in terms
of supreme greatness."

Maria Callas is a fighter. She conducts her campaigns
on many levels, and her weapons encompass a remarkable
range. To achieve her objectives she can be fierce and unyielding in her determination. But there are times when
she changes her tactics and, to succeed, brings into play
her most powerful weapon: an enormous amount of personal charm.

At a dinner dance given at the Waldorf-Astoria for
the benefit of the American Hellenic Warfare Fund, Maria
found herself face to face with Elsa Maxwell. Hollywood
magnate Spyros Skouras made the introductions. The ensuing dialogue, as retold by Maxwell, is one for the history
books.

Elsa: Madame Callas, I would have imagined myself to be the
last person on earth that you would have wished to meet.

Maria: On the contrary, you are the first one I wish to meet
because, aside from your opinion of my voice, I esteem
you as a lady of honesty who is devoted to tell the truth.

"When I looked into her amazing eyes, which are brilliant,
beautiful and hypnotic," recalled La Maxwell at another
occasion, "I realized she is an extraordinary person."

This new Callas conquest was to bring far-reaching
changes, though the two new friends could not plan on another immediate meeting. Christmas was nearing and, although Maria had to return to the United States in January to appear in court in Chicago, she and Battista decided
to spend the holiday season in Milan.

On the morning of their departure, December 21st,
Maria, very chic in a plum-colored dress and mink hat,
with Toy on her arm, and accompanied by Angelo Sereni,
her New York attorney, appeared to testify at New York's

Supreme Court in the Bagarozy lawsuit. This long-lingering case was nearing a showdown, but the final outcome was not yet in sight.

While occasional news items had appeared about the suit in New York and Chicago papers, little was known about developments behind the scenes. It was no longer Bagarozy vs. Callas. As far back as May, 1953, Bagarozy had assigned his claim to a third party named Barnett Glassman, since he lacked the funds to face extended litigation.

In a memorandum supporting a motion for summary judgment, Maria's attorneys stated that the lawsuit was nothing but a scheme "of systematically harrassing defendant for the purpose of inducing her to pay some wholly unjustified tribute, rather than incur the substantial expense of multiple litigation." In support of this assertion, attorney Angelo Sereni contended, on Maria's behalf, that a similar lawsuit brought against Nicola Rossi-Lemeni (another eminent artist formerly under contract to Bagarozy) had been settled in 1954 by the payment of $4,000, in sharp contrast to the claim against Callas of $300,000.

Sereni's move was effectively countered, and nothing happened that December morning to bring the case any closer to its final settlement. However, Maria was determined to fight to the finish. She insisted that Bagarozy, having done nothing to further her career, failed to live up to *his* contractual obligations. "My husband owns me as a manager," she declared in court and, later again, for the benefit of the reporters.

That same afternoon, Maria and her entourage left New York by plane. By an odd coincidence, one of her fellow passengers turned out to be none other than ex-Metropolitan baritone Enzo Sordello. The two artists met face-to-face, and Maria coolly returned the baritone's Merry

Christmas greeting. But when he came nearer, smiling, with an extended hand, she flatly refused the handshake. To the reporters who witnessed it all she readily explained: "I don't like that man to take advantage of my publicity."

"What did you think of your publicity in New York?" one of them asked.

"I think it's been wonderful. But this is lousy."

And with this succinct declaration she turned around, joined her waiting husband, and boarded the plane.

During the restful two weeks that followed in Milan, Maria set her definite schedule of performances at La Scala, where her return was awaited for the concluding half of the season. It was also during this brief sojourn that she accepted an offer from the San Francisco Opera. On January 3, 1958, she mailed a letter to Kurt Herbert Adler, San Francisco's General Manager, in which she confirmed a series of appearances for September and October.

Immediately after the Christmas holidays, Maria also managed to find time to dictate her "personal story" to Anita Pensotti, a staff writer of the magazine *Oggi*. The story was published during January, 1957, in five fascinating installments. The familiar combative spirit pervaded the closing page of these recollections:

"I shall soon return to La Scala to sing in *La Sonnambula, Anna Bolena,* and, finally *Iphigenia in Tauris.* I know that my enemies are ready for me, but I shall fight to the best of my ability. I will not disappoint my public which loves me, and whose esteem and admiration I am determined to keep."

Two peaceful Italian weeks were followed by two hectic ones in the United States, necessitated by the scheduled Chicago court action. To make this unwanted journey worthwhile from the artistic and financial viewpoints, Maria had accepted an engagement for a benefit concert in Chicago, to be given by the Alliance Française for Hungarian Relief.

Three days after her return to New York, on January 11, 1957, a new chapter unfolded in the blossoming Callas–Maxwell friendship. The two ladies met again at the Waldorf, as stars of a regal pageant dreamed up by a public relations firm for the annual ball given by the Hospitalized Veterans Service. Maria came costumed as the exotic Empress Hatshepshut of Egypt. The regal vestments of Catherine the Great bedecked Elsa Maxwell's generous contours, and other imperial ornaments were worn by Faye Emerson and Arlene Dahl.

"It seems we are going to be friends," reported Elsa in her column with uncharacteristic understatement. She was already planning a fancy dress ball in Maria's honor for the coming season of Venice high society. But, with all her effusions over her great new friend, Elsa still found time to reaffirm her love and affection for "the golden voice of Renata Tebaldi."

The Chicago concert on January 16th was Maria's first appearance in the city of her greatest American conquest since the fiery farewell of 1955. She returned with no bitterness in her heart, she assured her many friends, only affection and gratitude for the city's devoted public. But, and about that she was just as emphatic, she would not sing again under the same management that "betrayed" her. When the "process servers incident" was inevitably brought up, she was able to discuss it dispassionately with the press. "Sometimes I do get angry. Temperament on the stage benefits the theater. I am otherwise a calm person. Am I not?"

The concert itself reminded many of the splendid seasons of 1954 and 1955. It was no accident. Glamorously attired in a red velvet gown, Maria began the program with

Maria Callas and her husband, Giovanni Battista Meneghini, in the
garden of their Milan home. This picture was taken in October, 1957.
(Photo by Pix, Inc.)

Maria is an accomplished pianist. Apart from studying her roles, she frequently plays for her own enjoyment. Here she is seen in a relaxed musical moment at home. (Photo by European.)

Maria is posing with her favorite poodle, Toy, in the living room of her two-story Milan home. Both pictures on this page were taken during December, 1956, following her first Metropolitan season. (Photo by European.)

An enthusiastic cook, Maria is proud of her "American" kitchen. This photograph was taken in January, 1957. (Photo by European.)

The Meneghinis in one of the many happy moments in their ten-year married life. (Photo by European.)

At the "Angel Ball" in Chicago, November 1, 1954. From left to right: Rossi-Lemeni, Dario Soria, Elisabeth Schwarzkopf, L. J. Brown of E.M.I., Maria Callas, Walter Legge, Victoria Serafin, Giovanni Battista Meneghini, George Callas, John Woolford of Angel Records. (Courtesy of Dario Soria.)

At the party in Maria's honor following her Metropolitan debut of October 29, 1956. With her: Dario Soria. (Courtesy of *Opera News.*)

George Callas greets his daughter upon her arrival at New York's Idlewild Airport in November, 1957. Mr. Callas, a pharmacist, has been a New York resident since 1923. (Courtesy of Angel Records.)

Marlene Dietrich, a great Callas fan, visited Maria in her dressing room at her Metropolitan debut. They are looking at Maria's favorite good-luck piece just before the performance. (Photo by European.)

President René Coty of France congratulated Maria Callas during the intermission of the great gala concert at the Paris Opera on December 19, 1958. (Photo by Wide World.)

Another congratulation. This time by former President Harry S. Truman at Maria's Kansas City concert of October 28, 1959. (Photo by UPI.)

All smiles as Maria meets with British conductor Sir Malcolm Sargent at a gala concert which was televised from London in October, 1959. (Photo by European.)

Great sopranos and great friends. Elisabeth Schwarzkopf and Maria Callas at the Milan recording of Puccini's *Turandot* in July, 1957. (Courtesy of Angel Records.)

one of Amina's gentle arias from *La Sonnambula,* after
which she displayed the sharpest possible contrast in
Turandot's steely, imperious "In questa reggia." Excerpts from her most memorable Chicago successes, *Norma*
and *Trovatore,* followed to show the city what it was missing. The evening ended with the irresistible pièce de ré-
sistance, Lucia's "Mad Scene." If Maria needed reassurance that she was not forgotten in Chicago, that evening
proved it. The old magic was still there.

Ironically enough, Maria's projected court appearance, which was indirectly responsible for her long-awaited
return to Chicago, was postponed. A new date was set for
the fall, to coincide with her San Francisco engagements.

Without any further delay, therefore, the traveling
Meneghinis flew back to Milan in time to witness the world
première at La Scala of Poulenc's *Dialogues des Carmé-
lites* on January 26th. Resplendent in a chinchilla coat,
wearing large emeralds and diamond-studded eyeglasses
at the reception given in the composer's honor, Maria attracted a great deal of attention from the onlookers, whose
comments covered a remarkable range of human reactions.

The time of her rejoining La Scala for the scheduled
three gala productions was not far away. But first Maria
had to fulfill an important London engagement, which included her return to Covent Garden after a four-year absence, and the first of the projected five operatic recordings
for that year.

Her very appearance caused a sensation. Londoners
with vivid memories of her massive, columnar figure were
astounded by the sight of the svelte, stylish visitor, looking as if she had just stepped out of *Vogue's* pages. But
along with the fervently expressed compliments were the
secret concern and the unspoken doubts: "How would she
sing? In the absence of those unsightly but reassuring

sixty pounds, where would those remembered tones of opulence originate?''

The reassuring answers came with the first performance of *Norma* on February 2nd. The voice had lost a few shades of its erstwhile brilliance and penetrating strength, but it had become more even, was controlled with more assurance, and was particularly appealing in its warm, vibrant lower register. Her technique, her musicality, her shaping of Bellini's sweeping phrases, and her command of the ornamental and bravura passages were as awe-inspiring as ever. Two thousand Londoners, casting aside their traditional reserve, applauded ecstatically and shouted *Brava Divina* between acts and at the end of the performance.

On February 6th, when *Norma* was repeated, the frenzy grew to even greater heights. After the second-act duet ''Mira o Norma,'' which was sung by Maria and Ebe Stignani with a perfect blend of virtuoso accuracy and inspired lyricism, the applause assumed such torrential proportions that conductor John Pritchard was unable to continue. After a pause of contented indecision, there was only one thing to do. The two artists linked hands before the footlights, Pritchard gave his signal, and Covent Garden witnessed its first encore in twenty years. The two singers were in tears when it was all over. It was an unforgettable occasion.

Solo curtain calls are not in disfavor in London. Maria's were true to her best form, each one a performance in itself. Coming out for the first, after a well-timed delay of just a few seconds longer than her colleagues, there was that expression of modest amazement. Her subsequent returns were never the same, not even by accident. Each bouquet of flowers received with a rare combination of grace and theatrical flair; courtesy, smiles and flowers

to colleagues; finally, the affectionate clutching of a solitary rose to her heart, and, after a moment of hesitation,
its return with a graceful fling to the delighted, gasping
audience. The reaction was more or less hysterical, "but
no more than the performance deserved," remarked the
British magazine *Opera.*

David Webster, Covent Garden's director, lost no time
announcing Maria's re-engagement for the following
season.

After those two evenings, the recording sessions of
Rossini's *The Barber of Seville* in E.M.I.'s Kingsway
Hall studios seemed calm and businesslike by comparison.
The Scala cast of the previous season's production had
been imported to London for the purpose, with Luigi Alva·
and Tito Gobbi in the male principal roles. Alceo Galliera
conducted London's renowned Philharmonia Orchestra—
Tullio Serafin was still a "persona non grata."

Before returning to Milan, Maria and Battista surveyed her summer itinerary: Vienna, for a short engagement as Traviata under von Karajan's baton; Athens, for
two concerts under the auspices of the famous Athens Festival; and Edinburgh, for a series of *Sonnambula,* as part
of La Scala's elaborately planned guest engagements.
After that—America! It seemed like an exciting series; in
reality it turned out to be even more action-packed than
anybody could have anticipated.

Maria's triumphant return to La Scala after an unusually long absence found her, on March 2nd, in excellent
voice. The opera was *La Sonnambula,* in a repeat of the
highly praised, dreamlike Visconti production of 1955.
Observers who had originally found her characterization
somewhat affected, now discovered a new dimension of
naturalness and increased sensitivity in her portrayal.
Nicola Monti and Nicola Zaccaria were the male principals.

While the remarkably homogeneous cast continued performing the opera, Walter Legge and EMI's peripatetic engineers set up shop in the theater to perpetuate the production on records under Antonino Votto's direction.

April brought the traditional Fair to Milan, many thousands of visitors, and, to La Scala, a spectacular new production of Donizetti's *Anna Bolena.* The choice of opera was by no means natural; *Aida, Tosca,* or *Trovatore* would have been more appropriate to the "tourist trade." But La Scala offered Callas in the title role, an all-important factor which compensated for the opera's unfamiliarity.

Anna Bolena was truly unfamiliar, even to Italians. Donizetti's first successful opera, introduced in 1830 with Pasta and Rubini in Milan's Teatro Carcano, it had seen only a handful of performances since the composer's death more than a century ago, and none at all in major theaters. The 1957 production was the kind only Italy can give to an Italian opera, with a splendor characteristic of La Scala at its best.

A particularly fortunate circumstance was the choice of the conductor, Gianandrea Gavazzeni, Italy's foremost Donizetti scholar, who was not overawed by the long-dormant score to the extent of overlooking its weaknesses. Applying a firm but respectful editing hand, he eliminated some banal and arid stretches and brought the music vibrantly to life.

In this opera, Donizetti had the librettist, or rather English history, on his side. The tragic story of Anne Boleyn and Henry VIII is made of strong dramatic stuff, and the historical liberties in which librettist Romani had indulged could have offended only British sensibilities.

Luchino Visconti was the director again. This time his efforts pleased most of the critics. It was remarked, however, that on many occasions he concentrated on the central figure of Maria Callas to the detriment of the somewhat neglected subordinate characters. If this was so, his guilt was no greater than Donizetti's, for *Anna Bolena* is primarily a one-woman show.

La Scala's 1957 production offered Nicola Rossi-Lemeni as a strikingly Slavic-looking Henry VIII, Giulietta Simionato as the luscious-sounding Jane Seymour, and Gianni Raimondi, holding his own as valiantly as any modern tenor against the role of Percy, which had been fashioned for the superhuman voice of Rubini. It was a marvelous cast, but Callas was the show.

In its totality, *Anna Bolena* is not-quite-great Donizetti, but the opera's long final scene, in which the condemned Queen passes her last distraught and terrifying moments on earth, is among the finest pages he ever penned. It has everything a singing actress can ask for: complete domination of the stage, compelling dramatic opportunities, startling changes of mood, dazzling vocal pyrotechnics, music of melting lyricism, scorching passion, and heart-rending pathos. A fifteen-minute ovation greeted Callas after the final curtain of the April 14th *prima*.

"Would *Anna Bolena* enter the international repertory?" asked visiting English critic Desmond Shawe-Taylor. His own answer: "With Callas, yes; without her, or some comparable soprano of whom as yet there is no sign, no."

Anna Bolena continued to attract sellout houses during April and May. It also attracted Elsa Maxwell, at Maria's invitation. Photographers captured the moment when Elsa alighted from her plane at Milan's Malpensa airport and dashed into the waiting arms of the diva. Their fond embrace was accompanied by this caption in one local paper: "Ecco i due tigri." (Behold, the two tigers.)

Charmed by the attentiveness of her hosts, and more than
ever overwhelmed by her friend, Elsa exploded in her
column against "the evil web of invective that has been
woven around" Maria Callas.

Maxwell's remark was no idle gesture. Its special timeliness was underlined by the Vienna State Opera's announcement on May 4th that Callas's scheduled return to
the Vienna "Festwochen" was cancelled. It was not a matter of broken contracts, for no written contract existed,
only a verbal understanding between the Meneghinis and
Herbert von Karajan, born in the joyous and impulsive
aura of Maria's 1956 Viennese triumph. However, 1957
had brought a reappraisal of the situation, in the light of
which the 1956 remuneration of $1,600 per evening was no
longer considered sufficient to the hard-bargaining management firm of Meneghini & Co. Vienna could not afford
more—it had to do without Callas.

Spokesmen of the Opera subsequently announced that
Callas wanted $500 more. They denied the surging rumor
of a violent quarrel between the diva and Herbert von
Karajan. In fact, Vienna took its disappointment over the
Callas cancellation with an equanimity becoming a city
that has survived a siege by the Turks, two World Wars,
and the Russian occupation in its long history. The "Festwochen" went on without Callas. Virginia Zeani of La
Scala sang *Traviata,* though, judging by the critics, not
very well.

Elsewhere, however, the event caused stronger repercussions. One wild report depicted an enraged von Karajan
tearing up the nonexistent contract before the diva's eyes.
In the world of opera, on and off stage, melodramatic gestures and hysterical behavior seem to be the only way to
face the issues, as some observers would have it. Yet this

particular issue involved little more than the cold facts of supply and demand; a business venture which failed to crystallize, to the mutual disappointment of both parties.

Emotions, of course, always play a substantial part in such situations, for the public mind does not take kindly to an artistic personage who is all business. But, in the world of Maria and Battista Meneghini, money *was* very important. She was the world's most sought-after operatic artist, and she knew her value.

At that stage of her career, Maria was no longer interested in increasing the number of her yearly appearances. In this instance, perhaps, she had miscalculated, believing that her demands would be ultimately met by Vienna. Even then, she was as justified in insisting on her requirement as was Vienna in refusing it. Were her demands too high? In the world of opera they were the maximum imaginable under the circumstances. By the prevailing standard of remuneration joyfully paid to such other practitioners of the vocal art as, say, Elvis Presley, a mere pittance. Be that as it may, the worldwide publicity resulting from the Vienna affair was singularly unfavorable.

La Scala's season was drawing to a close with the third and final "Callas production," Gluck's *Ifigenia in Tauride*, a lavish and majestic affair which gave such visual pleasures the critics felt it should have been presented much earlier in the season. Only four performances could be given under the circumstances.

Ifigenia is really *Iphigénie en Tauride,* an opera set to a French text based on the Euripides drama. Its story is so completely devoid of sexual passion that when the opera was first presented in 1779, it was noted with some consternation that the word "love" did not even appear in the libretto. Despite this added handicap, the opera is not forgotten, though its presentation is rather infrequent (Victor de Sabata conducted a Scala production in 1936 with Maria Caniglia).

Maria, dressed in baroque costumes of silk and brocade, made a stunning appearance in the title role. Musically, the part lay in her comfortable middle register. It imposed no taxing demands on her technique, and thus enabled her to concentrate the many channels of her art on infusing dramatic meaning into Ifigenia's stately narratives and declamations. Critic Eugenio Gara argued that in Visconti's staging and under Nino Sanzogno's direction some of Gluck's forceful drama had disappeared but, he added, "Maria Callas stayed with Gluck. She remained a vibrant, impetuous Ifigenia while the others pastoralized."

Elsa Maxwell flew in again from Paris, in time for the dress rehearsal. She joined Ghiringhelli and the Meneghinis for dinner, and subsequently devoted an entire long column to Callas, relegating the counts and princes that normally inhabit her European chronicles to only passing mention. Having heard only expressions of praise about her friend from Ghiringhelli, the loyal Elsa again vented her anger on Maria's puzzling unpopularity in many circles: "Someone somewhere is spreading poison about one of the most touching individuals I have ever known. I am going to track them down wherever they may be. Nothing can destroy the supreme art of Maria Callas."

After fond goodbyes, and reassurances of another meeting before long in Venice, Maxwell returned to her neglected counts and princes, and Maria completed her remaining appearances in the Gluck opera, with which La Scala's season came to an end.

Her sixth consecutive season at La Scala was crowned by a distinction coveted by all Italian artists. On June 21st, the honorary title of *Commendatore* was conferred upon

Maria Callas by President Gronchi at the recommendation of the Minister of Education, Aldo Moro, in recognition of her artistic achievements. Maria was proud and happy, and rightly so. Very few women had ever received this honor, Toti dal Monte alone among female opera singers then living.

In July, La Scala was on the move again, this time for a short engagement at the newly built, ultramodern opera house of Cologne. Maria, with the inseparable husband and inseparable poodle, went by way of Paris, where the now inseparable Elsa was waiting to reciprocate her friends' Milanese hospitality.

The three days following the Meneghinis' arrival in Paris grew into an almost uninterrupted, and certainly unforgettable, dream-world roundelay. There were visits to fashion salons and society parties, cocktails at the Baroness Rothschild's, dinner at Maxim's, sipping tea with the Windsors, going to races with Aly Khan, bumping into Elsa's ubiquitous princes and counts every which way, with a sprinkling of the more esoteric brand of royalty and maharajas fortunately present to keep the company from lapsing into routine.

After those three days, the Cologne appearance was, perhaps, something of an anticlimax to the Meneghinis, though hardly to their hosts. Maria's arrival, on a bright Fourth of July, was proclaimed by the local *Bildzeitung* with the headline: WORLD'S MOST EXPENSIVE VOICE ARRIVES! The echo of the much-publicized Vienna cancellation was still noticeable.

To the amazement of the press, however, Maria received reporters graciously and answered all questions with endless patience. At the Hotel Excelsior, where the party arrived to discover that the Meneghini suite was not yet ready for them, Maria flashed an easy smile and ac-

cepted the management's offer of a temporary room with
a complete absence of prima donna antics. There was nothing particularly newsworthy or praiseworthy in her behavior, but many observers found it so in the light of the
publicity that had preceded her visit.

In the afternoon, Maria and her husband visited the
opera house. The building had been hailed by some experts
as the last word in functional design but, as is the case with
unconventional and daring structures, it was not built to
everyone's taste. Superintendent Maisch was, naturally,
eager to hear the opinion of a famous diva.

"How do you like the theater?" he asked.

"I don't know. I haven't seen it yet" was the totally
unexpected answer. Meneghini quickly explained, as best
as he could, the case history of Maria's extraordinary
myopia.

Cologne was overwhelmed by La Scala's performance, and Maria was praised extravagantly. But the choice
of the opera proved inauspicious. In Germany, *Die Nacht-
wandlerin,* which is the rather less euphonious German
equivalent of *La Sonnambula,* was practically unknown.
Neither Bellini's music nor the visual aspect of the production succeeded in convincing the patrons that the
opera's obscurity was unwarranted. But German audiences have always responded enthusiastically to authentic
Italian performances of Italian opera—something they
are very seldom exposed to—and La Scala's 1957 visit provided such a happy occasion.

Following Maria's return to Milan, the strenuous pace
of her schedule continued with two operatic recordings at
La Scala. Puccini was the composer of the month, with
Manon Lescaut and *Turandot* on the agenda, both scheduled for recording during the last three weeks of July. But

the big news was the reappearance of the familiar figure
of Tullio Serafin on the podium. Since their reconciliation
at a quiet meeting earlier that year, the relationship between Maria and her old mentor had become as warm
as ever.

It was particularly gratifying to have Serafin preside
over *Turandot*. The opera brought back many old memories, hours spent together in dedicated study, triumphs
shared in Venice and Verona in the faraway years of 1948
and 1949. During the peak years of her career, however,
Maria was no longer seen in Puccini's last opera, nor did
the recording succeed in reviving her interest.

Few operatic sopranos would call Turandot their
favorite role, and Maria Callas is no exception. The
Chinese princess is a cold, heartless figure who sings cold,
heartless music. Puccini, who was said to have been in love
with the immortal females of the operas he composed,
lavished all his affection on the touching, suffering Liù,
the opera's "other" soprano. Poor Liù does not get the
hero, but hers is the glory of Puccini's vibrant, heart-
rending musical inspiration, and the audience's sympathy.
The libretto bestows the bliss of one of opera's handful
of happy endings on Turandot—a privilege for which
her character is ill qualified—but poetic justice prevails in
the cruelly difficult and strenuous demands of Puccini's
music. To Maria Callas, the role represented a challenge,
and she acquitted herself with characteristic aplomb in her
recorded performance, though no longer with the easy
opulence in the high register which she had possessed when
Turandot was still one of her "specialties."

The Liù of that recording was Maria's good friend
Elisabeth Schwarzkopf. It was their first joint recording,
and the two artists had a marvelous time of it. Calaf, the

Unknown Prince, was Eugenio Fernandi who, after this auspicious disc debut, began a successful career at the Metropolitan.

Di Stefano was Maria's partner in Puccini's *Manon Lescaut*. It was their tenth recorded collaboration. No others have followed to date. The name part of this opera, like Mimi and Nedda, is one of Maria Callas's "recorded roles." She has not yet portrayed it in actual performance. Her recorded interpretation in 1957 was a penetrating character study, revealing, in its carefully pointed-up musical subtleties, her thorough study and complete understanding of Manon's impetuous personality. Vocally, however, she was not always in her best form. Maria was not pleased with the end result, and gave only a reluctant approval to its belated release late in 1959.

Four operas already recorded in 1957, one yet to come. This, undoubtedly, was Maria's "recording" year. Because of these exhausting commitments, because of the prolonged American tour and her late rejoining of La Scala, because of the extraordinary engagements undertaken for the summer, it turned out to be in all respects, a very trying, very difficult year.

In late August, Maria Callas returned to Greece, for the first time in twelve years, to fulfill an engagement for two concerts as part of the annual Athens Festival of Music and Drama.

She went with a strange mixture of feelings. In a sense it was a homecoming, for Maria Callas, a woman of many moods, is also a woman of many homes. In some of her moods she is an American. Born in the United States, she has retained American characteristics indelibly planted during her New York childhood. She travels with an American passport and returns frequently enough not to feel out of place in American surroundings. But she has

spent too many important years away to have retained a
deep sense of belonging. Italy is her artistic home, and art
is the only thing in life to which Maria has been beholden
with consistent, undeviating allegiance. Having been married to an Italian, keeping an Italian home, achieving an
institution-like status in Italian social and artistic life
have identified her, beyond the formal requirements of
citizenship, with the consciousness of her adopted country.

Yet, underneath the American and Italian elements in
her background, there were moods, and many, in which she
felt completely identified with Greece. The awareness of
cultural and linguistic tradition, the strength of her Orthodox religion gave this feeling substantial foundation. But
even stronger was the bondage born from the unforgotten
experience of sharing the bitter war years with the Greek
people.

Greece was proud of Maria Callas, but the local press
greeted the diva's arrival with no evidence of affection.
The widely publicized break between Maria and her mother
had been commented upon more extravagantly in Athens
than in any other part of the world. Evangelia Callas was
an Athens resident during these years. She saw to it that
the press was well supplied with details of the famous friction. No attempt was ever made on Maria's part to deny
any of the allegations, to defend herself, to present her side
of the story. It was a private matter concerning her and her
family, she insisted. The fact that her mother had never
considered it as such made no difference as far as she was
concerned.

To make matters more complicated, Maria's return to
Greece was seized upon by the opposition party to create
a political issue in the hope of causing the downfall of the
Karamanlis government. According to information circulated by the opposition, Callas's fee for the series of two

concerts amounted to $9,000, an exorbitant figure for a country that found the road of post-war reconstruction arduously difficult.

Hoping to avert further deterioration of sentiment, Evangelia and Jackie Callas were persuaded by a government agency to take a trip to the United States. They were no longer in Athens when Maria and Battista arrived.

It did not take long for Maria to size up the situation. Unfortunately, she arrived in a rundown, exhausted condition which was aggravated by the sudden change into Athens' hot, arid climate. Realizing that she could not perform to the best of her abilities, Maria decided to cancel her first concert scheduled for August 1st. To make matters worse, her decision was announced only one hour before curtain time, which caused a frenzied reaction from thousands of spectators.

All the persuasive powers of Giovanni Battista Meneghini were needed to placate the press and smooth the atmosphere. He rose to the task. After all, he said, artists were human beings subject to illness and indisposition. Why not consider the extreme pressures under which artists have to live, and which make them even more accessible to the dangers of mental and physical exhaustion! How can an artist be attacked for the enormity of her fees, and then attacked for refusing to perform for such fees knowing that she could not measure up to her own standards and the level expected of her?

Five evenings later, Maria Callas appeared before an antagonistic audience in the huge open-air amphitheatre. She gave an exacting program, and sang like a fury possessed. It was the tour de force of her Metropolitan debut all over again. When the concert ended, there was no sign of hostility. Athens was proud of Maria Callas, period. Premier Konstantin Karamanlis, who must have interpreted the torrential applause as a vote of confidence in his teetering government, personally requested Maria to return to the Greek capital as soon as possible.

In keeping with her established *modus operandi,* Maria made no commitments. Her immediate schedule of engagements was already crowded enough. La Scala's projected journey to the Edinburgh Festival, where she was to be one of the central attractions, was only a few weeks away. Without delay, the Meneghinis took leave of Athens and returned home after a brief but restful stop at Ischia in the Bay of Naples.

When Maria returned to Milan in early August, her physician, Dr. Arnaldo Semeraro, found that she was suffering from a serious nervous exhaustion, caused by overwork and fatigue. He advised against the Edinburgh trip and strongly urged that Maria take a complete rest for at least thirty days.

With the day of departure approaching, Meneghini lost no time to inform Luigi Oldani, general secretary of La Scala, that, in view of her condition, Maria could not make the trip. But Oldani would not consider such a lastminute change of plans. The opera in question was *La Sonnambula.* Its title role, he argued, was identified with Callas, her appearances had been promised to England and extensively publicized; a substitute would be out of the question. Besides, Oldani added, "Maria will be all right. She can do wonders."

Thus, against her doctor's advice, out of a feeling of obligation to La Scala, and mindful of the possibility of the damaging consequences that could follow another cancellation, Maria departed for Edinburgh. The traveling group, consisting of casts for four operas, included conductors Votto, Sanzogno, and Gavazzeni and a large contingent of singers. Renata Scotto, a very promising young

coloratura soprano, was taken along as a possible emergency substitute, in consideration of Maria's delicate
health.

The first *La Sonnambula* was broadcast. Maria
sounded tired, and she was decidedly in poor voice. A
British doctor, summoned to examine her, recommended
that she withdraw. Having come this far, however, Maria
was determined to take part in the four performances
specified in her engagement. Her second evening (August
21st) went much better. Thereupon Oldani made the announcement that an extra performance of *La Sonnambula*
would be given on September 3rd.

At this point, Maria Callas decided to draw the line.
Loyalty is fine, she said, but there must be a limit. Oldani's
arguments to the contrary, she declared categorically that
she would not participate in the fifth performance. By the
third evening, suffering from the damp, chilly weather, her
vocal form had reached its lowest level; the performance
was almost disastrous. Recovering somewhat for her final
appearance, on August 29th, she gave her best vocal effort
—her dramatic conception of the role was highly praised
throughout the engagement—though, unfortunately, the
entire performance suffered from the agonizing misfunc-
tion of the Festival's lighting system. After that tempestuous evening, true to her earlier announcement, she had had
enough.

The Mayor of Edinburgh and his wife came by to wish
her well before the Meneghinis departed. The sympathetic
views of England's music critics were summed up by
Albert Hutton in *Music and Musicians:* "... one was glad
for her sake when she departed for the warm south."

But music critics don't influence public opinion. The
British papers, for the most part, seized upon the occasion
to expose another "Callas walkout." The condition of her

vocal powers, of her health, was entirely ignored, and so was Maria's insistence that she had carried out her contractual obligations. By the time the Meneghinis reached London, the news was out in the Italian press as well: the tempestuous diva had caused another scandal, this time disgracing Italy's leading lyric theater.

Maria and Battista were heading for Venice, to the great party Elsa Maxwell was organizing in Maria's honor. After the unceasing strain of the months behind her, a little fun and carefree relaxation was exactly what she needed. She was seriously concerned about her health and the engagements awaiting her in the fall. So much so that she cabled the San Francisco Opera's General Manager, Kurt Herbert Adler, on September 1st to have a substitute ready in the event she should be unable to make her American journey.

La Sonnambula went on in Edinburgh on September 3rd, and Renata Scotto, till then a comparative unknown, embarked on her way to stardom with a captivating portrayal of Amina. The same day Maria arrived in Venice and was promptly engulfed by the international set. Elsa Maxwell, however, did her no service with this gushing disclosure in her column: "I have had many presents in my life ... but I have never had any star give up a performance in an opera because she felt she was breaking her word to a friend. ..."

Elsa, of course, outdid herself with the ball. According to her own inimitable description: "I have never given a better dinner and ball in my life. It had a flare of such joy and happiness. I played the piano and Callas sat on the platform by me humming 'Stormy Weather.' Even two princesses who hated each other were found exchanging smiles while another comtesse who couldn't remain in the same room with Merle Oberon stayed until 5 A.M."

It was *that* kind of a party.

Two days later, the gay company assembled on the *Christina,* the fabulous yacht owned by Aristotle Onassis, the multimillionaire Greek shipowner, another of Maxwell's great friends. Onassis had long been an admirer of his famous Greek compatriot. This was the beginning of a celebrated friendship.

It was a high-spirited, relaxing, fully entertaining week Maria and her husband spent in Venice, the kind no one would begrudge a tired businessman, or even a tired opera singer. But with the name of Maria Callas, public opinion had been accustomed to associate different kinds of standards. For an artist who had just "walked out" on La Scala for alleged reasons of health, she was found looking much too vigorous and carefree in the news photos which began circulating in the world press illustrating the gay doings at Elsa Maxwell's ball or showing the diva holding court among the celebrity set against the sparkling sand and striped cabanas of the Lido.

Returning to Milan on the eighth of September, Maria found an atmosphere of almost frightening chilliness. Still believing herself completely in the right, and refusing to admit any acts of disloyalty toward La Scala, she sought contact with Antonio Ghiringhelli, demanding that the theater make a public announcement to clear her name. Ghiringhelli refused to take a public stand.

The ensuing days unleashed a mounting avalanche of events which caused Maria's publicity to grow steadily and progressively worse.

Maria's doctors—she consulted a specialist in addition to Dr. Semeraro—persisted in advising her against the projected American journey and informed her that stage appearances were out of the question. Citing her condition and the expert medical advice she had received, Maria

cabled the San Francisco Opera on September 13th that she
would be unable to appear at the scheduled time, but offered to be present for the October portion of the engagement.

San Francisco's Kurt Herbert Adler flared up into a
colossal rage. There were only two weeks before the evening of the projected Callas debut. Adler knew about the
Edinburgh episode, had seen the generous pictorial coverage of the Maxwell ball. The mental association with the
Athens and Vienna cancellations was inescapable. He
announced to the press that the Callas debut was off and
quickly engaged Leyla Gencer for the part of Lucia and
Leonie Rysanek for Lady Macbeth. At the same time, he
referred the case of Maria Callas to the Board of the
American Guild of Musical Artists for arbitration. The
Guild decided to act on the case as soon as Maria Callas
could appear to testify.

When news of Adler's action reached Maria in Milan,
she showed remarkable composure. Although it was
rumored that an adverse ruling from AGMA could mean
suspension, she felt she had all the medical certificates
necessary to prove that her good will was beyond question.
Besides, she declared for the benefit of the press, ''artists
are an international treasure. Impresarios should realize
this and understand the situation.''

But the ''situation'' had already progressed to a point
beyond understanding. In such a predicament, an alert
personal press agent could have presented the issues in
more sympathetic colors. But Maria Callas, behind whose
incredible celebrity and press coverage the world had
always suspected the lurking shadows of press agentry,
actually had no such means at her disposal, not even an
American representative to speak up in her favor.

A few days after the break of the San Francisco story,
the web of harmful publicity tightened even closer around

the figure of Maria Callas. While San Francisco was seething, the diva went through a week of rigorous sessions to complete her fifth recorded opera of 1957, Cherubini's *Medea*. It was produced by the Italian Ricordi firm in collaboration with Mercury Records of America. All preparations, of course, had been made long before recording time. Maria had to face two alternatives: cancel the recordings and be blamed for one more cancellation, or go ahead with the plan, and be blamed anyway. Under the circumstances, she decided to go through with the sessions.

But after September 19th, with the conclusion of the *Medea* recording, Maria finally treated herself to the long rest her doctors and her husband had long been urging her to take. This temporary retirement from the limelight brought about a welcome hiatus in what had seemed to be an endless barrage of news releases about her past adventures and future plans.

While Maria rested, Renata Tebaldi fired off a few politely phrased but nevertheless well-aimed salvos in a series of Italian magazine articles against her erstwhile great friend, Elsa Maxwell. The inevitable reply followed with Elsa's firm reiteration of absolute loyalty and devotion to Maria Callas.

With the arrival of fall, San Francisco had brought its turbulent season to a close. The Chicago Lyric opened on October 11th with Verdi's *Otello,* putting forth the remarkable trio of Mario del Monaco, Renata Tebaldi, and Tito Gobbi. Tullio Serafin who, of course, had conducted Maria's *Medea* recording in Milan, revealed himself in the Chicago pit on opening night, energetic and authoritative as ever. Tebaldi rejoined the Metropolitan in early November, but the sudden death of her mother forced her to cut short her season and return to Milan.

Maria Callas arrived in New York on November 5th.

The primary cause of her visit was non-musical—the final showdown in the seemingly interminable lawsuit. To make up for this unwelcome obligation, and to justify her trip on artistic grounds, she accepted an engagement to open the season of the newly formed Dallas Civic Opera Company.

The emergence of oil-rich Dallas as an important factor on the world's operatic map was the doing of former Chicagoan Lawrence Kelly. A bitter courtroom fight arising from the Chicago Lyric's deficit-ridden 1956 season had separated the Fox–Kelly managerial combination and had left Carol Fox there in firm control. Kelly and Rescigno teamed up again and, with encouraging public support and the prospect of the spectacular Callas, succeeded in launching their initial "season" in Dallas in such an impressive manner as to produce an enthusiastic civic reception and a guarantee of continuing the venture for years to come.

In 1957, the "season" consisted of two evenings of Rossini's *L'Italiana in Algeri* starring Giulietta Simionato, preceded by a gala concert by Maria Callas. Maria's presence guaranteed worldwide attention and a most auspicious beginning. The event shattered all box-office records for a solo appearance in Dallas and took in a Texas-sized $17,000. It was billed as a "benefit" concert. While box-office statistics were cheerfully promulgated, the Callas honorarium remained a carefully guarded secret.

Whatever it was, however, Maria had earned it. Looking her most glamorous in a gold silk dress, she opened her concert characteristically with Constanze's fiendishly acrobatic aria "Martern aller Arten" from Mozart's *Abduction from the Seraglio,* one of the most difficult pieces of music ever written for the human voice. Following a similarly rigorous fare (arias from *Macbeth* and *I Vespri Siciliani*), she ended the program, after an intermission

change into a dramatic black velvet dress, with the Tower
Scene from Donizetti's *Anna Bolena*. This may have been
the first time that this music was sung in the United States.

Four days before the joyful junction of Callas and
Dallas, on November 17th, the announcement was made
that the Callas–Bagarozy lawsuit had finally been settled.
It was an out-of-court settlement; the terms were not made
public. Maria had little to say about it except to express
relief: "I am tired of being a courtroom character."

The brief American journey in November, 1957, accomplished both its artistic and legal mission with notable
success. A longer stay, embracing Maria's Metropolitan
engagement, was still a long way off, since she was not
expected there during the Met's opening months. On the
other hand, opening nights awaited her this time *both* in
Milan and Rome, for the new operatic season in Italy
coincides with the end of the calendar year.

Looking back on stormy 1957, remembering Sordello,
Vienna, Athens, Edinburgh and contrasting these memories with the carefree days of Paris and Venice, the
triumphant moments of Dallas, and the welcome disappear-
ance of the long-hovering legal shadows, Maria Callas
could have easily told herself: "All's well that ends well."
Perhaps, she may have thought, a period of calm was finally
dawning after the passing storm. Perhaps the new year of
1958 would bring about far-reaching changes, with a hint
of hope for less feuds and more peace of mind, less crises
and more diversions.

1958 did bring far-reaching changes, but not the kind
she hoped for.

CHAPTER **11**

The Roman Scandal

> Anna
> *Se meritai quest'onta*
> *giudica Tu . . . o Dio*
> DONIZETTI—ANNA BOLENA

By contrast with the effusive enthusiasm of Texas, Maria found the chill of Milan hard to bear. La Scala, from Ghiringhelli down to the minor functionaries, treated her with stony indifference. An atmosphere of uneasiness surrounded her visits, not at all like the stimulating preopening preparations of past seasons.

Edinburgh was still fresh in everyone's memory. In spite of Maria's reiterated stand about the unjustness of the accusations leveled against her, the hostile feeling in and around La Scala remained unchanged. She was still accused of disloyalty to the institution and of having breached her obligations. The one person who could have cleared her name by openly confirming the facts as Maria had presented them, Superintendent Ghiringhelli, remained silent.

Toward the end of November, rehearsals began in preparation for the opening production of the 1957/1958 season, Verdi's *Un Ballo in Maschera*. Maria, down to an all-time-slim 117 pounds, had to make last-minute costume adjustments to make up for a loss of weight that caused serious concern among her friends. If their concern was for her physical condition, they were worried needlessly. She was in excellent health. Her spirits, her nerves were another matter.

An aura of irritability hung over the rehearsals, tempers often verging on the breaking point, although major crises were averted. As Giuseppe di Stefano, the tenor star of the Verdi opera, and Maria rehearsed the lengthy love duet in *Ballo's* second act, the lack of conviction with which they sang their ardent vows was all too evident on both sides.

By opening night, however, the opera had crystallized into a characteristically brilliant and exciting Scala production. Margherita Wallmann's staging startled the audience with the austerity of its settings, in stern evocation of American pioneer life. But, whether placed into its rightful historical setting of eighteenth-century Sweden, or into the pseudo-American world of colonial New England where the censorship of Verdi's time had forced it, the story of *Un Ballo in Maschera* is equally unconvincing. Its ultimate success is in the hands of the musical interpreters.

Inspired by the thrill of the occasion and sparked by Verdi's inflammable music, this time Callas and Di Stefano had no trouble whatever in summoning the required ardor for the second-act love scene. Maria sang with an inner

fire and intensity reminiscent of her greatest triumphs,
shining particularly in the touching "Morrò, ma prima in
grazia" of the third act. She looked stunning in her costumes, which contrasted rather sharply with the austere
surroundings. The persistent rumors about her vocal decline evaporated before the impressive evidence to the
contrary. Di Stefano, also in excellent form, Giulietta
Simionato as Ulrica, and Ettore Bastianini as Renato contributed nobly to the evening's glories, which were witnessed by President Gronchi and the customary gala
audience.

The Verdi opera was the only winter production scheduled for Maria Callas that season in Milan. She appeared
in several repeat presentations in December, and spent her
days preparing once again for Bellini's *Norma,* in which
she was scheduled to open Rome's opera season on January 2, 1958.

Although Italy's two leading operatic theaters are
forever engulfed in bitter rivalry, their programming
schedules are wisely arranged in such a fashion that the
top Italian singers can contribute their talents to both institutions. Maria, who had made her Roman debut in 1950,
was seen frequently on the famous lyric stage of the Italian
capital during the first three years of her La Scala association. In more recent seasons, however, the demands of
her American commitments had repeatedly interfered with
her accepting Rome's invitations.

Absent from Rome since that tempestuous *Medea* of
January, 1954, which had given her a great triumph and
also some undesirable publicity, Maria was delighted at
the prospect of returning there in one of her favorite roles.

Norma was a Callas portrayal which Rome had already admired in 1953. Now, five years later, Maria was
gratified to find the same fellow-artists who had appeared

with her in the earlier production: Fedora Barbieri, Franco Corelli, and Giulio Neri, and the same conductor, the Roman veteran Gabriele Santini.

Maria and Battista arrived in Rome on December 26th, after having spent a quiet Christmas in Milan. Rehearsals began the following day under the best possible auspices. But the genial mood was soon dampened when Barbieri suddenly became ill with influenza. The part of Adalgisa was taken over by Miriam Pirazzini.

At first everything went remarkably well. At the rehearsal on December 29th, however, a slight pain developed in her throat, and Maria spent the next day resting in her suite at the nearby Hotel Quirinale. Refreshed, and in excellent vocal condition, she sang in full voice at the dress rehearsal on the last day of the year, so much so that the cautious Santini had to ask her to conserve her powers for the performance. At 9 P.M. that evening, Maria sang "Casta Diva" on a New Year's Eve television broadcast. After the broadcast she and Meneghini joined a small circle of friends for a champagne celebration at the "Circolo degli Scacchi" which lasted until a little after 1 A.M.

When Maria awoke on the first morning of 1958, her voice was gone. With opening night only thirty-six hours away, she could barely whisper. Meneghini called one doctor after another that holiday morning until finally one could be persuaded to come over. Frantic calls were also put through to the management of the Opera.

Sanpaoli, artistic director of the Rome Opera, rushed over in the afternoon, looking understandably agitated.

"How are you? How is your voice?" he asked.

"Bad. You'd better see to it that a substitute is ready."

"Substitute?" gasped Sanpaoli incredulously. "Impossible. This is no ordinary evening. This is a gala opening! The house is sold out, and the public paid to see and hear Callas!''

Indeed, it was no ordinary event. The President of the Italian Republic was expected, with his wife. Seats were sold at the exorbitant level of 24,000 lire ($40) top. There was no time to engage a substitute, and the cancellation of the performance was inconceivable.

The Meneghinis and the worried director sat around in gloom while Maria sprayed her throat and swallowed the prescribed sedatives. Finally, the three reached the inevitable conclusion that Maria would have to go on with whatever voice she would be able to summon. Even Meneghini agreed, for all his concern about Maria's well-being, that under the circumstances this was the only solution.

Maria retired early and awoke the following morning in what appeared to be a vastly improved condition. Her voice seemed to be returning. She was filled with optimism.

As the day progressed, however, it became evident that the improvement was only the temporary result of medical treatment. She was still in no condition to risk the crucial test of an evening of *Norma*.

Maria continued taking her medicines dejectedly and applying hot compresses while muttering prayers and waiting for a miracle. When evening fell, the Meneghinis were filled with forebodings of disaster.

It was opening night in Rome, 9:00 P.M., January 2, 1958. The Rome Opera was filled to capacity. Elegant Romans settled into their expensive seats and cast respectfully curious glances toward the luxurious privacy of what was once known as the royal box in the days when the house was still called the *Teatro Reale*. That night it harbored the figures of President and Signora Gronchi.

Nobility and officialdom, socialites and students, tourists and starlets contentedly shared the comforting thought of being able to afford the most expensive entertainment and the most imposing social event of the day. They also shared a blissful ignorance of the turmoil and heartbreak backstage.

The RAI network broadcast the opening. All Italy was listening:

"Norma viene . . . e la stella di Roma sbigottita si copre di un velo. . . ." ("Norma approaches, and the star of Rome veils itself in terror") intoned the chorus of Druid priestesses heralding the prima donna's entrance.

And Norma came, unfurling Bellini's majestic, menacing phrases:

"Sediziose voci, voci di guerra avvi chi alzar s'attenta. . . ." ("Who dares to raise seditious, war-like voices, to question my words that foretell the ordained fate of Rome?")

From the opening phrase Maria Callas knew that she was fighting a losing battle: her voice, or what was left of it, was going rapidly. The audience immediately sensed trouble. The expensive seats began to creak, the patrons muttered, exchanged worried glances, and some glowered ominously.

Maria could barely get through the taxing measures of "Casta Diva." The rousing *cabaletta,* which in other times had always been her peerless tour-de-force, now sounded tired and uninspiring. There was a mild applause, all but lost in mounting noises of displeasure.

The first act seemed interminable to Maria. When it was over, and the curtain fell, she rushed back to her dressing room amidst angry shouts of "Go back to Milan!" "You cost us a million lire!" In good voice, at her consummate best, Maria Callas would have been acclaimed for her great contribution to Rome's operatic glory. Now,

in her moment of weakness, she suddenly became an alien,
an outcast, a property of Milan, and the rivalry between
the two theaters burst open in all its cold fury. The reference to her fee, though ill-tempered, was accurate. The
gala audience was not getting its money's worth.

Rudeness and fierce demonstrations do not, as a rule,
frighten Maria Callas. Throughout a stormy career, she
has shouldered a generous share of them. Hisses and boos
enrage her, but fortify her as well, and fill her with determination to outdo herself, to fight back with her only
weapon, her art. But that night her voice was not there to
protect her. She was defenseless.

Closed in her dressing room, shivering with exhaustion, hoarse and growing weaker by the minute, she made
her decision. She would not return for the second act.
Norma was finished for her that evening.

The word spread through the corridors of the theater.
Carlo Latini, the Superintendent of the Opera, came, followed by other officials, Santini, the conductor, Margherita
Wallmann, the stage director, all offering words of encouragement, reminding her that the most trying moments
of the opera were behind her, begging her to continue.
After sober reasoning failed, they tried to appeal to her
emotions, to her pride, to her patriotism and respect for
the Head of State, summoning all the powers of Italian
eloquence and the full gamut of the Italian temperament.
It was useless.

Desperation then compelled the suggestion that she
should go back and walk through the part, declaiming the
words instead of singing. It would save the evening, some
argued. That kind of a violent disgrace to Bellini's music,
Maria retorted, would be unthinkable. No, she could not
return. Let the theater put on a substitute!

There was no substitute.

Long intermissions are not unusual in Italian theaters, particularly on opening nights. The audience rather likes them for the opportunities thus afforded for self-admiration, for lavish parades of eye-filling diamonds and décolletages. But after thirty minutes of inaction, the uneasy feeling began to spread around that something was not in order. The continued presence of the Presidential couple served to allay the fears for a while longer.

Finally, after forty-five minutes of waiting, came the laconic and incredible announcement through the loudspeakers: "The management is compelled to suspend the performance for reasons beyond its control."

After a few seconds of disbelieving, stunned silence, the dignified gathering erupted into a din of unbecoming catcalls—all aimed at Maria Callas. Heated arguments ensued, fists were raised toward the stage, angry shouts reverberated through the plush interiors. There was no sign from the management to explain, to calm the nerves, to confront the public in any way. President and Mrs. Gronchi had departed.

When the initial wave of their anger was spent, the crowds slowly filtered out of the theater, forming a menacing block around it. Motorized policemen arrived to establish order, but the demonstrators moved on to surround the Hotel Quirinale. The name of Maria Callas was on all lips. "What a *scandalo!*" "What a *disgrazia!*" "What an affront to the Head of State!"

The diva had left the theater through an underground passageway, accompanied by Meneghini and Elsa Maxwell, who had kept her company in the solitude of her dressing room. From her hotel suite, Maria listened to the curses, the angry shouts that persisted long into the night.

Rome had not had such a fiery evening of music since Nero's famous violin recital.

It was a full-blown, spectacular scandal in every sense of the word. All the cares of the world suddenly vanished from the Italian headlines to make room for a thorough-going coverage of the Opera's scuttled opening. This time, implied the scathing tone of most commentators, La Callas had gone too far. . . .

The parade of demonstrators continued in front of the Hotel Quirinale all through the following day.

Maria rushed away a letter of apology to President Gronchi and his wife, and received almost immediately a reassuring and most sympathetic telephone reply from the First Lady. Other messages, cables, and telegrams poured in, even a telephone call from Dallas, and heartening expressions of solidarity from such colleagues as Giulietta Simionato and Graziella Sciutti, conductor Gavazzeni, and old friend Luchino Visconti. But these manifestations of friendship and confidence were dwarfed by the persistent fury of the press and the implacable outcry of popular opinion.

Nor did it help matters when Elsa Maxwell, carried away by the concentrated attack on her friend, delivered herself later that day of an angry harangue in which she called the Italian press a bunch of barbarians. Only Maxwell's expeditious departure for the United States averted further deterioration of the mess into an international incident. All Italy was, of course, engulfed by the uproar. In Milan, a fist fight broke out in the smart Biffi Scala restaurant when a loyal Callas fan dared to raise his voice against the prevailing public sentiment.

While the storm raged, the diva remained secluded in her hotel suite. The doctors confirmed her condition as a throat inflammation accompanied by hoarseness and a "lowering of the voice," a fairly common phenomenon among singers. Aside from publishing the medical reports,

Maria saw no need for discussing the incident with the press. She firmly believed that the clear proof of her illness would vindicate her in the eyes of the public. But the agitation had long passed the point where it could be assuaged by a mere medical bulletin.

On the evening of January 4th, instead of the scheduled first repeat of Norma, the Rome Opera held another "opening." Another soprano, the generously proportioned Anita Cerquetti, was rushed in from Naples to take over the role of Norma. She came with the courteous dispensation of Ghiringhelli, who allowed her to pass up a Milan engagement in deference to the rival theater's critical need.

The Rome Opera was again filled to capacity, the audience just as well dressed and almost as tense. Foreign Minister Giuseppe Pella represented the Italian government and, this time, he and the rest of the assemblage were treated to a complete *Norma*. Rome wanted a triumphant opening very badly. When it was over, there were twelve curtain calls, and fervid cries of "Viva l'Italia!" "Vivan le voci italiane!"

Two days later, when the fury had died down somewhat, the press began to re-examine its one-sided attitude about the "Callas case." "How could a theater of such prestige and such a roster of artists approach an opening without a qualified understudy?" asked Rome's influential daily *Il Tempo*. It was a good question. Superintendent Carlo Latini attempted several explanations, but none of them convincing enough to escape severe criticism.

Nor can such absence of foresight be justified on any grounds. In recent times, the Metropolitan Opera was able to press three tenors into service for that many acts to save a performance of Wagner's *Tristan und Isolde*. It is hardly conceivable that Rome could not have found an adequate Norma to save *its* performance and to avoid the resulting huge embarrassment.

As the enforced rest, and the medical treatment began to show their effects, Maria declared herself fit to undertake the remaining two performances of her engagement, which were scheduled for January 8th and 11th.

The Opera's management, however, was not only unwilling to accept her offer, but published a statement disclaiming responsibility for her return "in the light of the present state of tension and the possible disturbances which might damage the institution, as well as law and order." Armed with this ominous declaration, Latini obtained a ruling from the Prefecture of Rome which closed the theater's doors to the controversial diva.

It was a highly debatable action on the management's part, motivated undoubtedly by the theory that attacking was safer than being attacked. It brought forth this disapproving comment from *Il Tempo:* "This case was created by the absence of a qualified substitute in the time of need. The management's proccupation with washing its hands like Pontius Pilate of the whole affair, and its referring the decision to the Prefect, has enlarged the issues to unlikely dimensions."

The "dimensions" were extraordinary indeed. Even the Italian parliament resounded with animated discussions of the "caso Callas," accompanied by fervent debates of such allied issues as the rivalry of Italian theaters, wasteful managements, and excessive power enjoyed by operatic stars. Deputy Bozzi took Callas to task primarily for her slight against the Head of State, while Deputy Bonfantini went after the management of the Opera with similar sternness.

"Let Callas have tantrums, let her have her volatile

moods," editorialized Rome's *Momento Sera,* "Art needs caprice." A liberal view such as this illuminates the fact that even sympathetic observers preferred to treat the episode as a result of capricious action. Somehow the very essence of the case, namely that an artist was truly indisposed, as shown not only by medical evidence but also by the unmistakable display of her enfeebled voice before nearly four thousand spectators, made no impression whatever.

Fedora Barbieri, one of the many artists approached by the press for an opinion on the case, testified that Maria's voice had appeared strained even during rehearsals. She also pointed out another plain truth: "If Callas withdrew it could not have been out of caprice. She must have known that this interruption could have turned out only to her disadvantage."

What could Callas have gained by the walkout? She had already enjoyed publicity to a sickening degree. At any rate, publicity of the kind that grew out of the episode could hardly have been desirable. She had nothing to gain, and everything to lose, most specifically four million *lire* in fees.

She was, on the other hand, guilty of poor judgment. With all the public sentiment against her, she could have still triumphed over the situation by facing the audience and explaining her predicament. Aided by the force of her personality and superior theatrical ability, she could have turned the tide in her own favor. Even later, after leaving the theater, she could have appeared on television, possibly with that engaging little poodle on her arm, to give her side of the story. American history has established proof that far more embarrassing situations can be explained in a similar manner. Maria Callas chose, instead, to remain silent. Facing the audience, she insisted, was the management's responsibility. Technically speaking, she was right, but Carlo Latini—lacking the Callas charm, talent, and personality—could hardly have saved the situation, nor did he display the required courage to even attempt it.

Faced with the Management's steadfast denial of Maria's right to return, the indignant Meneghini retained the prominent Roman attorney, Ercole Graziadei, and threatened with a lawsuit. Spokesmen for the Opera instantly retaliated with a similar announcement. But after conferences that lasted several hours on January 8th, the lawyers mutually agreed not to press legal action at that time.

On the morning of January 9th, Meneghini sadly announced to the assembled reporters at the hotel: "There is nothing for us to do here any more." Maria came down from her suite shortly thereafter, dressed for travel. She posed patiently for pictures, but gave no interviews. Finally, as the moment of parting came, she expressed her thanks to the thousands of fans who, in spite of all agitation, assured her in person, by mail, and by telegraph, of their sympathy and continued affections. An hour later, Signor and Signora Meneghini were on their way home.

Thinking back on the nightmare-like ordeal, Maria saw herself victimized both by circumstances and by a cruel and vindictive public opinion. The violent demonstrations that had taken place before the Hotel Quirinale reminded her of the lynch mobs she had read about in her American childhood. There was nothing for which she could reproach herself—she had acted in a manner to uphold art; rather than give an inferior performance she had preferred not to sing. Explaining the situation to the audience was the manager's responsibility, the same way as a host would not expect his cook to apologize for an unsuccessful dinner. Yes, she had followed what she firmly believed to be the only true and honest course. The over-whelming majority did not see the issues that way, but this circumstance failed to weaken her conviction.

With the most agonizing experience of her artistic life behind her, it was the same strong-willed, proud, and obsessively perfectionist Maria Callas who returned to Milan.

Milan and Rome may be adversaries in Italian oper-atic life, but officially neither stood on the side of Maria Callas in the year 1958. Friends and well-wishers showered the Meneghinis with their attentions upon their return, but not a sign of welcome issued forth from La Scala.

Un Ballo in Maschera was given on the evening of the 9th, the opera for which Anita Cerquetti originally had been engaged to substitute for Callas during the latter's Rome Opera stint. Even though Cerquetti was now in Rome with Ghiringhelli's blessings, and Callas was available in Milan, no one seemed to take notice, and a young and fairly unknown soprano was asked to take over the role of Amelia.

Of course, Maria's return to Milan was far from un-noticed. A councilman of the city by the name of Gian-franco Crespi assured himself of a day in the limelight by a public inquiry to the Mayor of Milan: "What caution will be taken to avoid incidents here such as recently oc-curred in Rome as a result of a famous singer's undue behavior?"

In the light of such display of animosity, a prolonged absence from Milan seemed to Maria like an act of Provi-dence. Her schedule called for a three-month tour abroad, mainly in the United States. She was not due back at La Scala until April, at which time she was expected to wind

up the season in Donizetti's *Anna Bolena* and Bellini's
Il Pirata.

April seemed very far away, and by all indications,
Ghiringhelli displayed no sign of interest in Maria's current, or even future, plans. On the contrary, while Maria
was preparing for her transatlantic journey, she learned
from the news reports that two sopranos had been engaged by La Scala, possibly with these two operas in mind.

On the morning of January 16th, Maria Callas, husband Meneghini, their maid, their poodle Toy, two mink
coats, and seven pieces of luggage boarded a plane at
Milan's Malpensa airport. This time Maria was relaxed,
almost cheerful: she informed the press that she was
eagerly looking forward to an enjoyable and comparatively restful stay in the United States. When the plane
landed in Paris a few hours later, she was deeply moved
by the sight of a throng of flower-bearing admirers. Then
she continued her trip to Chicago, by way of Montreal.

CHAPTER 12

Life in the Headlines

Giulia
Ma dove io porto il piè?
SPONTINI—LA VESTALE

On the evening of January 22, 1958, less than three weeks after the stormy Rome walkout, Maria Callas was back at the scene of her unforgettable triumphs, the Chicago Civic Opera House. She was to give another benefit concert for the *Alliance Française*. Once again she faced a huge audience stirring in their expensive seats. How would they receive her?

The answer came when she stepped on the stage. The audience gave the long-missed favorite a ten-minute standing ovation, another massive display of Chicago's unchanging affections. It mattered little that she was in far from her best voice. For that delirious crowd, she could do no wrong.

Chicago's musical press, traditionally pro-Callas, was divided. "Her voice . . . seems to have aged ten years in one," reported Roger Dettmer, one of Maria's most outspoken partisans. Yet to Claudia Cassidy, the same concert was still a demonstration of "Callas in full glory."

Critical comments aside, it was a triumphant evening, financially as well as musically. The *Alliance* collected $12,000 for its worthy cause. On top of this, the Callas honorarium was an eyebrow-raising $10,000, an amount not officially confirmed, but quite feasible at the steep box-office rates.

Delighted by her Chicago reception, which gave her spirits a much-needed lift, Maria flew to New York the following day and set up headquarters at the Waldorf-Astoria. It was there, on the evening of January 24th, that she appeared before a nationwide audience on Edward R. Murrow's television show "Person to Person."

Although the following morning's New York *Herald Tribune* summed up Maria's performance as the "epitome of moderation and easy-going good humor," it was a rather uninspiring interview, presenting neither participant in best form. Maria Callas, the audience learned, was very serious about her art; she was not born in Brooklyn though she did have many friends who had come from there; she was fond of television but seldom went to the movies for fear of catching a cold. As for the host, a man of searching mind and wide-ranging interests, the interview left no doubt whatever that music was not one of them.

The fifteen-minute program did, however, present its millions of viewers with the image of a serious, thoughtful, and remarkably courteous—to the point of stiffness—human being. Here was a woman who had nothing whatever in common with the fire-fuming dragon that lived in stormy headlines and in the fantasies of gossip columnists.

She was simply an opera singer proud of her art and eager to please her public at her impending return to the Metropolitan.

On the morning of January 27, 1958, however, Maria's entire Metropolitan engagement seemed in doubt. This was the day she had to appear before the American Guild of Musical Artists as a result of the charges brought against her by Kurt Herbert Adler of the San Francisco Opera. An unfavorable ruling by the AGMA Board could have resulted in the suspension of all her future American activities.

Accompanied by her husband, Maria arrived at AGMA's New York office on the corner of Broadway and 60th Street fetchingly attired in a beaver cape and matching hat. She also wore an unusually earnest expression, and briskly walked into the waiting room without pausing to talk to the assembled reporters. The hearing, which began almost immediately, lasted two hours. The twenty-member board examined the case in great detail, listened to testimony by both Callas and Adler, and studied the voluminous medical evidence Callas presented.

After weighing all factors, the Board concluded that Maria had breached her San Francisco contract by her failure to appear, but accepted as mitigating circumstances her ill health and her offer to fulfil at least the second half of her contract. It was also established, in Maria's behalf, that she did not appear anywhere else while she was contractually bound to San Francisco.

"BE IT FURTHER RESOLVED," concluded AGMA's somewhat redundant communique, "that the conclusions reached by the Board as contained in the above resolution shall, by their own terms, constitute a reprimand to Maria Meneghini Callas."

Although the ruling was an undeniable blot on the

Callas escutcheon, its significance amounted to little more than a warning. That she was able to emerge from the meeting's initially hostile atmosphere with no more than a reprimand can be attributed to the force of her personality. Her judges, however antagonistic some of them might have been, were for the most part colleagues in the performing arts. It is not altogether surprising that they were moved by her persuasive statement of her case. One member of the Board, a fellow opera singer, admitted later to have been strongly impressed by Maria's firm and courageous stand for the rights and privileges of the artist versus the management—a course of action often desired by but seldom open to performers of lesser stature.

The clouds that threatened Maria's second Metropolitan season had cleared away. She was ready to face the New York audience again.

Three operas had been contemplated for her: *Lucia di Lammermoor* and *Tosca,* in productions already familiar from the previous year, and *La Traviata,* in the Tyrone Guthrie staging first mounted in honor of Renata Tebaldi during the previous season. Maria was greatly annoyed by the fact that Bing could not give her a new production in spite of her undeniably huge box-office appeal. *La Traviata* was almost new, to be sure, but it had been created for Renata Tebaldi, a circumstance that was hardly conducive to Maria's appreciation.

However, faced with the immutable realities, Maria laid aside her personal disillusionment. She wanted to sing in New York. Knowing that her somewhat tarnished popularity was in need of renewed lustre, she approached her new engagements with a firm resolution to outdo herself.

The first day at work brought disappointments. For *La Traviata,* no longer considered a new venture, the management had scheduled only a limited number of rehearsals. That the star was entirely new to the production, that she was unfamiliar with the settings, that she had never sung previously with the other principals *on any stage* before, complicated the situation somewhat; but the Metropolitan had its rules and its severe difficulties—the diva would just have to solve her own problems herself.

She did the best she could. Working on the Met's "stage roof," in the absence of the actual stage facilities, using elementary or improvised props, marking out the limits of the stage, and relying on her ever-present Battista for visual cues, Maria familiarized herself with the routines sufficiently to give an impressive account of the role at the dress rehearsal. As always, she radiated far more confidence than she actually possessed. Deep down inside, she was concerned about misjudging distances and getting lost on the stage as a result of her myopia. She awaited February 6th, the day of her debut, with a growing uneasiness that bordered on fear.

She need not have worried. That evening began with the most glowing reception ever given her by the New York public. When the curtain rose and her slender figure was sighted as Violetta, it seemed that the applause would not allow the performance to get off the ground. It is true that the demonstration was unduly extended by hotheaded zealots whose actions inevitably led to disgusted grumblings by a large number of patrons. (The latter group was, for the most part, neither pro nor anti-Callas. It had simply come to the theater in the hope of hearing Verdi's music.) But, for Maria, it was inspiring, nevertheless.

Once the music did get under way, she managed to earn every decibel of her extravagant reception. Maria Callas lived the part more convincingly than any Violetta in recent memory. She also paid meticulous attention to

the composer's sensitive markings—an indulgence shared
by few interpreters of the part.

There were no mishaps on the stage, and the audience
remained completely unaware of her anticipated fears.
Even the consistent off-pitch singing of Daniele Barioni,
her tenor partner, which all but ruined the important first-
act duets, failed to upset Maria's profoundly artistic and
thoroughly compelling achievement. "She commands the
attention of all who regard opera as something more than a
concert in costume," wrote Irving Kolodin in *Saturday
Review*.

As always, there were a few voices of dissent. "All the
tenderness and brilliant acting in the world cannot com-
pensate for the lack of a true and beautiful voice," was the
summation of Paul Henry Lang of the New York *Herald
Tribune*. But this did not dim the over-all glow.

After the final curtain, Maria's frenzied admirers applauded for almost thirty minutes and made her come out
again and again. "I am numb, I am numb," she muttered
in complete exhaustion as she finally retired, surrounded
by her husband, her father, and the obviously pleased
Rudolf Bing, "I can't believe it finally happened."

As could be expected, Maria had a new tenor to sing
duets with when she repeated *La Traviata* four nights
later: Giuseppe Campora. Apparently, the management
believed in variety, or perhaps it was anxious to show off
its rich tenor harvest of the season. Whatever the cause,
Maria was given two more tenors for *Lucia di Lammermoor,* her next opera. On the evenings of February 13th
and 20th, her Edgardo was Carlo Bergonzi, on the 25th,
it was Eugenio Fernandi.

She delivered Donizetti's music "with a comprehension of musical meaning usually reserved for the best

players of Chopin's Nocturnes," in the words of Irving
Kolodin. She did have some trouble with the high E flat at
the end of the Mad Scene; it is an extraneous note which
some sopranos sing to keep "tradition" alive, others to
show off their agility and to embarrass their rivals, and
still others to bedazzle the public and thus deflect attention
from the empty, superficial glitter of their interpretation.
If any artist could get by without that stratospheric note,
it is Maria Callas, for she has consistently revealed
beauties and poetry in the part which elude many of her
rivals. But the defying note always looms before her like a
forbidding Alpine peak, and Maria Callas is not one to
shirk the challenge.

Every "Callas evening" that season was *sold out* at
the Met. As for the nonmusical events of Maria's New York
stay, they, too, held their share of excitement. Elsa Maxwell, her neighbor at the Waldorf, outdid herself to organize parties on behalf of her favorite artist. For her, Maria
was the "diva divina," the "prima donna of the world."
By then, La Callas had become an accredited member of
the international set who moved about in the company of
ambassadors, aristocrats, and other celebrities with a natural ease. Battista Meneghini, of course, tagged along
everywhere. It was a long way from the home-cooked meals
of the Chicago days!

Aside from managing Maria's social life on such an
exalted level, Maxwell also devoted her enormous energies
to the task of upholding her friend's reputation against all
attacks.

"Why should a woman, capable of so noble an expression in the classic arts, be tortured by a destiny that
makes her happiness almost impossible? Her mother, I
believe without a question, has been the cause of this situation." Thus spake Elsa in one of her columns.

Evangelia Callas had again established residence in New York after returning from Greece during the fall of 1957. She was now divorced from her husband, and no contact existed between them, in spite of numerous mutual friends. The same friends had also made some attempts toward reconciling mother and daughter, but all efforts proved fruitless. Maria was unwilling even to discuss the possibility of reconciliation. In fact, the whole subject was seldom if ever touched upon even in her private conversations.

On the other hand, Maria was on the best possible terms with her father. George Callas, getting on in years and no longer in good health, was still working as a pharmacist in a New York hospital. Maria's occasional visits brought warmth and excitement into his lonely existence, and he frequently appeared at the Metropolitan, at the management's standing invitation, to watch his celebrated daughter. A reserved, taciturn man, he resented all intrusions into family matters; he gave no interviews, but left no doubt in anyone's mind that in the controversy involving mother and daughter he stood firmly and with utter conviction on Maria's side.

No such reluctance governed the actions of Evangelia Callas. She was generous with interviews and commented on Maria's actions with an eager flow of information, generally uncomplimentary. For some entirely unfathomable reason, she even turned Maria's age into a subject of dispute by announcing to one surprised interviewer, contrary to the facts, that Maria was the older of her two daughters. No wonder that even the most seasoned observers were baffled by the difference between the real and publicized image of Maria Callas.

"You seem like a perfectly normal, nice guy. Why have so many people, including myself, been influenced to believe otherwise by the bitter press you've had? Don't you think you ought to hire a public relations man?'' The inquirer was Hy Gardner, columnist of the New York *Herald Tribune.* The meeting occurred at one of New York's posh restaurants, where a St. Valentine's Day luncheon was given by publisher Henry Sell on February 14th in Maria's honor.

''I don't see any reason to have to employ anyone to defend me. I am an artist. What I have to say, I sing. Greeks never stop fighting for what they know is right.''

''I came to lunch expecting to meet a cold, tempestuous but talented female ogre'' summed up Gardner in his column, ''and found instead a warm, sincere, handsome and down-to-earth human being, a real live doll.''

On February 26th, Maria and her father appeared on Gardner's television program. This time, as a result of the columnist's informal approach, more of Maria's human qualities emerged. But in spite of Gardner's efforts to look into the mother–daughter relationship, Maria maintained firm silence on that painful subject.

She was freely talkative, on the other hand, about the Rome incident, revealing among other things that one functionary of the Rome Opera had gone so far as to recommend that she stage a collapse during the second act of *Norma* as a desperate but ''dignified'' way out of that evening's predicament. Maria also had words of the fullest devotion for her husband, and reminisced very fondly about their first meeting in Verona, which was, in her own words, ''love at first sight.''

George Callas contributed a few halting but dignified observations, full of paternal pride and praise. All in all, it was an absorbing human interview in contrast to the formalized slickness of the previous ''Person to Person.''

Unfortunately, the Callas–Gardner friendship was

shortlived. Later that year, with her mind occupied with
things other than diplomacy, Maria somehow managed to
drop a slighting remark about her erstwhile interviewer.
Gardner thereupon devoted a stinging column to the former
"real live doll" and has not stopped taking periodic pot-
shots at her ever since.

Shortly after her TV appearance, Maria wound up
her Metropolitan engagement with Puccini's *Tosca,* opposite Richard Tucker, on February 28th and March 5th. The
second performance was praised to the skies by the critics.
It was one of those unusually inspired musical evenings
when everything clicked happily from beginning to end.
This was a galvanic *Tosca,* with the electric charge of inspiration constantly passing between three superior musical
artists (George London was Scarpia), sparked by the live-
wire conducting of Dimitri Mitropoulos.

Although this had been a happy season for all concerned, Maria and Rudolf Bing were unable to reach an
understanding with respect to her 1958/1959 engagement.
This chagrined the management somewhat, for it had
always been Bing's policy to promulgate the theater's
future plans at the end of each season.

Maria insisted on getting a new production. Verdi's
Macbeth was the opera both she and Bing agreed upon.
But disagreements persisted between them concerning
other roles. No final solution was reached, and the
Meneghinis departed for Italy with only one firm commit-
ment: that Maria would return in the fall for her third
Metropolitan season.

After a few days rest in Milan, they flew to Madrid
where Maria gave a rather uneventful concert, and thence
to Lisbon, for two evenings of *Traviata* on March 27th
and 30th, during the international gala season of Lisbon's
Teatro San Carlos.

"CALLAS—UNLIKEABLE WOMAN, GREAT ARTIST" head-lined Lisbon's *Diario Popular* upon the diva's arrival. But when she departed four days later, she left only admiration in her trail. The audience remembered her unforgettable portrayal. Her fellow-artists, the Spanish tenor Alfredo Kraus and the Italian baritone Mario Sereni, were completely disarmed by Maria's insistence on sharing the ovations with them. Umberto di Savoia, Italy's dethroned monarch, was one of the many dignitaries who came to express his personal appreciation.

Thinking ahead, as a good impresario should, Artistic Director Donati of the San Carlos Theater immediately suggested a splendid production of *Norma* with Giulietta Simionato in the role of Adalgisa for the next season. He received an encouraging but inconclusive smile from the diva, the habitual Callas gesture of "wait-and-see" generally reserved for such hastily tendered invitations.

On their way back to Milan, the Meneghinis spent a few hours in Brussels between planes, long enough for an excursion to the nearby chateau at Ixelles, where Maria Malibran once lived and where she lies buried. There Maria Callas spent a brief interlude honoring the memory of her nineteenth-century artistic predecessor whose many roles she had inherited and returned to currency after decades of slumber.

On the first day of April she was back in Milan, ready to rejoin La Scala for the two months still remaining of the theater's 1957/1958 season. Her first visit within those hallowed walls left no doubt in her mind that she was still a very unpopular person there.

A few days later, when she met Ghiringhelli face-to-face for the first time in months, the Superintendent pointedly ignored her. For the next several days, they would meet almost daily at luncheon, a few yards apart within the cozy intimacy of the Biffi-Scala restaurant, without a sign of greeting passing between them, without a word of recognition.

One thing that remained unchanged between April, 1957, and April, 1958, was Donizetti's *Anna Bolena*. That memorable Callas triumph of the previous year served to reintroduce her in Milan after a four-month absence.

The *prima,* on April 9th, was Maria's first public appearance in Italy since the Roman scandal, and tempers were still hot. Two hundred policemen had been mobilized to maintain law and order in the event of an "emergency." The ominous atmosphere was generally more reminiscent of a state of siege than of a gala operatic evening.

Inside, hostility was in the air. Maria's first entrance was greeted by stony silence—she was on trial, with the audience–jury prejudiced against her. But Callas thrives on such situations. She played the part of the injured and persecuted queen with a conviction and comprehension of which only an injured and persecuted queen is capable, with "a new kind of sadness, a pathetic tenderness of pure Donizettian inspiration," in the words of critic Eugenio Gara. When it was over, the house nearly exploded. Nobody talked about the Rome walkout anymore. That evening, the Callas crown shone with the old glitter.

Maria drove home from the theater in a quiet glow of contentment, happily reliving her triumphant moments before an audience that had been bent on her humiliation. With the applause and the *bravas* still ringing in her ears, she arrived at the Via Buonarroti. There an incredible sight shocked her back to reality.

The entrance of her beautiful home, the outside walls, the threshold, door, windows, all were smeared with dung and covered with obscene writings—wanton and vandalistic traces of vengeful and diseased minds. Maria entered the house pale and trembling, and broke into bitter tears. Was it worth it? She may have won another battle on stage, but her enemies did not forget. The "hissing snakes" could strike in many ways!

The following day, Meneghini reported the case to the police, and demanded protection against such insults and damages. His telephone call brought no satisfaction, his letter was not even acknowledged.

On April 12th, three nights later, La Scala gave the traditional gala to commemorate the opening of the annual Milan fair. In bygone years, the occasion had inevitably called for a "Callas opera," and it was understood when the plans had been formulated for the season that *Anna Bolena* would be given that night. While Maria was away, however, those earlier plans were abandoned. Instead, the world premiere of Pizzetti's *Murder in the Cathedral* took the evening's honor. Maria did not even receive the courtesy of an official notification.

Anna Bolena was given five times that spring with thunderous success, always to sold-out houses. The loyalty of her admirers, success, and recognition had their occasionally comforting effects, but the gaps between these gratifying moments seemed unduly long, and Maria found the atmosphere inside the theater, with its tension near the bursting point, virtually unbearable.

Fortunately for her peace of mind, she was able to submerge herself in new outside interests. Meneghini, whose only active business in these days, apart from managing his wife's career, lay in real estate ventures, had bought a summer estate on the Sirmione peninsula, near Lake Garda, in the early days of 1958. Before departing on their American tour, he and Maria had spent many hours planning the complete transformation of that cozy lakeside retreat. While they were away, architects and decorators were hard at work on the remodeling job.

In May, Sirmione was showing encouraging signs of emerging as a worthy adjunct to the Meneghinis' luxurious Milan home. Maria and Battista continued to supervise details of the construction, discussed the choice of decorations, enjoyed long walks in the estate's rambling gardens, and fondly looked forward to early June when all work would be finished and they would take possession of that restful paradise. Maria hoped to spend many peaceful weeks between her tours in the solitude of Sirmione. Meneghini, who at heart had never removed himself very far from his nearby paternal Verona, shared her longing.

Early May brought the season's final production: Bellini's *Il Pirata,* the last in the lustrous string of half-forgotten works from the age of the "bel canto" brought to new currency through Callas's revitalizing artistry.

Rehearsals began to the accompaniment of persistent rumors that the diva's association with La Scala had come to an end. When the confirmation came, it surprised no one. Maria openly declared that the hostility of Ghiringhelli's management had made her situation untenable. Her artistic conscience and dignity compelled the only possible decision: she would leave La Scala after the fifth and final performance of *Il Pirata.* She would return again, and gladly, but it would have to be under a different administration.

Il Pirata saw the light of day in Milan in 1827, and had not been given there since. It is not a masterpiece. Perhaps in 1827, when the legendary Rubini sang the principal tenor part of Gualtiero, the Pirate, with that phenomenal range and power of his, the opera's weaknesses were less evident. Franco Corelli, who inherited the part's

cruel *tessitura,* was no Rubini, not even a Gigli—who had
sung Gualtiero when the opera was revived in Rome and
Palermo on the occasion of the Bellini centenary in 1935.
But he did as well with this unenviable task as any modern
tenor would have, and better than most. In contrast, Maria
Callas felt right at home with Bellini's florid musical
tapestry—the part could have been written for her.

During the first two acts of the *prima,* on May 19th,
Maria had to fight a certain lack of audience response, and
her voice did not immediately find the needed warmth and
roundness of tone. But her unerring mastery of style and
often breathtaking agility, coupled with the force of her
magnetic presence on the stage, again worked wonders. The
ice was completely broken in the final act where, as in *Anna
Bolena,* the composer rewarded his soprano with striking
vocal and interpretive opportunities to convey countless
shades and degrees of grief. Maria's rendition of the
melancholy aria "Col sorriso d'innocenza" fell upon the
auditorium like audible tears.

The day of *Il Pirata's* fifth and final 1958 performance
arrived on May 31st. It was no longer a secret that it would
be Maria Callas's last appearance at La Scala for a long
time. The fact, however, that Maria had undergone a minor
operation during the preceding week, and that she had
sung on two evenings against medical advice, was kept a
well-guarded secret. The theater had a substitute available,
but Maria could not risk a cancellation in the face of her
hostile press and her strained relationship with the
management.

In the final scene of *Il Pirata,* Imogene, the heroine,
bemoans the fate of her captured lover, Gualtiero. In her
grief, she sees a vision of a frightful scaffold rising before
her eyes, a terrible reminder of the fate that awaits her
beloved. "Vedete il palco funesto," ("Behold that fateful

scaffold"), sang Maria Callas on the night of May 31st,
and as she sang her swan song to La Scala, an ironical smile
crossed her lips and her arms pointed toward the proscenium box.

The word "palco" has another meaning in Italian,
that of a theater box. In this grandiose manner, to the
music of her beloved Bellini, Maria Callas pointed out, for
all to see, that her departure from the leading theater of
Italy was motivated by the occupant of that "fateful box,"
Antonio Ghiringhelli!

Ghiringhelli had his own big moment a little later.
While Maria was still on stage, responding to the persistent ovations of her saddened but nonetheless enthusiastic fans, the iron curtain suddenly descended, signaling
the abrupt end to all bows. A group of husky firemen materialized from nowhere, determined to empty the theater in
the most forceful manner imaginable.

Shocked but undeterred, the faithful fans regrouped
themselves before the stage entrance. When Maria emerged
and joined her waiting husband, they showered both with
flowers and followed them all the way to the entrance of
the nearby Savini restaurant. Two hours later, when the
Meneghinis reappeared on the Galleria Vittorio Emanuele,
some of the fans were still milling about. "Come back
soon!" "La Scala needs you!" they shouted, with other
expressions of continued admiration and loyalty.

So ended seven grand seasons in Milan. Twenty-one
roles in one hundred fifty-seven performances had brought
Maria Callas's art before La Scala's demanding audience.
By whatever standard, those seven years must go down as
a triumphant episode nearly unparalleled in La Scala
history.

Callas contributed interpretations that set a new level
of musical and dramatic excellence; she acquainted the

world of music with forgotten masterpieces which would have been left slumbering had it not been for her animating art. She brought urgency and excitement to the theater, reminiscent of older, livelier days. Her appearances attracted capacity crowds and made new friends for opera.

Not all her achievements were felicitous, however. Her presence also sparked rivalries, enkindled the flames of jealousy, enlarged the habitual petty intrigues into occasionally warlike proportions. But the seven years behind her were seven great years for La Scala, and for the world of opera.

Above all, they were great for Maria Callas. She loved La Scala, where she had risen to the top of her profession, and which had surrounded her with a lavishness and artistic largesse no other opera house could have been able to match. She loved the excitement of La Scala evenings, and loved its feared, demanding, selfish, yet peerless, audience. It was a severe shock to end it all on such a bitter note, particularly since the break was provoked only by a clash of personalities, in obvious disservice to art. But so it had to be.

Callas and La Scala, two institutions once united in a combination as near-perfect as the anagram formed by their names, went their separate ways after May 31, 1958. "I take with me the hope to be able to appear again on that stage in the future, under more favorable circumstances," declared Maria in her parting statement to the Italian news agency ANSA.

The laconic Ghiringhelli darkly hinted to the press that the day would come when *his* side of the story would be published. (The day never came.) For the moment, he contented himself with the philosophical dictum: "Le prime donne passano, La Scala resta." ("The prima donnas pass, La Scala remains.")

Far from taking such a light view of the situation, *Oggi's* music critic, Teodoro Celli, declared that with the departure of Callas, La Scala suffered the loss of "a unique and irreplaceable art." But, he added, "an artist with her spiritul courage will overcome this sorrowful separation from the theater to which she has for such a long time given her best. She will be able to await patiently the time when a change of conditions will assure her happy return."

Would the departure of Callas mean the return of Tebaldi? This was the question that opera aficionados immediately began asking among themselves. Reporters went a step further; they asked Renata herself who, as it happened, had just returned to Milan, fresh from a triumphant guest appearance in Vienna.

Tebaldi's reply astounded some, disappointed many, including Ghiringhelli, but it did credit to her own sense of fair play. In the controversy between Callas and the management she sided, quite plainly, with Callas. "After what has happened between the management and my colleague," she declared, "my return would be certainly misinterpreted. I sing only for artistic reasons. It is not my habit to sing *against* anyone."

Serious lovers of opera, who had long regretted the prolonged rivalry between the two gifted artists and who had always maintained that both should be seen at La Scala year after year, considered Tebaldi's declaration an encouraging sign. Foremost among these was Emilio Radius, the Milanese magazine editor, who throughout the years of rivalry managed to retain the trust and friendship of both divas. He thought that the time had arrived for a reconciliation.

The first step, sounding out Maria and Battista Meneghini, brought the most encouraging results—both were willing to meet with Renata in private, as an initial gesture toward resuming a friendly relationship. Radius immediately contacted Tebaldi, but there he met with disappointment. Although Renata assured him that she was harboring neither animosity nor bitterness toward the Meneghinis, she thought it wise to refrain from the emotional strain of the meeting. Persuasion did not help. The meeting hopefully scheduled for the early days of June did not materialize.

As summer approached, Maria's Italian career stood at a standstill. Next season, she would not be seen in Italy's two greatest opera houses. For her, the loss resulting from the break with Rome and Milan was primarily emotional and psychological. It was not, essentially, a material loss. Maria Callas could under no conditions be thought of as an unemployed opera singer. In America, in many theaters of Europe, she could pick her own engagements.

She was, in fact, negotiating her first American concert tour with impresario Sol Hurok at that very time. But traveling about the world and making new conquests were not the answer to the loss of her domestic roots, which Italian operatic life, and Milan in particular, had come to signify.

A short week after her final *Il Pirata* at La Scala, Maria was back where she had always been received with open arms: London. This time she came for a longer stay, to participate in a gala season in celebration of the Covent Garden centenary.

The London papers had been cheerfully announcing the arrival of the "tigress," the sobriquet attached to her name after the Rome scandal which found particularly joyful acceptance in London and Paris. Perhaps it was because of the tone of the newspaper reports, perhaps she remembered the one-sided treatment she had received from the press after the Edinburgh episode—Maria was in no mood for interviews.

On June 10th, the centenary was celebrated with a brilliant gala evening in the presence of Queen Elizabeth, Prince Philip, twelve members of the royal family, members of the British cabinet and the diplomatic corps, and representatives of high society. Besides Maria Callas, Margot Fonteyn, Joan Sutherland, Blanche Thebom, and Jon Vickers participated in the concert. Maria sang Elvira's "Mad Scene" from Bellini's *I Puritani* and completely won the audience.

The austere appearance of a frail, gentle Puritan maiden, evoked with the assured mastery of the Callas stagecraft, presented a startling contrast to those free-wheeling press accounts about the bloodthirsty tigress. After the concert, Maria and Meneghini were seen in a radiant mood at a late supper with Lord and Lady Harewood and conductor John Pritchard.

On the night of June 20th, Maria began a series of five performances in Verdi's *La Traviata* in which Cesare Valletti and Mario Zanasi were her partners and her Chicago and Dallas associate, Nicola Rescigno, was the conductor. She was not in good voice, nor did she appear in the best of health.

A doctor was placed at her disposal every night she appeared, and on several occasions she had to take injections between acts. As always, the compelling dramatic force of her characterization held the audience in an iron grip, but most of the critics were disappointed. One resolute exception was Harold D. Rosenthal, editor of the English monthly *Opera,* who gave a virtual sigh-by-sigh account of Maria's famed portrayal.

According to Rosenthal, her fine-spun "Dite alla

giovine" in the second act was "a moment of sheer magic," the end of Act III was sung "as if Violetta's heart was truly breaking," and she died at the end "with a glaze over her eyes, a standing corpse."

Before the end of her Covent Garden engagement, Maria also appeared briefly on television. Asked to comment on her approach to Violetta, she told the audience that her aim was to create the image not of an opera singer but of a sick woman dying of tuberculosis.

With the London engagement behind her, Maria began a three-month uninterrupted rest, a luxury she could indulge herself in for the first time in nearly a decade. It was a marvelous summer.

Sirmione came up to all expectations. The romantic charm of the town itself, which dates back to the first century B.C. when Catullus immortalized its beauty in his poems, the comfortable villa surrounded by winding trails, restful lawns, hedge rows, flower beds, and waving carpets of Maria's favorite roses, the colorful lakeshore panorama —all breathed an aura of long-sought peace.

Maria rested and Meneghini plotted the fall and winter campaigns. With the opportunities lost in Italy, his attention naturally turned to America. It was a foregone conclusion that they would spend the main part of the season across the ocean. Maria's Metropolitan engagement was to begin in January, which would allow her ample time to undertake the nationwide concert tour organized by Sol Hurok, coinciding with her second season with the Dallas Civic Opera, which was to open in late October.

The concert tour and Dallas were no problem. The dates were worked out between the "managers" to mutual satisfaction. With the Metropolitan, it was another story.

Maria was thrilled by the prospect of appearing, at long last, in a brand-new production. The choice of opera,

Verdi's *Macbeth,* was also felicitous, as the role of Lady Macbeth held enormous appeal for her from the vocal as well as the histrionic viewpoint. The opera had never been given at the Metropolitan before, yet another favorable factor to stimulate Maria's interest. But beyond *Macbeth,* Maria and Rudolf Bing still could not reach an understanding with respect to the approaching season.

Bing had wanted Maria for a series of twenty-six performances in three operas—*Macbeth, Tosca,* and either *Lucia* or *Traviata.* For the first time, this long contract would have included appearances on the Met's transcontinental tour. But Maria would not commit herself definitely. The one thing she was definite about was that she was determined not to be seen in the Met's shabby production of the Donizetti opera another time.

Summer was passing, the Metropolitan was anxious to formulate final plans, but manager and prima donna were making no headway in their negotiations.

September came, and the Meneghinis traded the shady solitude of Sirmione for the colorful hubbub of Venice for a short week of entertainment, in preparation for the approaching season of musical and traveling turmoils. Then they continued on to London for a recording engagement.

In contrast to the unprecedented accumulation of studio activity during the previous year, 1958 had been relatively quiet. The termination of Maria's association with La Scala was a major factor. Her recordings had been marketed by E.M.I.–Angel under the official La Scala emblem; such a combination was no longer possible after the break—La Scala and Callas had to plan their future recordings independently.

Although the situation had thus become somewhat complicated, it was by no means critical from the practical point of view. It simply meant that Maria's recording headquarters would be transferred to London. There, Walter Legge's pride and joy, the topnotch Philharmonia Orchestra, was always available, and E.M.I. was more than willing to assemble the best possible casts (including La Scala members and conductors) for any major undertaking involving Callas.

In September, 1958, however, there was no need to organize an opera company, because Maria and Walter Legge decided not on complete operas but on two discs of aria collections, both utilizing the Philharmonia Orchestra under the baton of Maria's new conductor-in-attendance, Nicola Rescigno, and a group of English assisting artists.

The contents of both discs were chosen with admirable judgment. "Callas Portrays Verdi Heroines" contains extended dramatic scenes from three operas of the Callas repertoire she had not, theretofore, recorded: *Macbeth, Nabucco,* and *Don Carlo,* and from the Verdi opera which has regrettably eluded her so far on the stage: *Ernani.*

The second collection, which in America was misleadingly named "Mad Scenes," includes the final scenes from Donizetti's *Anna Bolena* and Bellini's *Il Pirata,* Maria's last triumphant roles at La Scala, and the "Mad Scene" from Thomas's *Hamlet,* a glittering tour-de-force from her concert repertoire.

In spite of some vocal unevenness, these two collections captured the crystallization of the Callas interpretive art. In particular, the two great scenes from *Macbeth* and the heartrending finale of *Anna Bolena* rank with her most spectacular demonstrations of penetrating character insight and compelling evocation of mood and atmosphere. The *Hamlet* "Mad Scene," a rather shallow and self-consciously exhibitionistic piece of music, fared not quite so well, proving that coloratura singing for its own sake is not an ideal medium for Callas. The *Hamlet* aria, which was sung in French, was, incidentally, her first recording in a language other than Italian.

Maria was extremely pleased with the London recordings, and with good reason. The fortunate few who managed to hear the two monologues from *Macbeth* on tape (the records did not reach the general public until months later) could easily foretell that the Metropolitan's forthcoming presentation of that Verdi opera with Callas and Leonard Warren, under Dimitri Mitropoulos's baton, would be an event not to be missed.

The opening of the 1958/1959 Metropolitan season was only three weeks away when Maria and Battista Meneghini, accompanied by Maria's secretary Teresa D'Addato and the peripatetic poodle, Toy, landed at New York's Idlewild Airport on the morning of October 7th. Maria's transcontinental tour was to begin four nights later in Birmingham, Alabama. Before continuing her journey, Maria was informed of the Met's projected schedule, which listed her seasonal debut in Puccini's *Tosca* for January 16, 1959.

The much-heralded premiere of Verdi's *Macbeth* was scheduled for February 5th. For the rest of February, the Callas performances were listed in this sequence: *La Traviata* on the 13th and 17th, and *Macbeth* again on the 21st.

Maria was in full agreement with the choice of operas, but immediately objected to the way Bing had programmed them, forcing her, as it were, to switch back and forth between two roles of such different vocal and dramatic characteristics.

Lady Macbeth requires a voice of dark quality, produced with penetrating strength; it calls for opulent tones and a gamut of dramatic expressions, from pensive whispers to piercing shrieks. Violetta, in the Callas interpretation at least, is a sick woman, and her pale, fragile figure should be reflected in a vocal quality to match. Besides, the first act of *La Traviata* requires a light voice of coloratura agility, in complete contrast to the big, passionate utterances of Lady Macbeth's music.

One glance at the program, and she knew that for her it was unacceptable. At the beginning of her career, when she went from Wagner to Bellini practically overnight, she would have undertaken the task without raising an eyebrow. It was different now. She was no longer building a career. On the contrary, she was determined to hold on to the one she had built by a decade of strenuous effort and self-sacrifice. Her voice had to be treated with good judgment and scientific care, and she knew, more than anyone, just what her capabilities and limitations were.

How different things were at La Scala, she remembered with some regretful longing. There an opera would be introduced on a certain day, repeated four, five times within the span of thirty days, and then put away for the season, making room for another production. No clashing contrasts, no undue strain on the voice, a better, more practical system all around. Even if it were true that Maria Callas had a shelf full of voices, as some critics have said, need she be compelled to exhibit her gifts by performing like a juggler?

Her displeasure with the Met's program provoked a critical situation. The Metropolitan's plans are made up months in advance. Roles had been assigned, commitments made, travels of artists arranged from far corners of the globe, all keyed to the complicated, perhaps imperfect, but already established schedule of performances. Drastic changes at that advanced stage were out of the question.

All Bing could offer was the suggestion of replacing *La Traviata* with *Lucia di Lammermoor*.

But, the gap that separates Lucia from Lady Macbeth is even wider than the already considerable distance between Lady Macbeth and Violetta. Bing's offer did nothing to remedy the situation, in Maria's opinion. Besides, she had already reached a point where she could no longer stand the sight of the same old *Lucia* sets, as she had said before.

Maria Callas left New York for her tour with the Metropolitan issue still unresolved, the theater in a dither over her refusal to confirm the proposed program schedule, and opening night drawing ominously close.

The first half of the Hurok-managed concert tour took the diva through Birmingham (October 11th), Atlanta (October 14th), Montreal (October 17th) and Toronto (October 21st), and ended with a south-westward swing to Dallas, for the two-week duration of that city's much-heralded, Callas-centered operatic season.

Throughout the entire concert tour, Maria sang the same program—a taxing but extremely effective sequence of arias from Spontini's *La Vestale,* Verdi's *Macbeth,* Rossini's *The Barber of Seville,* Boito's *Mefistofele,* Puccini's *La Bohème,* and Thomas's *Hamlet.* It was a wide-ranging representation of unusual versatility, embracing the dramatic, lyric, and coloratura repertoire. The surprising item on the program was the inclusion of "Musetta's Waltz" from *La Bohème,* because this part was never associated with the Callas career.

The fast-paced, exhausting journey came to a temporary halt with Maria's arrival in Dallas on October 24th.

The Dallas Civic Opera had taken big strides since its opening venture. Its second season was still a minuscule one—only five presentations in a two-week span—but the

publicity was greater than ever, local enthusiasm knew
no bounds, and, thanks to Lawrence Kelly's persuasive
ways with the local magnates, money gushed forth like oil.

This oft-vilified but nevertheless vital ingredient in
operatic productions helped to make international news
out of what under different conditions would merely have
been five performances of three operas. First of all, it
brought Callas, the world's most exciting and most expensive singer. Then, it allowed the productions—*La Traviata*
and *Medea* with Callas and *L'Italiana in Algeri* with Berganza—to be lavishly staged with the assistance of outstanding European and American specialists and guided
by the principle of creating something provocative and
memorable, letting the deficits fall where they may.

Franco Zeffirelli of Milan was engaged to stage *La
Traviata*. In his conception, which, contrary to Visconti's
at La Scala, remained scrupulously faithful to Dumas's
original setting of the 1850's, the entire opera was presented in a series of flashbacks. In the opening, Violetta
was displayed in full view, on her sick-bed, during the
poignant strains of the Prelude. Nicola Filacuridi and
Giuseppe Taddei were imported from La Scala to undertake the male leading roles in the Verdi opera's two
presentations.

For Cherubini's *Medea,* which was also scheduled
twice, Alexis Minotis of the Greek National Theater was
brought in to lend a style of authentic classicism to the
production. The costumes were painstakingly designed by
John Tsachouris from fabric woven in Greece. Broadway's famous Jean Rosenthal was engaged to style the
lighting. Jon Vickers and Nicola Zaccaria appeared in
the roles of Jason and Creon, respectively, and the brilliant
Spanish mezzo-soprano Teresa Berganza was Neris.

Miss Berganza was the star of the fifth operatic eve-

The price of fame! Wherever she goes, Maria Callas is besieged by reporters, photographers, and radio and TV newsmen.

As an international celebrity, Callas has been a frequent party-goer. Here she is embracing the hostess at party-giver Elsa Maxwell's "Ultra-mundane" party in Venice, September 4, 1957. (Photo by European.)

The Rome walkout! On January 2, 1958, Callas refused to continue the performance after the first act of Bellini's *Norma* at the Rome Opera House. Left waiting in the audience, among other notables, was Italian President Gronchi. Behind Callas are Miriam Pirazzini, Giulio Neri, and Franco Corelli. (Photo by Pix, Inc.)

Famous German sculptor, Fritz Behn, has made a career of modeling musical greats. When Callas objected to the size of the nose on the bust, he obligingly changed it. Munich, May, 1959. (Photo by Pix, Inc.)

Another party, this time at the Waldorf-Astoria, New York, November 21, 1958. This fete followed closely the cancellation by Rudolf Bing of Callas's Metropolitan Opera contract. Seen with her are Aly Khan, Noel Coward, and the ever-present Elsa Maxwell. As usual, husband Meneghini hovers in the background. (Photo by Wide World.)

The famous triangle of the summer of 1959. Aristotle Onassis, Callas, Meneghini. Scene: a gala party given in London by Onassis in the diva's honor. (Photo by Pix, Inc.)

The aftermath of the 1959 Mediterranean cruise. Even wearing dark glasses, Callas could not go out shopping without being observed and photographed. (Photo by Pix, Inc.)

The most important thing in Callas's life—her music. Always a thoughtful, conscientious artist, she is shown here during a recording session of her second *Lucia* in London, 1959. (Courtesy of Angel Records.)

ning, a single performance of Rossini's *L'Italiana in Algeri,* staged by Zeffirelli especially for Dallas in a production fondly remembered from the previous year.

In that entire company, there was not a harder worker than Maria Callas. She rehearsed every day of her two-week stay and set an inspiring example for all around her. Her colleagues were charmed, and the members of the chorus simply idolized her, whether working with her or just watching her from the wings. The board of directors and the scions of Dallas society were as thoroughly captivated with the prima donna as were the stage hands or the wardrobe mistress, who simply and affectionately called her "Mary" and would engage her in intimate conversation every afternoon over two cups of coffee in her dressing room.

Maria, in turn, was full of compliments for the dedication and artistic flair of Kelly, Rescigno, and their associates. Never during her American engagements had she been given so much in support of her own artistry. "In Dallas we are doing Art," she would say, remembering with a shudder some of the Metropolitan's aged productions.

On the night of October 27th, the Metropolitan opened its 1958/1959 season with Puccini's *Tosca,* with Tebaldi, Del Monaco, and London in the cast, Dimitri Mitropoulos conducting. All Rudolf Bing knew about Maria Callas was what he read about her Dallas activities in the papers. The impasse had reached a critical point, and an "either-or" decision had to be reached in a matter of days.

On the evening of October 31st, just before curtain time in Dallas for the opening *Traviata,* Maria received a telegram from Rudolf Bing. It contained an expression of good wishes, but concluded with the query: "But why in Dallas?" Maria did not send an answer.

That night, and at the second *Traviata* on November 2nd, the 4,100-seat State Fair Music Hall was filled with enthusiastic fans who adored the production and did not seem to mind very much that neither Callas nor her associates sang anywhere near their top vocal form. Responding to the cheers, Maria—always proud to call the Dallas achievements a triumph of ensemble effort—refused to take solo curtain calls, but her gallant colleagues succeeded in maneuvering her into a few, to the audience's thundering delight.

The first *Medea* was programmed for the night of November 6th. The previous afternoon, while the dress rehearsal was in progress, lightning had struck in the form of another telegram from Bing.

This time it was an ultimatum, demanding that Maria should indicate her consent to the Metropolitan's schedule by not later than 10 A.M., New York time, the following morning. Shocked by the insistent tone of the message, and much too involved emotionally in the preparation of *Medea,* Maria chose not to take note of what she termed Bing's "Prussian tactics." She continued the dress rehearsal until the late hours of the night, and retired, completely exhausted.

The following afternoon, at 2:20 P.M., a few hours before curtain time, Bing's third telegram arrived, notifying Maria that her contract with the Metropolitan was cancelled. Simultaneously, he released a statement to the press, and Maria Callas, after a short absence, was forthwith reinstated on page one.

"I do not propose to enter into a public feud with Mme. Callas since I am well aware that she has considerably greater competence and experience at that kind of thing than I have." So began Bing's formal statement. Its continuation, however, made it apparent that the

Metropolitan's General Manager had been overly modest in appraising his own polemizing talents:

"... I doubt if anyone will be surprised at the present turn of events. Although Mme. Callas's artistic qualifications are a matter of violent controversy between her friends and foes, her reputation for projecting her undisputed histrionic talents into her business affairs is a matter of common knowledge.

"This, together with her insistence on a claimed right to alter or abrogate a contract at will or at whim, has finally led to the present situation, merely a repetition of the experience which nearly every major opera house has had in attempting to deal with her. Let us all be grateful that we have had the experience of her artistry for two seasons; for reasons, however, which the musical press and public can well understand, the Metropolitan is nevertheless also grateful that the association is ended.

"The Metropolitan Opera fortunately has never been dependent on the talents, however great, of any individual artist. I could even name a number of very famous singers who thought they were indispensable and would now give their eye teeth to be back with the Metropolitan. So, on with the season!"

Maria was bewildered by Bing's action. As she explained to the press, she was in full accord with the Met's schedule. All she had asked was to cancel or substitute the two *Traviatas* scheduled for February 13th and 17th between two *Macbeth* performances to avoid the harmful consequences the sudden change might bring to her voice.

"I cannot switch voices. My voice is not like an elevator going up and down. . . . So Mr. Bing cancels a twenty-six performance contract for three *Traviatas*. And doing it today. . . . It might imperil my *Medea*. Pray for me tonight!"

That night, it seemed to observers that she was also singing for Bing, in addition to the more than four thousand Texans and assembled visitors. "In no other performance of our experience," wrote Emily Coleman in *Theatre Arts,* "has her production been steadier, her quality more rounded . . . her acting more plastic, and yet tastefully contained within a dramatic framework."

The second Dallas opera season was a huge success. The Opera's board of directors smiled at the deficit of $100,000 and immediately began discussing future ventures. Board chairman Leo F. Corrigan, a shopping-center and hotel tycoon with a reported yearly gross income of $75 million, pondered about a traveling production of *Medea* which, in his well-considered judgment, was "a wonderful show."

The ubiquitous Elsa Maxwell contributed even more fuel to Dallas's high-octane enthusiasm. And the triumphant Lawrence Kelly declared: "Callas has nothing to worry about. She has the world at her feet."

"Worried" was hardly the word to describe Maria's state of mind; "furious," would have been more appropriate. Now that the excitement and responsibilities of the season had ebbed, her controlled initial reaction to Bing's action was giving way to a flood of angry pronouncements.

"All those lousy Traviatas he made me sing," she exploded, "without rehearsals, without even knowing my partners. . . . Is that art? . . . And other times, all those performances with a different tenor or a different baritone every time. . . . Is that art?"

In a telephone interview with the Italian magazine *Oggi,* Maria illuminated in more detail the circumstances leading to the spectacular break. The repertoire dispute was not limited to the current season.

Looking ahead to 1959/1960, Bing had wanted Maria to spend a long season at the Met, but again offered her the same productions of *Lucia* and *Norma,* plus Rossini's *The Barber of Seville,* which held no appeal for her whatever. Maria had suggested Donizetti's *Anna Bolena* instead, the opera in which she had scored so spectacularly in two successive Scala seasons. "It is an old bore of an opera," was the way the Met's General Manager had dismissed the idea.

Bing's apparent lack of interest in what Maria considered her specialties, the "bel canto" operas of Bellini, Donizetti, Cherubini, Spontini, and early Verdi, had long been a painful thorn in their relationship. Nor did Bing show much more interest in Maria's suggestion to stage a more modern opera, like Giordano's *Fedora,* for her.

Conscious of the hard realities of opera production United States style, and without the munificence bestowed upon Milan's Ghiringhelli and Rome's Latini by a centuries-old Italian tradition that considers opera a proud national heritage deserving of far-reaching national support, Bing had been planning his seasons, year after year, around the unadventurous and safe core of the "box-office" operas. Furthermore, the Metropolitan had no production settings for the spectacular Callas specialties, nor was Bing certain that these half-forgotten works would meet with the right kind of acceptance in New York.

Bing ran the Metropolitan like a Prussian corporal, summed up Maria angrily in her *Oggi* interview, and in artistic matters he displayed an obstinate incomprehension. "For him *Macbeth, Lucia, La Sonnambula, Barbiere, Gioconda,* can just as well be all neatly lined up and placed side by side within the same category of interpretation."

In the United States, this new "Callas scandal" produced the expected wide-ranging repercussions. Washing-

ton music critic Paul Hume demanded Bing's resignation.
North Carolina's homespun essayist-philosopher Harry
Golden admonished the General Manager, in his jovial
fashion, for depriving the theater of such art and such
excitement.

On the other hand, several members of the Metropolitan issued statements upholding Rudolf Bing. The
most amazing among them was baritone Robert Merrill
who, in a short-order diagnosis, analyzed his colleague as
a "very afraid human being." Although Merrill had never
appeared with Callas, he nevertheless felt singularly qualified to express an opinion in the controversy, since he,
himself, had in the recent past been fired by Bing, and
subsequently reinstated after a public apology, for a
breach of contract.

In the crossfire of conflicting statements and opinions,
the editorial published in the November 15, 1958 issue of
Musical America managed to point up the complexities
and to illuminate the elusive truths of a controversy in
which both sides were right and both were wrong at the
same time:

"It is clear that she is an all but impossible lady to
deal with on a business basis. It is equally clear that she
is one of the most incandescent, and therefore most
fascinating, artistic personalities to be visited upon this
glamour-starved generation. Maria Callas is to opera
what Ted Williams and Mickey Mantle are to baseball—
high spirited, controversial, magnetic, and, at bottom, a
brilliant performer."

No mystery surrounded the seasonal habitat of
Messrs. Williams and Mantle on that day of November
15, 1958. But readers of that editorial, while agreeing
with every word, would have been eminently justified in
raising this question about Maria Callas: "Yes, she is a

brilliant performer. But, after Chicago, Vienna, Rome, San Francisco, Milan, and the Metropolitan, where will she perform?"

CHAPTER 13

Prima Donna at Large

Fedora
*Sento che qui comincia
un'altra vita in me.*

Giordano — fedora

However uncertain her immediate plans seemed following the Metropolitan's sudden action, Maria Callas was in no danger of unemployment. In fact, she was immediately deluged with offers, and so was impresario Sol Hurok, who managed her American tour.

One hotel in Miami Beach wanted her for a single appearance during Christmas week, and offered $5,000 for the privilege; a similar proposition came in from Hollywood. Probably, invitations of this nature would have never been extended to Callas, the opera singer. But now Maria Callas was a real "celebrity," in the Miami and Hollywood sense of the word, a front-page attraction

who also signified "culture." This magic combination
made her one of the hottest "properties" in show business.

Maria did not consider any of these more flamboyant
possibilities. But she did accept an offer from New York's
American Opera Society for a concert performance of
Bellini's *Il Pirata,* to be held in Carnegie Hall on January
27, 1959. Thanks to Rudolf Bing, the date was now free.
It gave Maria particular satisfaction to be able to bring
to New York one of her most successful portrayals, one
of the many which she had proposed to the Metropolitan
in the bygone months without ever capturing Bing's
interest.

Meanwhile, her transcontinental tour continued
through Cleveland (November 15th) and Detroit (November 18th). The storm that had been unleashed by her
Metropolitan dismissal redoubled the already widespread
interest in her appearances. In Detroit's Masonic Auditorium, an audience of five thousand, undoubtedly expecting a bundle of temperament on the strength of Maria's
press coverage, was startled when she came on stage, in a
golden gown, "a young woman with a school girl's shy-
ness," as the Detroit *News* put it.

Some Detroit critics found her vocal performance
uneven, but all were completely disarmed by Maria's
graciousness at her press interview. "What are your
plans?" they asked.

"Now I shall have time in Europe to make recordings,
to rest, and to study new roles. Art is everything, money
is nothing to an artist."

Giovanni Battista Meneghini never claimed to be an
artist. To him money meant something. Maria's Detroit
fee was $10,000 plus a percentage of the gross, the total
estimated at about $15,000. But it was a great show, and
she had fully earned it.

Back in New York on November 21st, Maria was just in time to attend a dinner party given by Elsa Maxwell in honor of the visiting Herbert von Karajan. Everybody who was anybody in music attended. The following evening Maria and Elsa were seen at the Waldorf in the company of Aly Khan and Noel Coward, among others, on the occasion of a dinner dance given by Earl Smith, United States Ambassador to Cuba.

Continuing her concert tour, Maria appeared in Washington, D. C., the next day before another glittering audience composed of high society and foreign dignitaries. At the dinner party which followed the concert, Hervé Alphand, the French Ambassador, paid fervent compliments to her art, whereupon Maria expressed great happiness at the prospect of her forthcoming first appearance in Paris, before the President of the Republic, at a gala concert planned for December 19th.

The Washington party was not without its unpleasant moments. Among the distinguished guests was the Italian Ambassador, Manlio Brosio, who had attended Maria's Metropolitan debut and had been the host at her first appearance in the capital in 1956. Then the Ambassador had been the embodiment of gallantry, full of appreciation for Maria's achievements in Italy's honor. Now, apparently, everything had changed. Ostensibly as a result of the Roman adventure, the presence of Maria and Battista Meneghini was ignored by the official representative of the Italian Government.

Maria's first American tour of ten engagements came to an end in California with a pair of concerts in San Francisco (November 26th) and Los Angeles (November 29th). With immense relief but in apparent good humor, Maria returned to her hotel after the final concert.

Before retiring, she sat around with her husband, her

PRIMA DONNA AT LARGE

secretary, Nicola Rescigno, who accompanied her through
the entire tour, and a few close friends, remembering the
many exciting moments of the tour, and also a few annoying and disturbing ones.

"It is not an easy life," Maria remarked.

"But you will always win, Maria," exclaimed one of
the faithful.

"Yes, I'll keep on winning," Maria replied. Then,
turning suddenly solemn and pensive, she added: "until
one day God kisses my voice."

The following day Maria and her entourage began the
long journey home. She was happy at the prospect of celebrating her birthday in Milan, and the comparative calm
of her schedule of engagements filled her with even more
contentment.

Apart from the Paris concert, scheduled for December 19th, her calendar only showed the Carnegie Hall
commitment in late January, then some recordings in
London. In between, she could look forward to long periods
of rest made possible through the concerted efforts of
Messrs. Latini, Ghiringhelli, and Bing. That was all right
with Maria. She was thinking of a peaceful Christmas
at home in Milan, and then of the bucolic pleasures of
Sirmione ....

The Paris concert was to be the usual splendid, expensive affair, with a notable difference. It was given as a
benefit for the Legion of Honor, and Maria's fee ($10,000)
was also donated to the cause. It was *the* event of the season. Seats went for as high as $85 a person (including a
lavish dinner which was to follow the gala, in the Opéra's
foyer). However, this did not discourage buyers. In a matter of days, all legitimate channels were exhausted, and
tickets could only be obtained through the black market.

Arriving in the French capital on December 15th,

Maria made an instant hit with the Parisians. After an exhaustive survey of the Opéra's acoustics, an inspection of its enormous stage, and a series of discussions with M. Julien, the theater's director, Maria confronted the press in her most convivial, affable mood, to assure them that "I will sing like I've never sung before."

On the night of December 19th, the great gala began exactly on time at 8:20 P.M. There was good reason for this unprecedented punctuality. The event was televised not only in France but in eight foreign countries: England, Italy, Switzerland, Germany, Belgium, Holland, Austria, and Denmark.

In the audience of three thousand sat President René Coty, whose arrival was greeted by an orchestral fanfare, members of the French cabinet, deputies from all parties who set aside their political disputes for the evening, ambassadors of the United States and Russia, and of other nations, General Norstad and Paul Henri Spaak, Jean Cocteau and Françoise Sagan, the Windsors and the Rothschilds, the elite of French artistic and theatrical life (the late Gérard Philipe was there, Michèle Morgan, Martine Carol, Juliette Greco, Brigitte Bardot), also the ubiquitous representatives of the international set, including Maria's Venice friends, the Greek shipowner Aristotle Onassis and his wife Tina.

Ministers and industrialists, ambassadors and bankers were among the disappointed thousands who searched in vain for tickets—there were only three thousand available for that many seats. Those unlucky enough to miss the spectacle, gathered before their television sets. Eight countries were watching.

The Opéra's Georges Sebastian conducted the overture to Verdi's *La Forza del Destino* for a thundering curtain-raiser. Then, to a roaring reception, the apparition

the French press called *le monstre sacré de l'Opéra* wafted
on stage in a gown of scarlet (the Legion's color), wearing
a Van Cleef and Arpels necklace cheerfully lent for the
occasion and worth more than a million dollars.

She also sang. First the "Casta Diva" from *Norma,*
with chorus, in which she was just beginning to find herself
vocally. But, if only her voice had obeyed her as much as
that on that fateful evening in Rome, she could have spared
herself a mountain of trouble. An excerpt from Verdi's
Il Trovatore followed, then Rosina's aria from Rossini's
The Barber of Seville. With each passing moment she grew
more electrifying.

Without costumes and scenery, relying only on her
ability to act with her voice and her innate powers of stagecraft, she established the right atmosphere, and her Rosina
was utterly disarming. After the second intermission, she
did have costumes and scenery; she also had the assistance
of the Opéra's leading tenor Albert Lance and La Scala's
great baritone Tito Gobbi, and with them she gave the
Parisians the second act of Puccini's *Tosca.* It was an experience to cherish, and the ovation that followed was
reminiscent of her zenith at La Scala.

Most of the press raved the following morning, as did
some foreign correspondents who, lacking the means and
the connections, had been forced to watch the proceedings
via television. But the Callas art has always inspired con-
tradictions—why, of all places, should Paris be the exception? Thus, critic Marie-Laure de Noailles thought "she
sang like a ventriloquist."

Maria conquered Paris. The Opéra's M. Julien
promptly aligned himself with Covent Garden's David
Webster on the select roster of opera directors who still
wanted Maria Callas during their regular season. Before
Maria left Paris, Julien had her promise to return in

December, 1959, to sing *Medea* on the stage of the Paris Opéra.

Even apart from her huge success and brilliant reception, Maria went away thoroughly captivated by Paris. At home again in Milan, where she spent Christmas in relative quiet, the memories of those hectic but immensely satisfying few days in the French capital went a long way to erase the shadows of the bitter Roman adventure that had begun the turbulent year of 1958.

Shortly after New Year's, the American public was given a glimpse of the prima donna in her Milan home. Maria agreed to participate in a one-hour televised musical discussion conducted by Edward R. Murrow in New York for the Columbia Broadcasting System's "Small World" program.

The other participants of the four-pronged discussion were the great British conductor Sir Thomas Beecham, speaking from Nice on the French Riviera, and the irrepressibly unmelancholy Dane, Victor Borge, who was picked up at Southbury, Connecticut. The United States audience saw the telecast on two successive Sundays, January 4th and 11th, in thirty-minute installments.

The program began most refreshingly:

Murrow: Tell me, Sir Thomas, how is the intellectual climate on the Riviera these days?

Beecham: There never was one and there isn't one now.

Murrow: Mr. Borge is talking from a chicken farm in Southbury, Connecticut. Victor, you're on a hot circuit to Milan and Nice.

Borge: Ed, you said Southbury, Connecticut. You didn't tell me where Nice and Milan is.

The stimulating discussion covered a wide range of subjects: the relationship of artists and audience, the responsibilities of serious artists, the attempted definition of a "serious artist," live versus recorded performances, the unpopularity of modern music, and opera in particular, translated operas, claques.

Maria was earnest, extremely formal, occasionally even ceremonious. Beecham, quick-witted and articulate as always, wore his proverbial irascibility like a coat of arms. Borge, the only one in the threesome to treat music with less than ritual reverence, contributed a refreshing stream of easygoing joviality between what occasionally seemed like two volcanos on good behavior.

Toward the end of the telecast, Sir Thomas recommended Handel's seldom heard opera *Hercules* to Maria's attention, calling it "the first music drama written in Europe." He then paid Maria the following compliment: "Only Madame Callas can sing the heroic, impassioned, and marvelous part of the wife of Hercules, Deianira. There's nobody else to do it, and if she doesn't do it I can't perform it."

On January 9th, before America saw the second part of the telecast, Maria returned to the United States for two more concerts under the Hurok management—St. Louis on January 11th and Philadelphia on January 24th.

The Philadelphia concert was another top-hat and diamonds benefit affair, occasioned by the 102nd anniversary of the Academy of Music. Maria's program consisted of arias from *Mefistofele, The Barber of Seville,* and *Hamlet.* The second part of the concert was devoted to Van Cliburn's performance of the Rachmaninoff Third Piano Concerto. Eugene Ormandy conducted the Philadelphia Orchestra. The ransom this time was established at a $100 top for orchestra seats.

It was January 27th, and time for the American Opera Society's concert performance of Bellini's *Il Pirata.* This was another "benefit," with tickets scaled up to $25.

By then the disturbing trend of Callas's new career as a prima donna at large had begun to crystallize: it seemed no longer possible to view her art without the ennobling though expensive halo of a "benefit performance." For those music lovers whose charitable urge was not matched by their affluence, she remained beyond reach.

Nevertheless, the American Opera Society had no difficulty whatever in filling Carnegie Hall's 2,800 seats for the first American performance of *Il Pirata* in more than a hundred years. If the audience was, in Howard Taubman's words, "inclined to be idolatrous," the diva did not let them down.

Without the benefit of scenery, she held them spellbound with the inventiveness of her art and the strength of her characterization. In good form vocally, she propelled Bellini's soaring, if unfamiliar, melodies with gradually lifting intensity toward the powerful final scene, which achieved its dénouement in the ideal tradition of the "ottocento": heroine and audience simultaneously took leave of their senses.

Maria wore a stunning white gown, the lights were dimmed, her assisting artists discreetly slipped into the background, and the atmospheric evocation of the opera's final heartbreaking moments was complete. To heighten the visual effect, Maria employed a thirteen-foot raspberry-red silk stole, with which she draped and shrouded and shielded herself, and around which she moved with the grace and agility of a Manolete. At the end—the expected pandemonium. The diva had to be rescued from her frenzied admirers after a series of bows which she shared with conductor Rescigno, tenor Pier Miranda Ferraro, and baritone Constantino Ego, who were imported from Italy for the performance.

Some New York critics actually voiced their thanks to
Rudolf Bing the following day for having unwittingly
caused this American renaissance of Bellini's long-dormant creation. The comments of avid Callasians, however,
were far less complimentary to the General Manager.

The next day, Maria Meneghini Callas, Commendatore
of the Republic of Italy, was honored by her native city.
It was a citation, presented by New York's Mayor Robert
Wagner, "to the esteemed daughter of New York, whose
glorious voice and superb artistry have contributed to the
pleasure of music lovers everywhere."

After this gratifying episode, Maria and her husband
departed for Milan. They were not present when Verdi's
Macbeth had its Metropolitan première on February 5th.
Leonie Rysanek made a good vocal impression, but fell
short of the dramatic ideal in the role which had been earmarked for Maria. However, the Verdi opera enjoyed an
excitingly successful run during the season. In the title
role, Leonard Warren, the Metropolitan's great baritone,
created what subsequently turned out to be the last contribution to his long list of memorable Verdi roles.

The provocative and potentially sensational casting of
Callas and Warren for the Macbeth pair remained an
unfulfilled dream, to the painful disappointment of the
connoisseurs. It would have been a stormy collaboration,
considering the two strong, unyielding personalities, each
driven by burning perfectionism. Sparks would have been
flying across the stage but, in the end, the artistic results
would have been equally electrifying.

A brief rest in Milan, and then London, for another
recording engagement. It was a leisurely stay this time,
since Maria's calendar was free.

Meneghini had been talking to impresarios from Germany, France, Holland, Spain, and elsewhere, but his terms were hard and, although he did set up a string of concert dates for the spring and summer, they were spread over a comfortable span. There was to be very little opera for the "Queen in exile"—a summer engagement at Covent Garden, and then nothing until the end of the year, when Dallas loomed again on the horizon.

During Maria's London stay, Covent Garden was readying its long-awaited new production of Donizetti's *Lucia di Lammermoor,* never much of a lasting hit in England. This time, however, the signs for a changing outlook were auspicious: Franco Zeffirelli gave the work some stunning settings, Tullio Serafin assumed the musical direction, and the gifted Australian soprano Joan Sutherland sang the title role.

Sutherland had played the minor role of Clotilda at the time Maria Callas made her London debut in *Norma* (1952). In the ensuing seven years, she had developed into an artist of considerable stature, with a spectacular voice. Maria came to the dress rehearsal, and showered enthusiastic compliments on her colleague and on the production in general. The London public agreed—the combined efforts of Sutherland, Serafin, and Zeffirelli turned the tide in favor of the Donizetti opera after the première of February 17th.

The occasion even prompted several British critics to admit that a widespread revision of attitudes was afoot toward Italian opera of the pre-Verdi era, a period which had enjoyed little sympathy previously from modern musical England. According to many commentators, a lion's share of the credit for this metamorphosis went to Maria Meneghini Callas—a tribute she still ranks among her most important achievements.

On March 11th, Callas began recording her own *Lucia* in London's Kingsway Hall. Although the original E.M.I.-

Angel version of this opera, cut in Florence in 1953, was
an excellent production which still sold well all over the
world, the rising stereophonic medium made a new version
a commercial, if not an artistic, necessity. Tullio Serafin
again conducted.

The veteran Ferruccio Tagliavini sang the music of
Edgardo in fervent romantic style, manipulating with consummate skill a voice that no longer possessed the range
and ring of old. The young singers assembled by Walter
Legge for the opera's remaining roles, on the other hand,
failed to measure up to the stature of the earlier cast. As
for Callas in the title role, dramatically she was as convincing as ever, and entirely beyond present-day competition. But her voice, for all the felicities of phrasing and
inflection, disclosed a pronounced stridency in the high
register, a frequent evidence of strain.

While the recording sessions were taking place in
London, a wild rumor swept through Milan that Maria had
suffered a heart attack. It was not the first time for alarming rumors; in Milan her sensational slimming-down had
been persistently attributed to a mysterious illness. This
time, however, the rumors seemed more ominous, and the
spreading panic finally prompted the Milan office of Associated Press to check London by telephone. There the
scouts found the diva in perfect health, not even tired, disposing of a steak dinner in the company of friends at a
fashionable restaurant.

After the completion of the recorded *Lucia,* the
Meneghinis said good-bye to their London friends, but only
for a short time, as Maria was expected back in early June
for her Covent Garden engagement, the highlight of London's opera season.

Now husband and wife were off to Paris for a tour of
business and pleasure. Business was quickly disposed of:
Maria agreed to make her operatic debut in *Medea* at the

Paris Opéra on December 11th, immediately after the Dallas season. The pleasures which followed were manifold: visits with enthusiastic friends, a look at the latest fashions, sessions with a famous magic-fingered coiffeur, and parties, and parties.

It was in Paris, on April 21, 1959, that Maria and Giovanni Battista Meneghini celebrated their tenth wedding anniversary with a sumptuous dinner at Maxim's in the company of friends, followed by a high-spirited stay at the Lido nightclub until four A.M. The occasion was commemorated in a press interview in which Maria attributed the major part of her success to her husband's devotion, faith, and tenacity.

Freely reminiscing about the difficult early years of her career, the time when she had been an insignificant singer and Meneghini an important and respected industrialist, Maria readily admitted that without her husband she never could have emerged from the ranks of the nameless. She went even further: "I could not sing without him present. If I am the voice, he is the 'soul.'"

Her free and easy Parisian sojourn ended with an annoying cold. This caused a two-week postponement of the German tour Battista had arranged several months before. Apparently, however, the management which represented her in Germany failed to make the necessary announcements concerning the postponement, because four different airlines claimed that the diva would grace their line with her presence on the day of her originally scheduled arrival in Wiesbaden. The crowds turned up as expected, but Callas did not.

Maria's health restored, her first concert tour in Germany began with a concert in Wiesbaden on May 10th. There were four concerts in ten days, all displaying the same program of spectacular and familiar Callas special-

ties, all conducted by the familiar figure of Nicola Rescigno,
all sold out far in advance at the by-now familiar extravagant prices. In Hamburg, where she appeared at a televised concert in the city's Musikhalle on May 15th, scalpers
got as much as $75 each for black-market tickets.

It was a flamboyant tour. Everywhere, Maria was
besieged by admirers and autograph hunters. Her car
blocked traffic wherever she went. Sightseeing on foot was
entirely out of the question. In each city, her luxurious
hotel suite was filled with flowers, and her thoughtful
managers saw to it that all her dressing rooms were dec-
orated with her favorite red roses. It was a heartwarming,
reassuring feeling to find undiminished the enthusiasm
she remembered from her earlier visits to Germany, but
many were the moments when Maria Callas would have
wished for a little more privacy.

The grand tour ended in Munich on May 20th with a
flourish: Maria was presented by her German admirers
with a luxury model Mercedes car. Here, too, she found
time to tell the press how much of her career was due to
the wisdom and devotion of Giovanni Battista Meneghini.

While Maria was touring Germany, the costumes and
stage settings of Dallas's *Medea* production docked at
Southampton, bound for trans-shipment to London's
Covent Garden. Appropriately enough, it was the *Queen
Mary* that brought them.

Behind this large-scale enterprise lay an inspired
barter concluded between two practical-minded operatic
impresarios, David Webster of London and Lawrence
Kelly of Dallas. In exchange for bringing the Texas-com-
missioned, Athens-created *Medea* production to London,
Dallas was to receive the widely admired Zeffirelli settings
of *Lucia di Lammermoor* for its coming November season.

The exchange, of course, involved more than scenery

and costumes. Both productions revolved around Maria
Callas, whose presence created the "necessity" which was
the mother of the two impresarios' invention. Alexis
Minotis and Franco Zeffirelli were to supervise personally
their respective stagings. Nicola Rescigno was to be the
conductor of both operas. Even the assisting principals of
the Dallas *Medea* would be part of the London presentation: Jon Vickers and Nicola Zaccaria. Everything was
scientifically arranged to keep both productions in the
Callas-centered "family," so to speak.

The news of the international exchange created quite
a stir throughout the operatic world, particularly in New
York, where many opera-goers felt that the Met could have
used both a new *Medea* and a new *Lucia,* to say nothing
of Callas.

The first of the five Covent Garden *Medeas* took place
on June 17th. It was another one of those diamond-studded,
formal-dress evenings, accompanied by stampeding cheers
and crowned by a shower of flowers, that only Callas was
able to bring about in that famous theater's recent history. Members of the Royal House, ambassadors, Lady
Churchill, and other prominent representatives of
Britain's first families lent one kind of pomp to the occasion; the presence of shipping magnate Aristotle Onassis
with his huge coterie of Monte Carlo celebrities and blue-
bloods provided another.

In far better vocal form than at her Covent Garden
Traviatas of 1958, Callas overwhelmed the audience with
the sizzling intensity of her characterization.

Cherubini's *Medea* had not been seen in London since
1870. No one in the audience was prepared to witness the
seething panorama of emotions with which Callas infused
the figure of that mythological monster. There was an
animal fierceness about her gestures, and an undying

hatred in her piercing eyes. A most miraculous clash of powerfully contrasting emotions seized her whole being in the crucial scene where she caressed her two children while her mind was already set on murdering them. The dramatic devices that evening included the use of a cloak which at times left only her penetrating, terrifying gaze to view.

"This 162-year-old opera stands or falls by the singers of its central part. With Callas on stage for most of three cruelly strenuous hours, it emphatically stood," summed up Eric Mason in London's *Daily Mail*. In the *News Chronicle*, critic Charles Reid sounded a note that had a reminiscent echo of the ecstatic Chicago days: "I came away wholly under her spell. None but Callas could achieve so supremely baleful a Medea to look at or a more cogent one to hear." And, to complete the picture, the inevitable dissenting voice, which this time belonged to Evan Senior of *Music and Musicians:* "She could sing divinely if she paid a little more attention to singing and less to acting. Opera demands a balanced measure of both."

The tremendous success of opening night called for a celebration. At this point, Aristotle Onassis stepped into the picture.

There were no half measures about this flamboyant, self-made man who owned a fleet of tankers and a controlling interest in the "Société des Bains de Mer," an unassuming-sounding enterprise which stands for virtually all of the lucrative activities in Monte Carlo. Maria Callas, a famous Greek, had achieved a great triumph. It was only fitting that another famous Greek, Aristotle Onassis, celebrate this triumph in a style Zeus himself would not have disowned.

The five thousand guests invited to London's Dorchester Hotel presented a dazzling sight. The spontaneous enthusiasm of Chicago's Angel Ball in 1954, even the glitter that surrounded the reception in Maria's honor at New York's Hotel Ambassador following her 1956 debut at the Metropolitan, all the previous festivities paled by comparison. Here she stood not only at the top of her profession, but also in the center of the swirling, intoxicating world of mundane society, a status she had not imagined for herself even in her most ambitious dreams. She had reached the summit, an unbelievable terminal for one whose journey had begun at Manhattan's Amsterdam Avenue.

At her side, Meneghini looked around him with uneasy glances. No stranger to luxury, he had enjoyed the pleasures of material wealth through most of his life. In time, a privileged social standing in his beloved Verona, then the honorary title of Commendatore, bestowing national prominence, had also become his. He was a figure respected in all Italy, not only as the husband of the celebrated Callas, but also as a man whose manifold activities had invariably spelled success: an industrialist, a concert and opera representative of the world's most coveted diva, a real estate investor with a steadily accumulating string of valuable holdings.

Giovanni Battista Meneghini was a millionaire, but one in the outdated sense of the word, one who was worth a few million dollars, or pounds, or perhaps a few dozen million liras in this new inflated world. What he saw around him—the Riviera set, the titled nobles, the international playboys, the debonair dispensers of inherited wealth—filled him with an uncomfortable feeling. Even a millionaire could feel small in the presence of that much lavishness showered on five thousand guests and, particularly, on the radiant guest of honor, by that embodiment of globe-girdling wealth, Aristotle Onassis. Giovanni Battista Meneghini pondered with a strange uneasiness as he remembered the famous line from Vergil that all Italians know from their schoolroom Latin: "timeo Danaos et dona ferentes (I fear Greeks bringing gifts)."

The big party broke up at 3 A.M. Maria and Battista were utterly exhausted, but their host, who appeared to thrive on such activities, preserved his undimmed vigor to the end. In the last minute, before the Meneghinis entered the elevator, he summoned a photographer for a series of pictures for what he called "the family album." No one could have foreseen at that moment that these pictures would eventually have an immensely wider circulation.

Before they parted, Onassis extended an invitation to the Meneghinis to join him and his wife on the luxury yacht *Christina* for its annual Mediterranean cruise. It would be a perfectly marvelous way to relax and get away from it all, Onassis suggested. Incidentally, he added, Sir Winston Churchill and Lady Churchill would be his other honored guests.

Maria was fascinated by the idea. Her husband, who had planned a less spectacular form of summer relaxation, was reluctant, but both assured their host of their deepest appreciation and promised that their final decision would be promptly forthcoming.

The Meneghinis left London at the end of Maria's five-evening Covent Garden engagement. They went by way of Brussels to Amsterdam, where Maria gave her first concert in the Netherlands, with Nicola Rescigno conducting the Concertgebouw Orchestra, on July 11th. She was in excellent form, and her program, containing excerpts from *Il Pirata, Ernani,* and *La Vestale,* was the highlight of that year's Holland Festival. A capacity audience of 2,400 stamped and shouted its approval.

After a long absence, Maria and her husband returned

to the familiar comforts of Sirmione on July 15th. Meneghini would have liked nothing more than to remain there for as long as possible. But Maria wanted the cruise.

Tina Onassis called them twice, urging them to accept, not to miss that splendid opportunity. When Meneghini was reassured that the *Christina's* unmatched facilities included a radiotelephone through which he could keep daily contact with his ailing eighty-four-year-old mother, about whose condition he was deeply concerned, the decision was made.

In Monte Carlo, on July 22nd, Maria and Battista Meneghini met Tina and "Ari" Onassis and Onassis's sister Arthemis, whom Maria remembered from her prewar years in Athens. Sir Winston Churchill and his wife arrived the following day.

Prince Rainier appeared at the docks to see off Monaco's distinguished guests. He told Maria about the unremunerative existence of the Monte Carlo Opera. Perhaps she would appear there some day, to lend the theater its much needed transfusion of excitement? "Possible," said Maria, who had come aboard the *Christina* with a vocal score of Bellini's *La Straniera* under her arm. "We'll talk about it during the cruise. There's enough time," added Onassis.

The fabulous *Christina*, with its 1,640 tons of solid luxury, its splendid treasures of Venetian and Byzantine art, its El Greco paintings, its gold and mosaics, its lavish bar and spectacular swimming pool, and its forty-three-member crew dedicated to the service of its world-famous guests, set out on the calm morning of July 23rd for the sunlit waters of the Mediterranean toward Nice and Genoa, its first ports of call.

CHAPTER **14**

Exit Meneghini

Mimi
Addio, senza rancor.
PUCCINI—LA BOHEME

The first few days of the voyage were calm. The *Christina* followed a leisurely course, casting anchor at Portofino, Capri, and Palermo for sightseeing trips, shopping excursion, visits, and cocktail parties given here and there in honor of the voyagers.

Maria did not get very far in her exploration of Bellini's *La Straniera*. She did the sights with Tina Onassis, attracting curious onlookers and photographers everywhere. Aboard, she was tense, her mind a maze of disturbing, confused, and conflicting feelings. Sir Winston asked her to sing just once. When he ran into a polite but definite "no," the subject was dropped, and the Great Briton returned to his cigars and to discussing navigation with his host.

Meneghini was unhappy from the outset—bored, restless, unable to participate in any discussions involving more than just a few words of elementary French. He felt out of place and wished that he had stayed home, near his ailing mother. He did enjoy the excursion to the Acropolis when the *Christina* reached the Greek seaport of Piræus. But then the sea grew choppier as the cruise continued through the hundreds of little islands in the Aegean Sea northward toward the Dardanelles, and the elements burdened his already sinking spirits with a nearly unsupportable weight.

To make it all even harder to endure, the forceful figure of Onassis, a man only nine years his junior, was growing constantly more dynamic before his weary eyes. There he was, issuing commands, charting the course, entertaining his guests, with a complete disregard of the elements, throwing his weight around like the Greek god Poseidon of ancient mythology.

The Greek landscape brought back vivid and often disturbing memories to Maria Callas. She was deeply shaken and disheartened by the sight of the misery that still beclouded the lives of the Greek mountainfolk. The always latent sense of kinship with the Greek nation that Maria had been carrying within her all her life was gradually flowering into a feeling of strong nationalism. An unfortunate incident served to build fire under this awakening feeling, and to turn her against her husband at the same time.

During one of the excursions, a group of Greek water carriers had been engaged. When the trip was over, and the carriers were about to be dismissed, Meneghini offered to pay their wages, but did so in a rather penurious fashion, which prompted Onassis to save the situation with a generous, even lordly—but for Meneghini immensely humiliating—gesture.

On August 7th, the *Christina* dropped anchor at the foot of Mount Athos, the 6,000-foot "Holy Mountain" which has been the site of convents for more than a thousand years, and a traditional place of pilgrimage for those of the Greek Orthodox religion. The following day, the Patriarch of Constantinople received the Meneghini and Onassis families. In proud and eloquent words, the Patriarch paid tribute to Maria Callas, "the world's greatest singer," and Aristotle Onassis, "the greatest seaman of the modern world, the new Ulysses," for the honors they had brought to Greece.

It was all Greek to Giovanni Battista Meneghini, but the solemnity of the occasion, the expression on Maria's transfigured face, the entire atmosphere shot through with its strange, Byzantine mysticism, filled him with foreboding. Meneghini was a perceptive man, and he knew Maria. Her behavior throughout the trip had indicated all too clearly to his sensitive eyes the true depth of an emotional crisis.

"It was an outburst of nationalism," Meneghini later reminisced with bitterness, "which left Maria with a visible mark of exaltation. She was no longer the same. How could I defend myself against the new Ulysses?"

The blow came on the night of August 8th, as the voyagers of the *Christina* were getting ready to attend a gala party at the Istanbul Hilton. Maria told her husband that all was over between them, that their marriage had come to an end because she loved another man—Onassis. That night, Meneghini stayed on board. Pleas, bitter outbursts, recriminations behind the closed doors of their luxurious cabin as the *Christina* turned southward the following day, back toward the Adriatic, left the basic issue unaltered: it was the end of a marriage.

Until the journey ended a week later, when the *Christina* gracefully sailed into the lagoon of Venice, the days

seemed endless to Battista Meneghini. Stunned into speech-
lessness, humiliated by the overpowering sense of his loss,
he was still unable to comprehend the reasons for Maria's
decision, or the violent swiftness with which it had happened. But the break was final, although, at that point, still
a secret kept within the triangle. When Maria and Battista
landed at the Milan airport, and descended from Onassis's
personal plane, the tense look on Meneghini's face was explained by the onlookers as the result of his mother's
illness.

On August 17th, Onassis appeared at the Sirmione
villa. For hours the threesome went over the same painful
ground, passionately and aimlessly. Clearly, their relationship was beyond explaining and beyond reconciliation. At
four o'clock in the morning, Maria and Onassis left the
villa. The break was complete. Maria returned to the Via
Buonarroti, where she remained in seclusion for several
days, and Onassis flew to Venice to rejoin his yacht and
his blonde wife Tina, who was undoubtedly waiting for him
with a few questions that had been accumulating in her
mind during his absence.

While the Meneghinis remained out of circulation,
with Maria in Milan and Battista in Sirmione, a news event
of a different nature was in the making. A reconciliation
between La Scala and its Queen-in-exile was considered
to be imminent. After an interruption of two years, during
which time Callas had recorded only in London, E.M.I.
was again busily setting up its equipment in the Scala
auditorium, in preparation for the recording of Ponchielli's *La Gioconda*. If Callas was again recording under
La Scala's auspices, concluded those in the know, the logical next step would be her return to the theater during the
forthcoming season. Big news indeed was in the making,

but, as things turned out, the reconciliation was completely buried in the explosion that followed a few days later.

On the afternoon of September 2nd, Maria drove to La Scala in her Mercedes. Alone. She was greeted effusively by her fellow-artists, by conductors Votto and Tonini, by members of the staff who had assembled for the first run-through prior to the actual recording.

But there was something unusual about her appearance, and it was immediately noted.

"Where is Battista?" someone asked.

"He stayed in Sirmione, to be near his mother. She is ill, you know."

The rehearsal pleased all concerned. Conductors, vocalists, and orchestra were asked to resume, this time before the microphones, three days later. Maria Callas, calm and businesslike as usual under such circumstances, drove away in apparent good humor.

The following evening: the explosion. Maria Callas and Aristotle Onassis were discovered at the Rendez-vous, an intimate nightclub away from Milan's social whirl, dining tête-à-tête, to the accompaniment of soft dance music by a five-piece orchestra. Photographers materialized out of nowhere, and while the music played and Maria and Aristotle chatted in seeming unconcern, telephones jangled and Milan's morning papers hastened to reset their front pages. At three o'clock in the morning, the celebrated couple left the Rendez-vous. Maria carried a fresh bouquet of red roses as she entered the Principe e Savoia Hotel on Onassis's arm. By that time their secret was shared with all Milan.

Next morning, the whole world knew it. Photographers and reporters surrounded the house on the Via Buonarroti and witnessed a parade of lawyers. The newspapers were having a field day with predictions, recollections, speculations, because no one could be reached for statements.

On the afternoon of September 5th, the recording sessions of *La Gioconda* began. This opera's throbbing strains had once supplied the romantic background to the budding Verona romance of Maria Callas and Giovanni Battista Meneghini. Now, twelve years later, the same opera was destined to ring down the closing curtain on that romance.

The first day's session lasted until midnight. What took place when it was over would have been worth a front-page headline under ordinary circumstances. However, with all the news space devoted to the marital tangle, only the musical world took notice: Antonio Ghiringhelli and his entire artistic staff greeted Maria in the vestibule of the theater's Via Filodrammatici entrance with beaming faces and outstretched hands. After a warm and friendly conversation, the group left in perfect harmony. Maria's reconciliation with La Scala had become official.

Friends of the theater, already gladdened by the recent announcement that Tebaldi would return for the opening of the 1959/1960 season, looked forward to similar news regarding Callas. But with the world press devoting acres of columns to the diva's marital problems, La Scala chose to remain aloof, and withheld the news of reconciliation.

On the evening of September 8th, while *La Gioconda* was still being recorded, Maria Callas made the following announcement to the press:

"I confirm that the break between my husband and myself is complete and final. It has been in the air for quite some time, and the cruise on the *Christina* was only coincidental. The lawyers are working on the case, and will make an announcement ... I am now my own manager. I ask for understanding in this painful personal situation. Between Signor Onassis and myself there exists only a profound friendship that dates back to some time. I am also in business connections with him; I have received offers from the Monte Carlo Opera, and there is also a prospect for a film. When I shall have further things to say, I shall do so at the opportune moment, but I do not intend to call a press conference."

This announcement prompted Maria's intimate friends to explain that her reconciliation with La Scala had been made possible by her newly gained "freedom." Much of Maria's past tribulations, they said, had been due to Meneghini's influence, his frequently poor judgment, and his difficulty in getting along with impresarios. Now that Maria was managing her own affairs, things would be different. . . .

Within a few hours after Maria's statement, the press also heard Meneghini's side:

"It is all true. The separation which means the end of our married life is irrevocable. I do hope that we can reach a mutual agreement, without rancor. The causes are very well known: the sentimental link between Maria Callas and Aristotle Onassis . . . I bear no bitterness toward Maria, who honestly told me the truth, but I cannot forgive Onassis. The laws of hospitality were sacred for the ancient Greeks."

That same day, Aristotle Onassis was sipping cognac at Harry's Bar in Venice. He was brooding, but made no attempt to avoid the inquiring reporters. Never allergic to publicity, he took their rapid-fire questions in his stride. He had nothing to do with the Meneghini's marital break-up, he insisted. "Of course, how could I help but be flattered if a woman with the class of Maria Callas fell in love with someone like me? Who wouldn't?" He only lost his composure when the questions turned to his wife Tina.

Tina Onassis had been the center of interest at the lavish party given by Elsa Maxwell the night before. She had given no evidence of grief or bitterness, but maintained absolute silence on the issue that kept Venice and the rest of the world buzzing. So did, not surprisingly perhaps but most uncharacteristically, her loyal friend and hostess, Elsa Maxwell.

Back in the friendly retreat of Sirmione, the erstwhile haven where reporters were never admitted, Giovanni Battista Meneghini freely discussed the affair, commenting with wistfulness, candor, and still a trace of disbelief on the "thunderbolt that wrecked his life." He was no longer the man in the shadows, the unseen hand that guided his wife to success. In this drama he was the unquestioned star, though his role, unfortunately, was modeled on the baritones in Italian opera, who hardly ever manage to end up with the heroine at the final curtain.

Meneghini's two younger brothers, who had been somewhat alienated from him during the years of his separation from the family business, now returned with the old solidarity and affection. So did many old friends from Verona, all singing the same tune: "I told you so." One erstwhile intimate sent a telegram: "Congratulations. You regained tranquility."

Meneghini's bitterness was mainly vented on Onassis —"That man with an ambition like Hitler, who wants to own everything, with his millions and his accursed cruise and his accursed yacht!" Toward Maria he was still loyal; he was desperately trying to probe beneath the reasons for her emotional crisis, and he blamed the critical tone of the Italian press for causing his wife to live in a constant state of tension.

However, for all his loyalty and devotion to Maria,

Meneghini was deeply hurt and shaken, and made no attempt to conceal his feelings. Contrary to the rumors which had hinted at a rift between them, contrary to Maria's own announcement about their disagreements, nothing had really prepared him for such a blow. He even recalled in one of his press interviews that Maria had once planned to retire to Sirmione some day and that her thoughts had advanced further into the future: she had wanted that quiet resort to be the final resting place where she and her devoted Titta would be together in all eternity.

In another mood, the saddened husband's thoughts turned to the past: "I created Callas . . . she was a fat, clumsily dressed woman, poor like a gypsy, when I met her. And now I hear that I am accused of having exploited her . . . she had nothing, and now we have to divide the community property . . ." Then, as his eye caught the aging poodle, Tea, who was left behind in Sirmione, he remarked with bitter irony: "You'll see, if everything will be split, and if we'll have to divide this poodle, Maria will get the front end and I will end up with the tail!"

While Meneghini talked, and all Italy listened, Maria sang. The recording of *La Gioconda* was completed on September 10th. The following day, Onassis's private plane picked her up at the Milan airport. Accompanied by sounds of general consternation, Maria returned to the *Christina*. Onassis's sister went along for this second phase of the voyage; the globetrotting poodle, Toy, represented the Meneghini household. Tina Onassis was in Paris, visiting her family and planning her future course of action. The world's press reported the drama's every move.

In Italy, the newspapers and magazines seemed to be writing about nothing else but the Meneghini–Callas–Onassis triangle, gleefully prognosticating an infinite variety of developments. Onassis may build a new theater for Maria, reported one source. He would finance her movies, stated another.

Evangelia Callas lost no time in joining the parade. In a particularly malicious two-page exclusive for the Milanese weekly *L'Europeo,* she categorically announced that Maria would eventually marry Onassis to further her limitless ambition. In New York, Hy Gardner quoted Evangelia in the following statement on September 11th: "I was the first victim of Maria. Now it is Meneghini. Onassis will be the third."

Keeping up the barrage of speculations and predictions, another unimpeachable social historian, Cholly Knickerbocker, gave this dissenting but equally authoritative verdict: "It was Callas who kept the publicity going and Onassis won't have an easy time losing her. But I will make a bet, that the future will still find Ari and Tina Onassis together—with Maria singing a loud solo."

For a while it seemed the deluge of words would never end. Then, on September 13th, the Russian Government, with the jubilant announcement that their sputnik had hit the moon, gave the world something else to talk about. Khrushchev landed in the United States for a visit that, for a while at least, monopolized the front pages in most parts of the globe. But in Italy, the two events still consumed newsprint at an approximately identical rate, and the summit meeting seemed to be taking place in the Mediterranean, not at Camp David.

The *Christina's* ten-day cruise was interrupted in Athens. There Maria boarded the Onassis plane for a quick flight to Bilbao, Spain, where she gave a concert to what was possibly the coldest reception of her career. Without wasting any time, and successfully eluding the photographers, she then flew back to Athens, pausing just long enough to dismiss Bilbao as a "silly little engagement," a remark which immediately unleashed a wave of indignation through musical Spain.

On September 22nd, the *Christina* came to dock in Messina, the Sicilian seaport, after passing through the strait that separated the fearful Scylla and Charybdis of mythological times. Aristotle Onassis did not need to fear the tempting songs of Circe that had nearly brought Ulysses to his ruin. On the contrary. He had his siren on his arm as they posed for the photographers, while Circe-Callas benignly informed the press: "There is no romance. Mr. Onassis and his wife are my very dear friends. I hope you will not wreck our friendship."

At that time, unsuspected by Maria, and possibly even by her escort, Tina Onassis was already in New York, with the two Onassis children, initiating divorce proceedings.

On September 23, 1959, Maria Callas returned to the world of music. Since her five London *Medeas* during June, she had given only two concerts—one in Amsterdam on July 11th, and one in Bilbao on September 17th. With all the front-page sensations, the world was beginning to forget that she was capable of making *musical* news as well. . . .

Not only the musical world, but Maria, herself, also needed reassurance. She welcomed the opportunity to erase the unpleasant Bilbao episode from her mind. It seemed particularly auspicious at that moment that this opportunity should occur in London, where the memory of her musical triumphs was still fresh, where her popularity still appeared undiminished.

"Be kind to me. I am in a very delicate situation. I have to work for my living." With these well-chosen words to illustrate the far-reaching changes in her life, Maria introduced her first London appearance without the guiding and supporting hand of Battista Meneghini. There was another startling change about her. When she faced the audience of three thousand in the Royal Festival Hall, she displayed none of her fabled jewels. One ring and one necklace were the austere status symbols of the new Callas, the working girl.

She sang near top form. When the concert was over "Maria Callas had London at her feet. It was one of the most dramatic and memorable nights in London's music," reported the *Daily Mail*. The "Mad Scene" from Thomas's *Hamlet* proved to be the highlight of the occasion. No major artist had presented that coloratura tour-de-force in London since the palmy days of Nellie Melba.

Although she was under contract to do another concert in London for television on September 29th, Maria flew to Milan for an urgent conference regarding the settlement of community property. There was no chance of a reconciliation with Meneghini, she declared to the press. The reason? "Discord and conflicting business interests."

On September 28th, Meneghini filed suit for legal separation "for reasons due to the fault of the wife." The hearing was scheduled to take place on October 24th.

Under the impact of this announcement, Maria was forced to postpone the London television engagement. (It took place later, on October 4th.) She also cancelled a Berlin concert which was scheduled for October 3rd. The latter event caused a great deal of consternation because an intensive promotional campaign had preceded the concert, and because adverse publicity had already been created by the elevated prices. Besides, Callas chose a week that was rather unfortunate for impresarios in Germany: Renata Tebaldi also bowed out of a Wiesbaden engagement which was to follow the Callas concert by two days.

News of the impending separation suit by the Meneghinis was presented in this ominous form to the selfçlaimed twenty million readers of his syndicated column on October 2nd by society reporter Cholly Knickerbocker: "The entire Onassis–Callas powder keg will explode when Giovanni Battista Meneghini sues his wife Maria Callas *on moral grounds* in Brescia, Italy. And in Italy this can *result in a jail sentence.* All in all it should make some pretty sensational reading."

But the breathless buildup was in vain. The explosion Mr. Knickerbocker's faithful readers had every right to expect never came. Maria's lawyers obtained an extension, and a new date was set for the Brescia hearing: November 14th. The postponement enabled Maria to keep the Berlin engagement on October 23rd, although it necessitated some changes in her forthcoming American tour.

She winced when she thought about her schedule— even without the threatening shadow of legal complications and all the strain and harassments, her American trip presented virtually unsurmountable problems of timing and a myriad of other complications. This time there would be no Meneghini at her side. She was her own manager.

Hoping for the best, with Toy as her sole traveling companion, Maria Callas left Milan. She flew by way of Paris toward her American engagements in Kansas City and Dallas, knowing that she would have to be back at the Brescia court on November 14th for a painful personal ordeal.

Her impending arrival signalled the opportunity for Elsa Maxwell to break her long, surprising, and punitive silence on the subject of the Callas crisis. After two years of loyal and enthusiastic drumbeating, often filling relatively uneventful gaps in Maria's career with streams of effusive and well-intentioned chatter, it had been a rather ironical twist of fate which imposed silence on Elsa's animated lips at a time when the world's press had an open season on Callas.

At any rate, on October 27th, Elsa—like her operatic namesake, Lohengrin's talkative bride—broke her silence with an oblique reference to Maria in her column without mentioning her name. "That much-heralded diva arrives in America," she began her say, and followed with a dialogue that had taken place a few days before between her and the New York Philharmonic's Leonard Bernstein:

> *Bernstein:* How do you feel about her?
> *Maxwell:* I don't feel anything.
> *Bernstein:* But you must take some stand.
> *Maxwell:* Do you mean morally or musically?
> *Bernstein:* Both.
> *Maxwell:* Musically, I can only say she is the greatest artist in the world.

Callas had lost her erstwhile place of eminence in Maxwell's column. The breathless superlatives previously lavished on her now were showered on Tina Onassis, as if to give final proof of where Maxwell's sympathies stood in the tangled affair.

On the morning of October 27th, Maria Callas landed at Idlewild. Dario Soria, no longer head of Angel Records but still a close friend, was on hand to spirit her into a limousine toward the Kansas City plane scheduled to take off from La Guardia Airport, some ten miles away.

It was not a simple operation. More than fifty reporters and photographers descended on Maria like disorganized rabble, popping flashbulbs and questions with a monotonous, noisy, rude insistence:

"What will happen at the trial?"

"Will you be reconciled with your husband?"

"Do you love Mr. Onassis?"

"Will you marry Mr. Onassis?"

Maria would have none of it. Asked about the future, she replied "I never make any plans." Truer words have seldom been spoken. Beyond that, she refused to discuss her private affairs. "I want to be left alone," she exclaimed to the Port Authority policemen who came to her aid. "Get these wires out from under my feet!" as she began to be hopelessly tangled up in the network of microphone wires. Finally, when nothing seemed to discourage or drive away the leeches, she screamed in a far less musical tone, but in a way to leave no doubt about the firmness behind it: "Lay off, will you?!"

The plane left with the diva, and the reporters went about their business in search of another prey. In the next day's press she was castigated for the uncooperative manner in which she treated "the same reporters to whom she owes so much and the same press which has built her into an international figure," in the scathing opinion of Cholly Knickerbocker, Maria's self-appointed prosecutor.

In Kansas City, the following evening, just before she was to begin her concert, the management of the Midland Theater received information that a bomb had been placed under the stage. Nevertheless, Maria insisted on singing the first number of her program, an aria from Mozart's *Don Giovanni*. When this was over, the white-tie, capacity audience was ushered outside. After a half-hour interruption devoted to a thorough search, the bomb scare was declared a hoax. The concert went on, and ended with a thunderous ovation. Former President Harry S. Truman and the Governors of Kansas and Missouri headed the list of attending celebrities.

After the concert, the evening's activities continued with a posh party in the diva's honor. Maria's role appeared in the press in carefully detailed but somewhat contradictory accounts. Undoubtedly, one of the proffered two alternatives must have been the truth:

New York *Journal American*
Maria Callas lived up to her reputation for capriciousness last night by standing up the Governor of Missouri and 800 of Kansas City's elite. The temperamental diva was just too tired to attend a champagne reception in her honor . . . . Gov. James T. Blair, his wife and the wife of Kansas City's Mayor waited in vain for the Great One to appear.

Time Magazine
After a thunderous ovation, Callas greeted Harry S. Truman with a courtly "I am honored," made her manners to Kansas Governor George Docking, even attended a post-concert party at the River Club where she danced with local millionaires and nibbled caviar snacks and the "Delice Callas" dessert . . .

The Kansas City concert took place under the management of Dallas impresario, Lawrence Kelly. At its conclusion, Kelly, conductor Rescigno, and their star attraction immediately emplaned for Texas to start preparations for Dallas's third operatic season.

Originally, Kelly had planned to present *Lucia di Lammermoor,* in the Zeffirelli production borrowed from Covent Garden, on November 6th and 8th, with Maria Callas in the title role. Maria's next appearances, according to the original plan, would have occurred on November 19th and 21st in the title role of Cherubini's *Medea.* In between, Kelly had scheduled two presentations of Rossini's *The Barber of Seville,* with Teresa Berganza as Rosina.

When impending maternity caused Berganza to cancel her engagements, Kelly obtained Callas's promise to take over the part of Rosina as well, in what would have been her first United States appearance in that role. This plan was frustrated by the decision of the Brescia tribunal, which summoned Maria back to Italy on November 14th. Thus Maria was faced with the prospect of appearing at the separation hearings in Italy between two pairs of extremely demanding operatic appearances in Dallas—all within the span of fifteen days.

Understandably enough, she was restless and impatient in Dallas during her first week, much less active in the many social affairs than in the previous season. But the city was on her side. Its press and public treated her with considerate understanding of her predicament and her state of nerves.

The first *Lucia* on November 6th, however, was a near-disaster. Even the customarily superb dramatic qualities could not deflect the audience's attention from the many vocal mishaps. The troublesome high E-flat in the "Mad Scene" was spectacularly missed.

Two girls from the chorus rushed to her side after the curtain fell. Maria was talking to herself furiously: "I had the note. I had the note. I don't know what happened." To prove the point, she hit five consecutive E-flats on her way to the dressing room. Regaining better control, she gave a much improved account of the role two nights later. She sang with assurance, omitted the E-flats, and it was all to the total gain.

While La Scala's Eugenia Ratti arrived in Dallas to rescue the Rossini opera from the threatened cancellation (she sang Rosina brilliantly), Maria flew back to New York on November 9th, on her way to face the separation hearings in Italy.

First, however, she had to face the New York reporters. They were just as numerous this time, and just as full of questions, but much better behaved. Maria rewarded them with a surprise announcement: while waiting between planes she had telephoned Rudolf Bing at the Metropolitan, she informed the press, and peace had been restored between them.

Did that mean that Maria would return to the Met? It was possible, she intimated, though for the moment her main concern was the impending separation trial. She also implied that legal complications might compel her to take an extended rest. Questioned about Onassis, she replied calmly: "He is one of my many friends in Europe." Then, as the reporters rushed to their telephones, she departed.

Bing confirmed Maria's story with a remark that was devoid of his customary wryness: "The return of a prodigal daughter is as welcome as the return of a prodigal son." He declined to comment on the theory that the reconciliation was brought about by Meneghini's removal from the diva's life. Nor did he foresee Maria Callas's return to the Metropolitan in the immediate future in view of the commonly known fact that the theater's programs were already established for the entire season.

On the morning of November 14th, Maria Callas and her husband, Giovanni Battista Meneghini, appeared before Justice Cesare Andreotti, President of the Brescia Tribunal. It was a great event in Brescia, a city of 100,000, an industrial center seldom involved in the imbroglios of the social and artistic elite.

Meneghini was the first to arrive at the courthouse. The assembled throng greeted him with hearty cheers. Without a question, sympathy was on his side. He was the wronged man, and, above all, an Italian who was abandoned by his foreign wife for another foreigner.

Maria arrived shortly thereafter, accompanied by her lawyer and her close friend, Giovanna Lomazzi. There was no emotion on her impassive face as she made her way to the court building through the curious, milling, but generally well-behaved crowd.

In accordance with the Italian law, Court President Andreotti heard Meneghini first, then Maria, then both,

in a final attempt to effect a reconciliation. Faced with
the hopelessness of the situation, the lawyers entered the
picture, and the long arguments to establish the property
settlement began.

It lasted six hours, but the end brought the parties
together in mutual understanding, which was the outcome
both husband and wife desired. The property settlement
left Maria in possession of the Milan townhouse and most
of her considerable wealth in jewelry. Meneghini kept the
Sirmione villa, and all other real estate holdings. Maria
was also assured the sole income from all future recording
royalties. Their paintings and art objects were divided.
Maria retained ownership of both poodles, Tea and Toy,
and Meneghini's earlier qualms about being shortchanged
in the settlement soon evaporated: the division was fair,
and evidently to his complete satisfaction.

Meneghini withdrew his original request that the
separation be granted through his wife's fault. It was
arrived at by mutual consent and in an atmosphere of
perfect amity. Husband and wife, the lawyers, and even
the press echoed the praises of Justice Andreotti's fair-
minded and effective handling of the ticklish case.

Immediately after the Brescia hearing, Maria flew
back to Dallas, slipping through New York practically
unnoticed, to fulfill her obligations for the season, the last
commitments accepted under the Meneghini "management." Lawrence Kelly and her many Dallas friends, delighted at the good news of the speedy Brescia settlement,
welcomed her with fervent affection.

In turn, Maria, although she had arrived only on the
day of the dress rehearsal, outdid herself in *Medea.* "Again
she gave us a Medea of tenderness, fury and impassioned
singing, and she was rewarded with standing ovations,"
reported George C. Leslie in *Musical America.*

After the second Dallas *Medea,* on November 21, 1959, Maria Callas removed herself from the vocal arena for the longest pause of her career. The proposed Paris appearance, set for December 11th, never materialized. She returned to Milan and immediately set the city buzzing with rumors of a reconciliation when Meneghini was sighted a few days later at what was now Maria's undisputed property on the Via Buonarroti.

It was only a meeting between friends. The occasion: Maria's thirty-sixth birthday. The thoughtful Titta arrived, preceded by the customary bouquet of two dozen red roses, and stayed for a leisurely breakfast. He tendered fondest birthday greetings, and received Maria's sincere good wishes for his own future. Then he accompanied Maria to Madame Biki's salon. The day began almost like old times. . . .

But there was no sequel. The rumors of reconciliation died down, to make room for other rumors. Giovanni Battista Meneghini returned to Sirmione, the idyllic retreat where the poet Catullus had penned his lyric poems and biting epigrams and had brooded about the vicissitudes of love.

At sixty-four, a man of worldly wisdom, Meneghini no longer rebels against the unalterable. Twelve years of glory and excitement have been his, and these are fondly and wistfully remembered. He has endured a fair share of vexations, feuds, and even scandals, and the thought that his future life will, in all likelihood, follow a calmer course fills him with a sense of relief. Meneghini is now a name the whole world knows, and finding himself in the Italian newspapers or magazines with or without any reference to Callas gives him a feeling of satisfaction. He reads avidly, follows the Italian and French press regularly. It has become a habit. In the past he would read them all, then he

would hide the meanest comments and the most savage
attacks to spare his wife's sensitivities, to keep the outbursts of temper to a minimum. He still follows that fascinating career with unchanging concern, and wonders,
with the rest of the world, about the course it will take.

But Meneghini's concern probes deeper. How long
will Maria Callas continue to be her own manager? He
knows that she cannot carry the burden alone. Who but a
devoted husband, who loves her, understands her, can pro-
vide the constantly needed encouragement and support?
Who will share her responsibilities, or be willing to relieve
her of them entirely, and, above all, who can step into the
many-sided duties and activities he, Giovanni Battista
Meneghini, carried out so expertly for more than twelve
years? Who will be able to serve Maria Callas with utter
selflessness?

On his frequent trips to Milan, Meneghini is besieged
with offers, and constantly approached by talented sopranos, tenors, and baritones in the hope that he will
"build" their career as he once did for Callas. His answer
to these hopefuls is always the same: "Just bring me one
who sings like Callas, who has a mind like Callas, a heart
and temperament like Callas, an ambition and fierce dedication like Callas, and leave the rest to me."

The world moves on, and opera moves on with it. St.
Ambrose Day, 1959, brought Verdi's *Otello* to La Scala,
with Mario del Monaco, Leonie Rysanek, and Tito Gobbi
as the principals. Two nights later, Renata Tebaldi returned in *Tosca*, after almost five years of absence. "A
state of delirium," reported *La Notte*. "We have never
heard Tosca sung so beautifully," exclaimed the critic of
L'Italia.

Eager eyes looked high and low for Maria Callas who
was rumored to be in the audience. She was not. Her

thoughts on this occasion were clearly stated to music critic Eugenio Gara in an interview that same week: "Now that Renata Tebaldi returns to La Scala, public attention should be focused on this important event without direct or indirect interferences of any kind. I have closed many chapters this year, it is my sincere wish that this chapter, too, be closed."

Indeed, many chapters were closed in 1959 for Maria Callas. For better or worse, Giovanni Battista Meneghini was out of her life. She made her peace with Antonio Ghiringhelli and Rudolf Bing. With no efforts to fan the flame, her protracted feud with Renata Tebaldi was reduced to ashes. Amity and calm loomed on the horizon at the threshold of 1960.

But what about the chapters yet unwritten?

Whatever the future holds for Maria Callas, the artist, it will be governed by the course of her personal life, that closely guarded, contradictory, and enigmatic part of her in which—headlines to the contrary—perhaps no one has yet fully shared. In a sense, it never has been a *personal* life, but one curtailed by driving ambitions, demanding standards, forbidding goals, and pressing obligations.

By 1960, it had again become a lonely life, for she found herself liberated, by her own choice, of the man who had asserted a subtle but powerful influence on its most significant period. Admirers may cheer, critics may rave, impresarios may surround her with roses or kiss her hand with obeisance—these gestures are all rendered to the coveted diva. Bereft of the splendor which spells personal glory and material gain to the legions that depend on her, the figure of Maria Callas stands alone.

Out of the relative silence and inactivity during most of 1960 will emerge a new period in Maria Callas's tempestuous life. Ghiringhelli counts on her to continue her association with La Scala in all its old glory, hoping for the return of the habitual *Esaurito* evenings which had fallen off alarmingly in Milan during Maria's absence.

The way is also open for Maria's return to the Metropolitan, which also needs her artistry if it cannot always satisfy her exalted standards. Time may have taught her a more patient understanding of the problems of opera production, American style. She may even, some day, return to Rome, if for no other reason than to give a new boost to the traditional inter-theater rivalry.

In all likelihood, the future will see a mellower Callas, an artist who can look back on an arduous road with the pride of accomplishment, and also with a retrospective view of contentment. Nor is the future likely to see a Callas enslaved by her career to the extent shown in its first twenty years. Her appearances are likely to be less numerous, though, it is hoped, planned with more circumspection and meaning than the events of her brief tenure as a prima donna at large.

"Benefit" concerts, vocal exhibitions in circus-like settings may bring on the pomp and the pompous, may shatter all records in box-office take, but they will not uphold the high standards of art, to which the valuable years of an incredible career were dedicated. On the contrary, they deny her interpretations to the multitude of opera lovers on two continents who value the same high standards just as highly, and who are anxious to share the enjoyments born of artistic creations on the Callas level.

She is still a young woman, and after more than twenty years of incessant and often self-denying struggles, she wants to live. The yet untold chapters of the Maria Callas story may bring about developments for which this chronicle may leave the reader totally unprepared. Part of these, one should like to hope, will enrich operatic history. Another part—of this there is little doubt—will continue on the front pages.

For essentially she is still the same Maria Callas of the impulsive bent, magnetic personality on stage and off. Above all, she is a woman endowed with an unshakable faith in herself. This inner strength is the key to her extraordinary career, and to her world-famous but often misunderstood personality.

CHAPTER 15

Portrait of a Prima Donna

Rosina
Mi lascio reggere, mi fo guidar
Ma se mi toccano dov'è il mio debole
Sarò una vipera . . .
E cento trappole, prima di cedere,
Farò giocar . . .
ROSSINI — THE BARBER OF SEVILLE

The designation of "prima donna," somewhat incongruous in our modern age, was virtually removed from circulation until the relatively recent emergence of Maria Callas. Whatever individual opinions may be of Callas as a human being, an artist, or a singer, she is a "prima donna" by universal consent. The controversies she inspires serve only to underline this fact. What, then, is a prima donna?

Singers have been a problem ever since the infancy

of opera. In a beguiling book called *Observations on the Florid Song,* the Italian teacher and composer, Pier Francesco Tosi, once exclaimed: "Who would ever think that a virtue of the highest estimation should prejudice a singer? And yet, whilst presumption and arrogance flourish, the more the singer has of amiable humility, the more it depresses him." Tosi's book was written in 1723.

"Presumption and arrogance"—let us simply call it conceit—is still the opera singer's stock in trade. It is the magic elixir that instills courage and self-confidence into the aspiring novice; the stimulant that fortifies against the hazards of an arduous road that seems to lead forever uphill; the reassurance in times of failure and frustrations; the shield against real or imagined threats from rivals and other "enemies." Once the summit is reached, conceit in the artist becomes a quality widely understood, and even respected. It surrounds the star with a happy halo of assurance; it protects her like an armor against ill-tempered criticism; and, in many cases, it provides the justification for illogical, irresponsible, or irrational behavior.

Conceit and talent make a spellbinding combination, but they do not always go hand in hand. "Presumption and arrogance" unaccompanied by a similar measure of talent produces obnoxious nonentities. Great talent, if unaided by self-strengthening ego, is doomed in a world where only the fittest survive. To reach the top, the singer must possess both these qualities. Add flamboyance, the third magic ingredient, and you have the basic requisites of the "prima donna."

Prima donnas are, as a rule, good singers, though, as history shows, not always extraordinary ones. What is an absolute must, however, is that they possess a kind of magnetism that attracts and holds attention and that makes them the focal point of stage action. A prima donna must

generate excitement by the sheer beauty or consummate
use of her voice, by an inborn theatrical flair, or by an impressive command of gestures and dramatic nuances that
make up an extraordinary interpretation.

But theatrical excitement is not enough. Prima donnas
are not expected to operate on the every-day level even
outside the theater walls. Perhaps because they project
opera's exaggerations and incongruities into their daily
lives, or because they live under the shadow of traditions
they feel compelled to uphold, or because they are simply
spoiled by a traditionally appreciative and tolerant public,
excitement—real, imagined, or fabricated—follows them
everywhere.

A true prima donna is a figure surrounded by legends
and half-truths that strain credulity and truths that are
sometimes downright incredible. She is a personage of
caprice and haughtiness, of restless, bold, and provocative
individualism.

These qualities seem more natural in the feminine
character, but, as Gatti-Casazza once observed: "all artists
have a feminine side." When we hear about a "prima
donna tenor," the term is not as paradoxical as it may
sound. However, theatricalism, vanity, possessiveness, and
hyper-sensitivity are more readily tolerated in the female,
who, even at her most tigerish, can retain a certain quality
of the touching and defenseless on occasion, while a hysterical, self-worshipping male is forever in danger of over-
stepping the thin line that separates the glamorous from
the ridiculous.

History has given us fascinating variations on the
same basic pattern. No less a musical figure than George
Frideric Handel heads the list of the long-suffering race
of opera impresarios driven to the limits of their endurance by the ladies of song.

Handel composed one magnificent air after another for the brilliant voice of Francesca Cuzzoni, only to be rewarded with torrents of abuse and temperamental fits. On one occasion, he seized Francesca bodily and came near to throwing her from a window before she yielded to his authority. Unable, finally, to cope with his terrible-tempered star, Handel began to favor Faustina Bordoni with his compositions, and thus triggered a rivalry compared to which present-day animosities amount to no more than spirited chatter. The two divas actually came to blows on several occasions, and since both commanded sizable throngs of partisans, the consequences were uproarious.

It was Bordoni, incidentally, who first demanded contractual assurance that her salary be the highest paid to any member of the company—a prima donna gesture still very much in fashion, two centuries later.

Prima donna notoriety reached its summit with Caterina Gabrielli (1730–1796), a child of the Roman slums who nevertheless ruled the stage with such grace and elegance that "the spectators could look at nothing else while she was in view" (Burney). Away from the stage, Gabrielli treated rich and poor alike with the same impudence and lack of propriety. She was imprisoned twice, each time for the same reason: gross insult, first to the Viceroy of Sicily, then, three years later, to the Infante of Spain. Popping up some years after that in the court of Catherine the Great, Gabrielli lost no time making eyes at Count Potemkin, the royal favorite, an indulgence which prompted a one-way ticket back to Italy. Gabrielli died in regal splendor, surrounded by a retinue of servants and an army of admirers.

Indomitable spirits like Cuzzoni and Gabrielli have long disappeared from the world of opera. But things were

seldom allowed to get too dull for long. Maria Malibran
and Henrietta Sonntag filled the first half of the nineteenth
century with romantic and adventurous escapades Hollywood might envy. (The fanciful and rather asinine gesture
of drinking champagne from satin slippers as a sign of
adoration was allegedly first offered in Sonntag's honor.)

After them, the prima donna tradition was upheld by
Adelina Patti with her private railroad car and fabulous
jewelry displays, Jenny Lind, glorified by Barnum's publicity stunts, the tenor Angelo Masini who traveled with
a retinue of ten, including his own cook, barber, doctor, and
lawyer, and who was in a habit of holding rehearsals in
his hotel room when he did not feel like showing up at the
theater, and Nellie Melba who once, by insisting on singing
Brünnhilde out of sheer caprice, managed, during the
course of one evening, to deprive the Metropolitan of
Nordica's services and to bring her own glorious voice to
near-destruction.

And those flaming, fantastic feuds! Cuzzoni with Bordoni. Malibran with Sonntag. Melba with Garden. Melba
with Calvé. Melba with Eames. Melba with Ruffo (men do
get involved, occasionally!). Garden with Cavalieri in
Chicago. Jeritza and Olszewska in Vienna. Fremstad and
Gadski on the verge of fighting it out right on the Metropolitan's stage during a performance of *Die Walküre* . . . .

Eccentricity and temperament, however, need not be-
cloud the issue. Every one of these artists was extraordinary in one way or another. They ranged from vocal
endowments of unique perfection (Melba) to commonplace
vocalism but great interpretive genius (Garden); from
visions of spectacular beauty (Cavalieri), to those of spectacular ugliness (Cuzzoni); from exciting stage personalities (Jeritza) to ladies of unemotional gentility (Eames);

from stunningly svelte figures like Geraldine Farrar to dumpy and grotesque ones like Luisa Tetrazzini. *Voilá,* the prima donna!

Some purists will argue that prima donnas are not only nonessential but downright detrimental to opera. They will cite the example of Toscanini, who once reminded Geraldine Farrar that the only stars he knew were those of heaven. Nikisch, Mahler, Strauss, giants of the baton, were also men of immense authority who ruled over singers with an iron hand. Opera, in the purist view, is a triumph of the ensemble, the perfect fusion of contributing elements, without the imbalance imposed upon it by an overbearing and unmanageable personality.

But there is another view. "The house is meant to be full and not empty," was Verdi's creed. He knew that to accomplish this prima donnas were indispensable. (He was married to one.)

Opera managers, always mindful of box-office appeal, have long recognized that these valuable properties must be treated with angelic patience, cherubic deference, and limitless diplomacy. Surrounded by such flamboyant specimens of the super-ego, walking the tightrope between explosive temperaments and artistic responsibility while staring down into an abyss filled with a demanding, insatiable public and carping critics, the impresario's task is clearly an unenviable one. But underneath that suffering exterior there beats the heart of a man who, once bitten by the opera bug, readily yields to his burden, greedy for punishment.

Opera is perhaps the art form that is most vulnerable to criticism, and the prima donna species is perhaps its most sensitive spot. Yet the species would have long been extinct had it not been for the smiling indulgence of the operagoing millions throughout the years for whom ex-

cesses held intolerable in next-door neighbors have signified fair exchange for the enjoyment of extraordinary
talent. Audiences are still the same, though today's more
knowledgeable opera-goer demands more of opera than
beautiful singing.

Therefore, it is not surprising that an artist of exceptional vocal gifts, whose fascinating temperament and
mannerisms sometimes recall the divas of old but who
thoroughly understands the demands of the modern theater, should take a powerful hold on today's public. Such an
artist is Maria Callas.

At her inspired best, Callas embodies the technical
mastery of a Sembrich, the temperamental intensity of a
Muzio, the fiery determination of a Malibran, and the
theatrical flair of a Patti—with an invigorating dash of
the Cuzzoni shrewishness. But with all that, she is a painstaking musician and a tireless worker with an all-consum-
ing drive for self-improvement.

Opera is a fiercely competitive business, and Maria
Callas has been, from the beginning, a fierce competitor.
Nothing ever "came easily" to her. Nothing but driving
ambition and unyielding will power could have helped her
over the forbidding initial hurdles. Childhood inhibitions,
her fear of multitudes, her feelings of inferiority about
her appearance were not the only barriers. All through
her career, to this day, she has had to combat the multitudes who have never accepted her unconventional vocal
endowments without major reservations.

Maria Callas could not build a career along conventional lines, on the foundations of what all critics would
unanimously call a "beautiful" voice, a voice of sensuous,
warm colors, rich and even in all registers, a voice of a
Rosa Ponselle or a Renata Tebaldi. Callas's path to the
top led through uncharted terrain where other sopranos

feared to tread. She had to confront more formidable challenges than those offered by the conventional repertoire; she had to extend the boundaries of conventional operatic art. To build such a career, she needed more than ambition and determination; she needed courage.

Versatility at its most daring was the first quality that attracted the world's attention to the uncommon talents of Maria Callas. Wagner one night and Bellini the next; the dizzy coloratura of *Armida* followed by the cataclysmic drama of *Medea*—the challenge was there, and the courage was there to meet it. But daredevil feats of this nature were the means, not the end. They were useful to catapult into world fame a talented young woman of prodigious though unconventional vocal gifts, one of yet unformed dramatic capabilities seriously hindered by an unappealing stage presence.

Once she triumphed over the weight problem, Maria Callas was freed of her most painful inhibitions. No longer was there a need to tackle *all* obstacles without regard to the consequences. The beneficial collaboration with Luchino Visconti gave new dimensions to her theatrical art. There was no need to sing Wagner any more. Callas found her most felicitous area of activity, the most rewarding outlet for her creative and re-creative talents—the operas of the "ottocento," the music of Bellini, Donizetti, Cherubini, Spontini, and early Verdi.

Today Maria Callas is proud to be considered, and with a great deal of justification, the modern equivalent of the great divas of the "ottocento"—Malibran, Grisi, and Pasta. Those artists, like Callas, sang *all* soprano roles, without regard to specialization, without deference to special technical hazards.

Yes, Maria Callas is a proud woman. Proud not only of her talent, but also of her contribution to operatic his-

tory, of the interest she has created all over the world in
neglected operas, of the new standards she has established
in operatic performance. "I have no rivals," she said in a
television interview in 1957. "Until other singers can sing
the way I do, act the way I act, do the operas of my repertoire the way I do them, I cannot have any rivals."

In another interview with a *Time* reporter a year
later: "My repertoire, by God's will and nature's blessing,
is complete. When my dear friend, Renata Tebaldi will
sing, among others, *Norma* or *Lucia* one night, then *La
Traviata* or *Gioconda* or *Medea* the next—then, and only
then, will we be rivals. Otherwise it is like comparing
champagne with cognac. No, champagne with Coca-Cola."

"Arrogance," Maestro Tosi, the sage of the 1700's
would say. But behind this militant facade still lurk the
deep-seated insecurities of childhood years; they never
leave Maria Callas. In addition to these, there is another,
professional, insecurity. Callas knows that there are among
her rivals those so lavishly endowed by nature's gifts that
they do not require her kind of dramatic genius. She must
fight them at the levels of her own strength—in the arenas
of musicality, of stagecraft, where she is driven by an
obsessive perfectionism, or, if need be, in polemics.

Because Callas is a proud woman, and because she
firmly believes that "artists are an international treasure," she demands to be treated with a great deal of respect. Often she has demanded far more than that, an
arbitrary power to make decisions without regard to consequences. Such power is, perhaps, satisfying to her
artistic creed and personal pride, but it can be a strain
on her relations with her associates.

However, the art of making music, in her eyes, tran-
scends all other obligations. This conviction has been a
contributing factor in giving Maria Callas some of her

most unfavorable newspaper headlines. Undoubtedly, a
more diplomatic way could have been found to handle the
Roman crisis, even after the unavoidable cancellation of
that fateful *Norma*. Nor was it absolutely necessary to end
her Metropolitan association in the manner she did, by
keeping the company hanging on a cliff, and virtually pro-
voking a radical action on Bing's part.

Yet, in all the major controversies involving Callas,
the real issues were never between right and wrong. Her
actions were nearly always justifiable, and in more than
one instance she was victimized by half-truths and a mis-
informed public. But Maria Callas sincerely believes that,
where diplomacy is needed, the impresarios should apply
it. This is the true prima donna way of looking at things.
Having the most important opera directors follow her
around the world waving tempting offers before her, as
they have always been doing, even in her "exile" days, is
not likely to bring lasting changes in the situation.

Much of her trouble with opera managements stems
from a very simple personal trait. Maria Callas hates to
commit herself in advance, hates even to make plans. Her
methods are impulsive action, instantaneous decision, and
no regrets. She refuses to think far ahead and finds it
difficult to accept the fact that opera companies and concert managers, by necessity, base their existence on advance planning. In her eyes, this facet of her personality
is not a fault. It is an absolute right, to be respected by
those wishing to secure her services.

Getting Callas committed to future engagements has
always been a formidable task, as managers of opera and
recording executives on two continents can testify. But
once she is committed, her word is her bond, misleading
headlines to the contrary. Her record at La Scala—one
hundred fifty-seven performances in seven seasons, and

only two evenings cancelled—speaks for itself. She does get ill on occasion, as do other human beings and even other operatic sopranos. In such cases, however, contrary to most other stars, Maria Callas is expected to call a press conference to give tangible proof of her state of health.

The Chicago Lyric Opera's Carol Fox probably spoke for the managerial fraternity when she declared that Callas "was difficult only before signing a contract." Once committed, she approaches her task with concentrated, undeviating seriousness.

Her dedication to work, her endurance and utter immersion in the total effort are proverbial. Unlike the traditional prima donnas and their Hollywood counterparts, Maria Callas is not one to make a ritual of late arrivals. On the contrary, she shows little consideration for time or fatigue. In terms of hours spent in preparation, and energy expended in the common interest, no opera company has ever received less than fair return for even the most extravagant fee paid to Maria Callas.

Vittorio Grassi, who as head porter at La Scala for more than thirty years has observed two generations of celebrated singers in action, once declared that no artist had ever arrived at the theater, even for rehearsals, with such manifest enthusiasm as did Maria Callas. The joy of singing, said Grassi, was always on her face.

This dedicated attitude is by no means common among opera singers. Many famous artists can get by with only the minimum number of rehearsals, secure in the conviction that they can still satisfy their public. These artists do not believe that the "all out" Callas effort is necessary to achieve high artistic aims.

It follows naturally that the Callas attitude toward rehearsals, her unsparing insistence on the highest possible standards, sometimes evokes a mixed reaction among her colleagues. Maria has lived with this phenomenon throughout her entire career, without any desire to compromise. On the contrary, she has always maintained that all artists should work as hard as she, thereby gaining the admiration of such perfectionists as Visconti, Zeffirelli, Serafin, Karajan, or Bernstein, and at the same time assuring herself of a certain amount of resentment from the dissenting colleagues.

"If the second tenor slips off for a cup of coffee and isn't there the minute he is needed, she'll tear the roof off," Rossi-Lemeni once remarked. Her feuds with Di Stefano and Christoff also began in the heat of pre-performance tension. But in contrast to the few, and oft-ventilated, feuds, Callas's relationship with the majority of her colleagues has been remarkably good.

Even allowing for the extra amount of tension generated by the Callas presence, there are many who admit its beneficial influence. Giulietta Simionato claims that she is constantly stimulated and inspired by working with Callas. Similar sentiments were expressed more recently by her London and Dallas colleagues, Nan Merriman, Jon Vickers, and Nicola Zaccaria.

Metropolitan Opera baritone, Frank Guarrera, who had never seen Callas until late 1959, turned up at her first Dallas *Medea* to see for himself "what the excitement was about." He sat in the front row, took a hundred pictures with his miniature camera, and came away transfixed by the impact of her characterization. "I would go anywhere, at any time, to see that woman perform," he was heard to exclaim afterwards. (It was the day of the Metropolitan-Callas separation, which lent a special timeliness to Guarrera's remarks.)

The seriousness and concentration which characterize Callas, the acting singer (not the "singing actress," a term

which has often been used as a politely implicit admission
of vocal deficiencies), has also been an earmark of her
recording career.

"We have worked together for eight years without a
cross word, and she has been for me the ideal collabora-
tor," states Walter Legge, director of Electric and Musical
Industries. "She is objectively self-critical and accepts
suggestions and criticisms for her work with the best will
of the world. She does not suffer fools gladly, and she ex-
pects from all those who work with her the same concentration that she brings to her own work. The refrain of
all our discussion during recording sessions is: 'Don't tell
me what is good—tell me what you don't like and why you
don't like it.' "

Legge has enjoyed Maria's trust and confidence to an
extent attained by no opera manager. All matters concerning repertoire have been decided between them either over
lunch or dinner. There have been no serious differences of
opinion and, certainly, no arguments. Whenever Legge has
attempted to talk her into recording songs with piano
accompaniment, Maria has resisted firmly. Her answer is
always the same: 'I leave that sort of thing to Elisabeth"
(Elisabeth Schwarzkopf, one of today's foremost *lied* interpreters, and Mrs. Walter Legge in private life).

The blissful relationship that exists between recording star and musical director need not imply that recording
Callas is an easy task. She appeared at one of her recording
sessions in 1955 and after a few measures she discovered
that she was not in good voice. The session had to be called
off at that moment; she would not continue. The fact that
her colleagues were eager to go on and that the huge La
Scala Orchestra had been engaged, and naturally had to
be paid for the day, meant nothing. It was a black day for
the Exchequer, but would it have been better to have con-

sented to completing a recording which was doomed to be inferior?

Another Milan recording session was responsible for a different, yet equally characteristic Callas story by William Mann in London's *Gramophone Record Review:*

"She was recording an opera at La Scala. During one of the sessions she experienced difficulty in hitting high A accurately and sustaining it without a crack. She asked Walter Legge, who was supervising the session, to telephone his wife, Elisabeth Schwarzkopf, in their hotel and arrange a rendez-vous after the session in the restaurant under the opera house. The two singers met there; the restaurant was crowded with diners and winers. Callas went straight to the point: 'Elisabeth, show me how you sing a top A in this passage . . . no, don't just tell me, show me.' Schwarzkopf protested, but eventually was forced to sing the note. And so, for half an hour or so, in the middle of an astonished public, the leading sopranos of Italy and Germany yelled top A's in turn and prodded one another in the diaphragm, the ribs, the small of the back, completely unconcerned with life about them."

Callas is devoted to her public, and forever concerned about being liked and appreciated. A complimentary or considerate remark by even the most casual autograph-hunter warms her heart. But few are the "casual" admirers in her court. She inspires fervent loyalty in her fans who accompany her in amazing numbers across Europe or America like a tribe of camp followers. She corresponds with many, sometimes through her secretary, sometimes by short, personal notes written in longhand. In either case, her communications have a natural, informal quality.

Several of the faithful in New York, Chicago, or London were thrilled by a wholly unexpected telephone call when the diva was "passing through." One bouquet of flowers accompanied by a warm-toned letter moved her so much during her 1958 Metropolitan stay that she rushed to the telephone to express her thanks to the sender. On another occasion, having received a fan-letter from a twelve-year-old boy in London, she contacted the family by phone and invited them to her hotel suite.

The diva who demands regal respect from opera managers is consideration and patience personified in the company of her loyal fans. She has a remarkable memory for names, a quality she has cultivated to counterbalance her concern about her myopia. Inadvertently slighting people as a result of poor eyesight was a source of constant worry in the past. One of the multiple Meneghini tasks was to be at her side on such occasions, to indicate with a delicate whisper or a subtle touch at the elbow the approach of this person or that. Contact lenses, disdained in the Meneghini days but now adopted, will henceforth guard her against these hazards.

After performances, Maria Callas goes through agonizing self-doubts. Has she given her best? Like most singers, she is troubled by the fact that she cannot hear herself sing, that she has no way of appraising the effect her voice makes in a large auditorium. When things don't go well, she need not be reminded. On such occasions she cries in her dressing room, out of helpless frustration and depression over the disappointment she has caused.

Even when she senses genuine success, she seldom accepts congratulations in a routine manner. She likes to discuss her over-all approach to the role, her vocal effects, and certain dramatic details. "Did you really like it?" "Which act did you like best?" "What did you think of the stage business in ...?" These are the questions with which she is likely to greet her admirers in the excited hubbub of her dressing room after a performance.

Although Maria Callas's life is wrapped up in music, her musical interest is not universal. Her fondness for the piano has, of course, played a great part in shaping her career. Respect for the "instrumental" technique stimulated her treatment of the voice as a sublime musical instrument. The voice, as Callas sees it, is capable of shadings of expression no musical instruments can match. But its emotional qualities must be balanced by an "instrumental" respect for the printed score, for the composer's intention.

This "instrumental" approach provides the key to the strict musical discipline of the Callas interpretations. It is interesting that Vladimir Horowitz, an avid admirer of "bel canto," is known to have carefully studied the singing style of such artists as Mattia Battistini, from whom a piano virtuoso could learn a good deal in matters of phrasing and subtle coloration. After all, was not Chopin also influenced by Bellini?

Apart from the piano's felicitous effect on her career, Maria Callas is a personage of opera. Symphony and chamber music have little fascination for her, she does not attend concerts, nor does she ever discuss any music other than opera. But once the subject centers on her specialty, there is nothing, from vocal exercises to stage props, from cadenzas to room acoustics, that escapes her range of interests.

What kind of a person is Maria Callas away from opera?

"She is a woman of strong feelings, her friendships and hatreds are absolute," Luchino Visconti once remarked. The observation is accurate insofar as the strong feelings are concerned. But the "absolute" friendships and hatreds do not endure. Callas is an impulsive woman and an inflammable one. Furthermore, she is blessed or cursed with a tendency to speak her mind plainly and without caution, letting the chips fall where they may. If the incendiary effect is thus unavoidable, the fire burns fast, and some of her most spectacular feuds have ended in quiet reconciliation.

Beyond a certain point of professional respect, Maria Callas does not warm up easily. The climate of an opera house is not, and never has been, ideal for the flowering of lasting friendships. Breathing the atmosphere of operatic rivalry, and having struggled so long and so hard to reach her present eminence, she has remained extremely sensitive to hostility, and imagines herself to be living in a world populated by enemies.

During the trying years of her career, Maria Callas must have known at all times where she was going and why. But *only* she knew. She has seldom confided in people, even her intimates. After ten years of marriage, when the break came with her husband, it stunned her father, her close friends, and her associates. Never had any of them had any cause to doubt that she and Battista had had a happy and harmonious relationship, for never had Maria seemed anything but an utterly devoted, considerate, and loyal wife.

In company, Maria Callas, the singer with a shelf full of voices, can display another shelf full of moods, now plain and unaffected, now stubborn and imperious, sometimes withdrawn and almost shy, sometimes joyful and even teasing. But essentially she is a very serious woman, lacks a real sense of humor, and has so far failed to convince any perceptive observer that she has ever known true happiness.

A consummate actress on or off the stage, she commands a full arsenal of feminine wiles, and sometimes radiates an incredible aura of defenselessness men find irresistible, though they should know better. Her keen mind, sharp powers of observation, and rare intuition have

helped her career immensely. Unaffected and completely
natural in speech (she is a fluent conversationalist in four
languages: English, Greek, Italian and French), she turns
scientific and analytical when the subject is opera or
singing.

Her information about musical happenings is always
up to date. She reads her reviews eagerly, and her secretary
and network of friendly correspondents see to it that *everything* comes to her attention. Friendly reviews and articles
are, of course, preferred. But Callas also listens carefully
to the voices of dissent. She follows with constant interest
the career and whereabouts of a great many other singers,
particularly sopranos. Apart from reading her own reviews, she is also very much interested in *theirs*.

Callas enjoys parties, and generally manages to dom-
inate them by the force of her personality and the natural
magnetism of her presence. Party-going, one of her few
mundane pleasures, was acquired in relatively recent
years. That and other aspects of her newly created luxurious mode of living give her a feeling of compensation for
the cheerless years of her youth.

The Callas wardrobe and the Callas jewelry have inspired many news comments. She never seems to wear the
same dress twice, owns about three hundred hats—including a few "wild" specimens for shock effect—at least six
fur coats, and 150 pairs of shoes. Red is her favorite color
but, in general, she is partial to strong shades and disdains
anything vague or wishy-washy. A characteristic trait of
her appearance, which reflects her changeable moods and
impulsive nature, is the frequent change in her hair style
and color.

The Callas of 1960 is a figure of high fashion and mundane elegance. Five years ago, she still amazed her friends
and associates by the gusto with which she could enjoy

simple pleasures, like kitchen gadgets, shopping in supermarkets or "five and ten" stores, or cooking at home.
Today, the whirl of high society allows her less time for
such enjoyments as her social obligations mount up with
their tempting though sometimes tiresome schedule.

But the change has not been *forced* on Maria Callas;
it has grown out of her determination to "get ahead," to go
on to ever greater heights. Whether her new way of life will
have a beneficial effect on her artistic career is open to
question. But then, as always, no one but Maria Callas
knows the kind of future she *really* wants for herself. "Like
all Greeks, I am something of a fatalist. I believe in trusting
God, preserving a clean conscience, and letting the future
take care of itself." This is her credo.

Looking back on her career, one is struck by its logical,
step-by-step pattern, leading with unbroken purposefulness
to the top. On her way, she struggled tirelessly and sometimes even ruthlessly, taking advantage of all the breaks,
absorbing the benefit of any influence that could help to
develop her artistic stature. Some say she has mercilessly
discarded all who have helped her. But it would be far too
simple, and wholly inaccurate, to explain the Callas career
in terms of outside influences. Above everything else, it was
built by herself, yielding notable dividends to all who have
assisted in the building. Helping Maria Callas to the top
was always a two-way affair.

The list must begin with the most important influence,
her mother, whose determination virtually forced her
daughter into a musical career. Mothers of famous operatic
personalities hardly ever became famous in their own
right. A notable exception, Evangelia Callas can now enjoy
the celebrity she always wanted. A bitter and painful road
has led to this goal, but obscurity would have been far more
frustrating to her determined personality.

Elvira de Hidalgo was an all-but-forgotten figure of the past when fortune swept that awkward Greek-American girl in her way more than twenty years ago. Callas has brought her teacher renewed lustre, and will make her name doubly immortal in the annals of opera.

Nor has Tullio Serafin's beneficial influence gone unrewarded. Through association with Callas, his long-established reputation as a great conductor has reached unprecedented heights. As for Luchino Visconti, his theatrical genius was a major factor in developing Callas into an exciting dramatic personality. She, in turn, expanded the director's vision and brought him triumphs in opera— an entirely new and challenging medium for Visconti.

What about Giovanni Battista Meneghini, the Veronese Pygmalion who could not keep his Galatea? Today he knows that it was only a career he sculpted, not a person. He gave Maria material security and guided her affairs with astuteness and complete dedication, if not always with a full measure of foresight and diplomacy. In doing so, he traded the sedate pleasures of provincial life for the excitements of the limelight and international prominence; his familiar cronies on Verona's Piazza Brá for the company of ambassadors, aristocrats, and movie stars. He gave up the possession of an industrial enterprise for the enviable if only transitional possession of Maria Callas. Losing that possession was an immense blow, but did he really lose more than he gained during the intervening twelve years?

Another major factor in building the Callas career was publicity. In the beginning it helped, and Maria sought it as any artist would. The Oscar Wilde epigram "the only thing worse than being talked about is not being talked about," is very much to the point in the world of art and entertainment.

But the Callas publicity became progressively out of

control and focus as she rose in the artistic world. Because
of her uncompromising spirit and habitual outspokenness,
because of her uncanny way of doing the unexpected, Maria
Callas has always had a unique news-making capacity. In
time, even this was not enough. The press developed a way
of goading her into making news. Wherever she went, reporters and photographers followed, flinging probing,
indiscreet, and impertinent questions, invading her private life. Frequently, she lost her composure (and who
wouldn't?), and countered with an intemperate or not fully
thought-out remark. Thus were some of the Callas headlines born.

During her German tour in 1959, she had to give up
her sightseeing tours because of the all-pervading presence
of the press. After her break with Meneghini, photographers followed her every move, and kept a round-the-
clock watch on her home. She was photographed while
doing her shopping for the household (dressed in an
austere black garb and wearing dark glasses, to no avail),
while mailing a letter, while talking to neighbors on the
street.

At the same time, in the absence of all authentic communication, the gossip mill began to grind, pumping into
millions of readers speculative, uninformed, and frequently
malicious tidbits about her life. What the general public
knows of Maria Callas today is, unfortunately, the distil-
lation of this mass of irresponsibilty. Publicity has helped
to make Maria Callas a "public figure," perhaps beyond
her artistic measure as an opera singer, but at the same
time—like the apprentice's broom—it has beclouded her
true significance by flooding her artistic contributions in a
tide of trivia and irrelevance.

Today it is difficult, even for the keen-sighted observer,
to separate the "artist" from the "personality." The total

image is a fascinating fusion of qualities, but careful analysis will detect in these qualities the magic ingredients
of a prima donna: talent, conceit, and flamboyance.

"Why is Maria Callas more famous than all operatic
artists today?" The question was put to Tullio Serafin who,
as a close personal friend and close associate in music,
could be assumed to be best qualified to answer it.

"Because she is Maria Callas."

The answer may not clarify the image, but no one has
yet come up with a better one.

CHAPTER 16

Maria Callas Speaks

Violetta
Io sono franca, ingenua . . .

VERDI — LA TRAVIATA

The following selected quotations from one of the most prodigiously quoted personalities of our time will serve to add more light and shade to the Portrait. They have been chosen from the following sources:

1. Interview with *Music & Musicians,* London, November, 1952.
2. Interview with Mary Jane Matz, *Opera News,* December 3, 1956.
3. Maria Callas's memoirs published by *Oggi,* January, 1957.
4. Conversations with Lawrence Kelly as recorded in Mr. Kelly's article in *Gentry,* Spring, 1957.
5. Radio interview, Philadelphia, August, 1957.

6. Radio interview with Norman Ross, Chicago, November 17, 1957.

7. Conversations with critic Eugenio Gara, as recorded in *Maria Callas* (pub. Kister, Geneva, 1957) and in the magazine *L'Europeo,* November, 1959.

8. Interview with New York *Post,* March 2, 1958.

9. "Small World," CBS Telecast, January 4 and 11, 1959.

10. Maria Callas's replies to questions asked by the author in connection with this book.

"There must be a law against forcing children to perform at an early age. Children should have a wonderful childhood. They should not be given too much responsibility." (6)

"I was always too mature for my age—and not very happy. I had no young friends. I wish I could go back to those days. If I could only live it all again, how I would play and enjoy other girls. What a fool I was!" (2)

"The most important room in my house is the music room, where I have my piano and where I work and practice. This room knows all my happiness and my anxiety when I am studying a role. After that room comes the kitchen, and I spend a lot of time there, cooking tasty things." (1)

"Heavens, if I had a reducing system I would not keep it a secret. I could become the richest woman in the world." (2)

"My poor sight gives me an advantage. I can't see the people in the audience who are scratching their heads while I am lost in my role and giving everything I have to the drama." (2)

"When I read the things they say about me, I laugh. I say merely the truth. That is my trouble." (2)

"I am not mad with ambition. I live, thank heaven, quite well, but I work for the love of working and not for money. I will admit that I am considerably helped by my tremendous stamina. I don't know its source, but it seems to keep me going on and on." (2)

"If I have stepped on some people at times because I am at the top, it couldn't be helped. What should I do if someone gets hurt—retire?" (8)

"Some say I have a beautiful voice, some say I have not. It is a matter of opinion. All I can say, those who don't like it should not come to hear me." (5)

"I do not intend to adjust the scores to the comfort of my voice just to be able to create a purer sound, a more beautiful sound in the external sense of the word." (7)

"I am happy with my studies of Concone and Panofka; for me these are not dry vocalises, cold sequences of chromatic scales, mordents and trills, but fantastic germs of melody, minute sketches of indefinable music." (7)

"Singing is not only vocal display. We singers are the first instrument of the orchestra." (6)

"Sopranos, like violinists, must be able to perform every kind of music. Those who cannot execute certain technical requirements should not sing, in my opinion."(5)

"Our duty is not to serve ourselves. We serve art and we serve the composers who were geniuses. We are not geniuses." (9)

"I am a very romantic singer. I sing the old music where the melody is good. The public has to have a tune to hold on. If the public cannot keep a tune in its head after they heard the opera, it means the opera is a flop." (9)

"Modern composers should really forgive me, because I don't really mean it that way, but I do not like modern music, because it's all complicated, and everything that is complicated today bothers me. You see, the people go to the opera to have a bath of beauty. Music should be a beautiful supreme tune—the great legato—the great melody ..."   (9)

"I get bored very quickly with any opera I sing after a few performances, and I like to go on to something new."   (2)

"The magic of *Norma,* the sublimity of its melody, remains always new for me. I feel the same way about Anna Bolena, Leonora, and all personalities that are strongly drawn and brought to life in melody."   (7)

"Donna Anna is a bore."   (4)

"All three roles in *Hoffmann?* My dear, would you pay me three fees?"   (4)

"Even the least utility man, even those who play the smallest parts and with whom I sang during my long career, have given me something and have in a certain way contributed to my artistic forming. In our work everybody, independently of the position they hold in the musical or artistic world, can teach you something which enriches your personality."   (10)

"Generally speaking, I do not like publicity. I never paid for having it. I consider publicity as something false which inevitably alters the features of truth. I do not think that publicity has helped me; on the contrary, it has contributed a good deal to creating the legend of a tiger-like Callas, whose portrait I refuse to recognize as myself."
                                                                    (10)

"We artists strive for years to establish our name. When, finally, fame follows us everywhere, we are condemned to be always worthy of it, to outdo ourselves in order not to delude the public. But we are only human, with the natural weaknesses."   (3)

CHAPTER 17

Portrait of the Artist

Norma
La mia voce tuonerà.
BELLINI — NORMA

Back in the early part of the eighteenth century, the era which by all evidence constituted the true golden age of singing, vocal artists recognized only one obligation—to sing beautifully. As opera developed, and the concentration on the dramatic element in singing became more paramount, there began a gradual decline in singing perfection. Pier Francesco Tosi was alert to recognize this phenomenon in 1723: "I do not know if a perfect singer can at the same time be a perfect actor; for the mind being at once divided by two different operations, he will probably incline more to one than the other. What a felicity would it be to possess both in a perfect degree!"

More than two centuries have been spent in search

of this elusive perfection, and the likelihood of ever attaining it grows dimmer with each passing generation. No wonder today's vocal purists, who deplore present-day imperfections, often gaze longingly into the past, citing the exploits of such bygone artists as Rubini, Pasta, and Malibran, who dazzled audiences more than a century ago.

We have, of course, no tangible evidence of the art of these legendary singers. But reading their contemporary critics will reveal the wisdom of Tosi's remarks. The perfect fusion of singing and drama was, already in the 1800's, an elusive myth.

This is the way Giuseppe Verdi, for example, remembered the unforgettable Maria Malibran: "Malibran? Very great, but not always. At times sublime, at other times eccentric. Her singing style was not of the purest; the voice was strident in the high notes. In spite of everything, a very great, a marvelous artist."*

Of Malibran's great rival, Giuditta Pasta, Stendhal left the following remarkable analysis: "One of the most uncommon features of Madame Pasta's voice: it is not all moulded of the same *metallo,* as they would say in Italy; and this fundamental variety of tone produced by a single voice affords one of the richest veins of musical expression. . . . Outstanding singers long ago demonstrated how easily an apparent defect might be transformed into a source of infinite beauty. . . . No voice whose timbre is completely incapable of variation can ever produce that kind of suffocated tone, which is at once so moving and so natural in the portrayal of certain instants of violent emotion and passionate anguish."**

Apart from being a keen analytical observation, this paragraph, written more than a century ago, defines with

* Verdi's letter to Count Arrivabene, December 27, 1877.
** From Stendhal: Life of Rossini, ©1957 Criterion Books, Inc.

startling accuracy the very characteristics of Maria
Callas's vocal art, down to the peculiarity of her mysterious, veiled or "suffocated" tones. This, of course, should
not be surprising. Callas not only sings the Malibran-
Pasta repertoire, but she is today what these great singers
were more than a century ago—an absolute soprano.

Remarkably enough, both Malibran and Pasta had
started out as contraltos and succeeded, with dedicated
effort, to extend their range upward to include notes up to
E flat above the staff. With such a remarkable extension,
and a technique to match, they were able to master *all*
music written by operatic composers of their age for the
soprano register. Bellini wrote the title roles of both his
La Sonnambula and *Norma* for Giuditta Pasta. That today
the former is considered a "coloratura" and the latter a
"dramatic" part is the result of the changes which have
occurred during the intervening decades.

No such distinction existed in Bellini's time, or even in
the 1850's when Verdi wrote his early operas. For, clearly,
only an absolute soprano can do technical justice to the
part of Violetta, which demands the agility and florid
abandon of a coloratura specialist in the first act, and the
emotional and coloristic varieties of a "lyric" and "dramatic" soprano in the succeeding scenes. Verdi wrote
Il Trovatore's Leonora for a similar type of multiple voice.
This voice must rise above the powerful ensembles, manage the dramatic, dark-hued "Miserere," and the florid
"Di tal amor" cabaletta of the first act, as well as the
exquisite "D'amor sull'ali rosee" of the last.

Absolute sopranos of the caliber of Malibran and
Pasta, rare to begin with, became even rarer as the second
half of the nineteenth century ushered in the era of vocal
specialization. Such an artist, however, was Lilli Lehmann,
who left audible proof of her mastery in an unparalleled

repertoire that included Isolde, Fidelio, Norma, Violetta, and all major Mozartian roles. But just how unique an artist Lehmann was among her contemporaries is borne out by the remarks of the most renowned opera critic at the turn of the century:

"Genuine technique is no longer a requisite for dramatic singers," lamented Eduard Hanslick. "Our coloraturas haven't the voices, and they can't act, our dramatic singers have no vocal technique." Lilli Lehmann was, in the opinion of Hanslick and everyone else, the exception.

Since Lehmann's retirement fifty years ago, opera has seen only one soprano with a similar grasp of the complete soprano repertoire: Rosa Ponselle, whose natural superiority in the big dramatic parts of the romantic operas (*Aida, La forza del destino, La Gioconda*) was supplemented by her triumphs as Violetta, Elvira in Verdi's *Ernani* (another characteristic Verdi part for at least "two voices"), Donna Anna, and Carmen. Ponselle was also the greatest Norma of her time, which is no coincidence at all since no one but an absolute soprano can hope to achieve true mastery of this most exacting of operatic roles.

Maria Callas is the absolute soprano of our times. She is not the most perfect vocal artist, nor is she unsurpassed in every one of her interpretations. It is easy to detect vocal blemishes or even interpretive shortcomings by holding up isolated moments of every one of her performances to microscopic criticism. Her art must be valued in its totality, and it can only be understood against the proper historical background.

For all its seemingly limitless potential, there are clearly marked boundaries to the Callas art. To understand her true significance, we must also define her limitations. Maria Callas is *not* a universal singer in the sense

BELLINI—*La Sonnambula*. Maria sang the gentle Amina in 1955 for the first time. The same Visconti production was revived for her in 1957. Nicola Monti was her tenor partner at the revival. (Photo by Erio Piccagliani.)

BELLINI—*Norma*. One of the great Callas roles, in which she made her London, Chicago, and New York debuts. Here she is seen with Giulietta Simionato in La Scala's 1955 production. (Photo by Erio Piccagliani.)

BELLINI—*I Puritani*. Callas triumphed in the taxing role of Elvira in Venice, Rome, and Chicago. Also in Mexico City, where this picture was taken in 1952.

CHERUBINI—*Medea*. A stunning Callas specialty, acclaimed on two continents. The picture presents her in the authentic Greek costume designed for the Dallas production in 1958. (Courtesy of Robert S. Clark, Jr.)

DONIZETTI—*Lucia di Lammermoor.* Giuseppe di Stefano and Maria Callas delighted operagoers as Edgardo and Lucia in Milan (1954), Mexico City, Berlin, Vienna, and on records. (Courtesy of Angel Records.)

DONIZETTI—*Anna Bolena.* Callas electrified Milan in this opera during two successive seasons (1956/1957 and 1957/1958). The Henry VIII in 1958 was Cesare Siepi.

GIORDANO—*Fedora*. One of the memorable Callas portrayals in the field of the *verismo*. From the 1956 Scala production. (Courtesy of *Opera News*.)

GLUCK—*Alceste*. Callas is a particularly gifted interpreter of Gluck's stately, massive vocal writing. As Alceste she was celebrated in Milan during the 1953/1954 season.

GLUCK—*Iphigenia in Tauris*. Her second Gluck role was the tragic Iphigenia, produced by La Scala in 1957.

PUCCINI.—*Madama Butterfly*. This photo was taken on stage at the Chicago Lyric, where Maria Callas portrayed Cio Cio San in 1955.

PUCCINI.—*Turandot*. An early Callas role and a famous recorded interpretation. (Courtesy of Angel Records.)

PUCCINI—*Tosca*. On stage at the Metropolitan, singing "Vissi d'arte," in February, 1958. Walter Cassel is the Scarpia. (Photo by Melançon.)

ROSSINI—*The Barber of Seville*. Callas created a highly individual Rosina for La Scala in 1956, and for the phonograph a year later.

ROSSINI—*Il Turco in Italia.* The temperamental Fiorilla was Callas's first comic characterization when this opera was first mounted in Rome in 1950. La Scala staged it again in 1955, with Nicola Rossi-Lemeni (shown here) as the picturesque Turk. (Courtesy of Angel Records.)

VERDI—*Don Carlos*. Maria learned the role of Queen Elisabetta di Valois early in her career, but first sang it in the Scala production of 1954. (Courtesy of Angel Records.)

VERDI—*Il Trovatore*. "Her Leonora was perfection," said Jussi Bjoerling, who was Maria's partner in Chicago's memorable production of 1955. (Courtesy of Angel Records.)

VERDI—*Macbeth*. Maria sang Lady Macbeth in Milan in 1952, but received far more publicity when she was prevented from singing it in New York during the Met's 1958/1959 season.

VERDI—*La Traviata.* A compelling and individual Callas portrayal. Here she is seen with Luchino Visconti, who directed the controversial but tremendously successful Milan production of 1955.

$\longrightarrow$

VERDI—*La Traviata.* Callas in the same opera at London's Covent Garden in June, 1958. She was also acclaimed in the part in Rome, Florence, Chicago, and New York. (Photo by European.)

VERDI—*Un Ballo in Maschera*. The stunning costumes Callas wore in La Scala's 1957 production of this Verdi opera contrasted sharply with the austere settings.

Lilli Lehmann was or Victoria de los Angeles is today. The realm of the lied, the art song repertoire, oratorios, and the music of the baroque period do not engage her interest. Even in opera, which is her *only* medium, her repertoire is no match in point of versatility for that of De los Angeles, who has excelled in Verdi, Rossini, and Puccini at one extreme, Mozart at another, Wagner at yet another, and all this without in any way lessening her undisputed hold on the operas of Gounod, Bizet, and Massenet, or the song literature from Schubert to Debussy. (Granados and De Falla are included as a matter of course.)

Maria Callas's significance clearly does not lie in versatility for its own sake. As an absolute soprano, she has the means at her disposal that would assure technical mastery of practically all operatic roles. But satisfying technical demands in itself was not her only aim. The Callas repertoire is composed of impersonations which have captured her sense of drama, human characters in which she can believe and whose feelings, emotions, reactions she can communicate through her interpretive art.

Such a character may be a mythological figure (Medea), a personage of history (Anna Bolena), or literature (Violetta), or the embodiment of the eternally feminine (Isolde). Happily in most cases the dramatic challenge is closely allied to great musical values. In some, the artist has chosen to bypass great music (*Don Giovanni*) in favor of mediocre musical values which nevertheless hold marvelous dramatic possibilities (*Il Pirata, La Vestale*).

Once an operatic character has captured her interest, Callas is able to "live the part" with a dramatic comprehension rarely displayed by opera singers. Her methods are not based on historical research or profound psychological dissections. With her extraordinary perception, she penetrates the role and reduces it to its essential human

problems. Her intuition seeks out the *woman* in the mythological surroundings of Alceste and Iphigenia, under the
regal vestments of Anna Bolena and Elisabetta di Valois,
in the boudoirs of Violetta and Fedora, or in the sheltered,
awakening femininity of Amina and Rosina. Once inside
the role, having grasped the essence of the character and
the forces of environment, she proceeds to build her own
conception, infusing the part with her personal insights.

At that point, her intensive musical study begins—a
search for musical cues to point up and to underline character traits and for opportunities to infuse musical notes
with the appropriate color or accent that will express a
limitless range of human emotions: anxiety, fear, shame,
venom, revenge, disdain, ecstasy, devotion, compassion.
This is the crucial point of conflict between the dramatic
and vocal arts. Singers are musicians first, and must always
be conscious of the dangers of overdramatizing their interpretations to the point of altering the musical design.
The art of "acting with the voice," of conveying these
subtle dramatic nuances by accents, shadings, and perceptive alterations of vocal color, is the only way to overcome
this danger. Mastery of this art is the true mark of a singing actress.

In the theater, when Callas is in top form, she moves
the audience with the cumulative grandeur of her interpretations. Except for her uncritical and mesmerized following, which is considerable, her hold on the audience is
seldom instantaneous. One is *not* overcome with the sen-
suousness and absolute purity of the vocal sound that explains the immediately spellbinding qualities of Tebaldi
or De los Angeles. But as the Callas performance gathers
momentum, and all elements of dramatic insight, magnetic
stage presence, creative intuition, and expressiveness
through acting with the voice fall into place, the force of

her interpretation sweeps along with the insistence of an avalanche.

On records, the effect is similar, though the absence of her striking stage personality is a factor to be considered. At the same time, one becomes even more aware of her expressive acting with the voice. Whether these qualities impress the considerable body of opera-lovers who go to the theater or listen to records "just to hear the music" is debatable. If the listener is unaware of or unconcerned with textual meaning, and looks for musical perfection in beautiful if sometimes impersonal or disembodied tones, then the essential interpretive qualities of the Callas vocal art fall on unresponsive ears.

On the other hand, to follow her performances with the score and thus to discover the dramatic rightness and musical faithfulness of her interpretations counts among the most gratifying experiences an opera enthusiast can enjoy. Needless to say, this is also the most effective way to highlight her respect for the composer's intentions, her meticulous regard for the score's dynamic markings, note values, special accents, and also her way with passages left unmarked by the composer in deference to the artist's creative individuality.

It is undeniable that the vocal art of Maria Callas has succeeded, to an unprecedented degree, in delineating human character and conveying emotions by purely vocal means. Her Medea, Norma, Lady Macbeth are strongly drawn, three-dimensional figures. There is a death-haunted, sickly quality about her Violetta from the outset, casting a shadow of tragedy over the opera's first act, which is not apparent in conventional interpretations. In the first act of *Madama Butterfly,* she sacrifices effective vocalism for its own sake to create the vocal image of a fifteen-year-old. In *Tosca,* which is one of her most grip-

ping recorded characterizations, she can create almost
tangible impressions of hatred, jealousy, and suffering.
Yet she eschews a sure-fire melodramatic effect at the end
of the second act. In place of the theatrical declamation
of the famous line, "E avanti a lui tremava tutta Roma,"
she sings these words on the reiterated C sharps as indicated by Puccini's score.

Every recorded interpretation yields rich varieties of
expressive nuances achieved through musical means and
placed at the service of character penetration. No singer
of this generation has shown greater respect for the text
than Maria Callas. Neither has any succeeded nearly as
well in investing not only isolated words but even syllables
with telling significance and, on occasion, breathing poetry
and eloquence into commonplace and uninspiring lines.

Her constant striving for expressiveness can occasionally lead to characterizations that are somewhat over-
drawn. It is safe to say that the range of dramatic expression Callas finds in Lucia di Lammermoor exceeds the
composer's and librettist's vision of this essentially un-
complicated heroine. Nor do the comic characterizations of
Rosina (*The Barber of Seville*) and Fiorilla (*Il Turco in
Italia*) represent the dramatic art of Maria Callas at its
most convincing, however replete they are with rewarding
musical and dramatic details. On the other hand, it takes
the Callas art to breathe humanity into Turandot's forbidding figure. Most sopranos are content with singing all of
Puccini's notes with a reasonable degree of accuracy—and
that is a feat in itself. Similarly, the transfigured intensity
she imparts to Gioconda's music in the opera's final act
seems to lift both character and music into Isolde's realm.
Here, too, we are dealing with what is termed as a "singer's opera," and *singing* the part beautifully would justly
satisfy all demands. What Callas supplies through con-

summate interpretive art is an unexpected and unprecedented *plus*.

The painstaking thoroughness and searching insight
she brings to her interpretations is revealed in the following recollection of Harold Lawrence, who, as musical
director of Mercury Records, supervised the recording
sessions of Cherubini's *Medea* in September, 1957:

"We were recording the scene in the opera's second
act, in which Medea, having just been banished from
Corinth, begs King Creon for one day's delay. Callas was
in fine form, and she sang Medea's plea meltingly. As she
came to the control room to hear the playback, we greeted
her with resounding *Bravas*. We replayed the scene, and
liked what we heard even more. But Callas had some reservations. 'It was very well sung,' she agreed, 'and it was
a moving plea. But something was missing. You see, at
that moment Medea already knows that she will utilize
that one day to carry out her bloody revenge. Her mind is
really on other things than pleading, and the music must
bring out that ominous undertone. I must do it over.'

"So she went back, and did the scene over just as beautifully. But this time there was an almost imperceptible
but nevertheless clearly menacing undertone to her singing. It was a spine-tingling experience."

Another illuminating story is related by Teodoro Celli
in his absorbing study of Callas's vocal art (originally published in *Oggi,* and reprinted in *Saturday Review* as translated by Herbert Weinstock). This relates to the recording
of Verdi's *Rigoletto* in which Celli was struck by the
peculiar accent Callas imparted to the word "Uscitene"
("Get out") in the second act where Gilda, at once carried
away and frightened by the Duke's amorous declaration,
begs him to leave the house.

"Well, that word from the already enamored girl re-

sounds in Callas's voice with a strange coloration, between
timid and ardent, a *mezza-voce* of private innocence. It
certainly expresses her infatuation, but I could not explain
its effect to myself. So I asked Callas why she had given so
very special accent to a word of apparently small importance. She replied: 'Because Gilda says *Get out* but wants
to say *Stay!*' How much acute psychological justice there
is in this intuition; how appropriate it is to the simultaneously ingenuous and passionate character of Verdi's
heroine and to the movement of the drama, and how revealingly it is realized by means of that chaste vocal color.''

Expressiveness is thus the key to the vocal art of
Maria Callas. It embraces intuition, inspiration, and artistic flair and discipline to carry out the composer's explicit
and implicit intentions. Whether or not her voice is beautiful *per se* is a matter depending on one's conception of
beauty in a vocal performance. Surely, there are moments
in Callas's singing that are beautiful no matter what standards are applied. Conversely, there are isolated passages
in her recordings (particularly in *Madama Butterfly,
Lucia,* and *La Traviata*) which are decidedly unappealing.
Ardent Callas admirers who fall into a trance at the mere
mention of her name will deny their existence and will
explain every muffled, strident, or unfocused note as having some hidden dramatic meaning. But this misguided
devotion is pointless and, furthermore, will do the artist
no service.

A highly controversial aspect of her vocal quality is
the characteristic veiled timber of her middle register.
Many critics have dismissed this as downright detrimental,
yet this misty quality is in fact a marvelous instrument to
express poignancy, to add a plaintive or melancholy coloration to the voice. Stendhal's comments about a simular
quality in Pasta's voice are confirmed by the recollections

of the English critic, Henry F. Chorley: "There was a portion of her scale which differed from the rest in quality and remained to the last 'under a veil.' " This quality is quite unique with Callas among singers today. The great baritone Titta Ruffo was able to produce similar veiled tones to color his singing with suggestions of sadness and melancholia. But while Ruffo could resort to this quality at will, and appeared to exert full control over it, with Callas it seems to be an intrinsic, mysterious component of the voice, not always fully controlled. Still, she has been able to transform this apparent defect, as Pasta did five generations ago, "into a source of infinite beauty."

In its physical and technical manifestation, the voice of Callas is a voice of compromises. Not being what we today commonly call a "dramatic" voice, it is not exceptional in volume, nor is it ideal for the robust accents demanded by such parts as Santuzza *(Cavalleria Rusticana)* or Maddalena *(Andrea Chénier)*. It is most certainly not a voice of lightness and transparency such as we have come to associate with singers specializing in "coloratura" parts. Consequently, it cannot toss off stratospheric notes with an absolute lack of effort, and it is seldom placed into the service of showy cadenzas and bravura effects for their own sake.

But these seeming limitations are, in fact, the characteristics of the absolute soprano. In dramatic parts, what the voice may lack in sheer volume is more than offset by flexibility, lyric grace, and coloristic variety. The superficial glitter of coloratura fireworks is replaced by tones that are full-bodied and strongly supported, by accents that are heroic and not fragile, by attacks that are bold and not warbling. To illustrate the difference, one can compare Callas's singing of "In questa reggia" *(Turandot)* with that of Birgit Nilsson or Eileen Farrell, or her Lucia with that of Roberta Peters or Renata Scotto. Whether the one or the other is "better" is a matter of individual preference, but the difference in vocal qualities and musico-dramatic approach is revealing.

Callas's vocal range extends from A below the staff (which she sings with a true mezzo-soprano's chesty quality in *Un Ballo in Maschera*) to an E flat above (in *La Traviata* and *Lucia di Lammermoor*)—over two and a half octaves. Although her command of the high register was spectacular in the early phases of her career, it is a well-known and certainly well-documented fact that this is no longer the case. The decline, as far as one is able to determine, began in 1954, and the coincidence of the artist's amazing slimming-down is too obvious to ignore. Conquering the weight problem was her greatest triumph, and a major factor in building her into a great singing actress. But, like all triumphs, it had to take its toll.

The erstwhile virtuoso command of the notes above high C is no longer there. She can manage the notes, but only with a strident quality that contrasts with the natural timbres of her voice. Music critics have often commented on this undeniable fact. What has been consistently overlooked is that Callas today retains exceptional control of what is generally considered the soprano register, the two octaves from middle C to C above the staff.

By contrast, truth compels the observation that some famous contemporary sopranos, though possessors of more sensuous and creamier vocal instruments, cannot match this extension. Though they can sing ravishing B flats, the high C and everything above it is beyond their effective range.

Apart from the "coloratura" sopranos who must be able to sing at least three tones above C to practice their trade, the only artists capable of navigation in the vocal stratosphere today are the heavy dramatic specialists, particularly suited for the demands of Wagner. Unfortunately, their particular gifts in this direction are frequently offset either by an unsupported or colorless quality in the middle or low register (Leonie Rysanek) or an absence of warmth and intensity without which characterization in Italian opera cannot be convincing (Birgit Nilsson).

Possession of all the notes comprising the soprano range and the art of suffusing these notes with a wide range of dramatic expression account for two major attributes in Maria Callas's vocal art. The other two qualities, which go hand in hand and which complete the picture, are technique and musicianship.

Her kind of vocal technique is the natural outgrowth of an absolute soprano. It bespeaks not only a mechanical command of scales, trills, mordents, and technical feats singers can master only by dedicated study, but also an ability to place technical accomplishment at the service of musical expression. To master the art of legato by emitting glorious arches of song is remarkable in itself, but to make these arches resemble a rainbow of vocal colors, or to achieve the kind of poetry Callas can breathe into Lucia's "Verranno a te" or Elvira's "Qui la voce" are the earmarks of superior vocal art, a magic combination of inspiration and respiration.

Examples of the way her technical command is adapted to musical exigencies are, of course, plentiful in the Callas recordings. A few remarkable instances will be singled out so that vocal connoisseurs can compare these examples with parallel recorded excerpts by other artists:

A good example for discovering that trills are far more than superficial embellishments is Leonora's "D'amor sull'ali rosee" in the fourth act of *Il Trovatore*.

Celli rightfully observed that these trills symbolize the heroine's anxiety and sorrowful longing, and this is the exact quality Callas conveys to the perceptive listener. A few moments later in the same act, Leonora sings the fiery cabaletta "Tu vedrai che amore" (a piece of music most sopranos choose to omit altogether, even on recordings). Here the plaintive Leonora is transformed into a woman of resolute heroism. The voice is hurled forth with an appropriately dramatic thrust, and the cleanly articulated chromatic runs (which are the probable reasons why this aria is in such disfavor with other sopranos) enhance the dramatic as well as the musical design with telling effect. Chromatic runs are tossed off with similar exactitude in *Norma's* first act (both in "Casta Diva" and the succeeding cabaletta, "Ah! bello a me ritorna").

But far more instructive than citing isolated examples is a closer look at Callas in the performance of an entire scene. Her recorded interpretation of the magnificent "Sleepwalking Scene" from Verdi's *Macbeth* (Angel 35763), for example, offers a concentration of all that makes up her vocal art.

Verdi spent three months rehearsing this music before the opera's première in 1847. He insisted, and he was right, that *Macbeth* would stand or fall with the success of this scene. This is the type of singing he wanted: "For Lady Macbeth I should like a harsh, choked, dark voice ... it should have something devilish ... the Sleepwalking scene must be acted and declaimed with a very hollow voice, otherwise it will have no effect."

It is night in Macbeth's castle. During the poignant and hauntingly atmospheric orchestral introduction Lady Macbeth enters slowly, walking in her sleep. She carries a light. Suddenly she puts down the light and rubs her hands, as if to rub something out:

The Text	The Interpretation
Una macchia—è qui tuttora ! *A spot —it is still here!*	vocal color appropriately dark.
via, ti dico, o maledetta ! . . . *Away, I tell you, o cursed spot!*	the peculiar Callas "veil" on *dico;* seething venom pervades *maledetta.*
Una . . . due . . . gli è questa l'ora ! *One . . . two . . . this is the hour!*	*una* . . . *due* sung on the score's musical notes, but with a distant, unearthly quality.
Tremi tu ? non osi entrar ? *Do you tremble? Are you afraid to enter?*	terrifying in *Tremi tu,* utter contempt in *non osi entrar,* ending in a choked outburst.
Un guerrier così codardo ? *A warrior who is such a coward?*	note sweeping legato.
Oh vergogna ! *Oh shame!*	*Oh* is accented for emotional effect.
Orsù t'affretta ! *Now, hasten!*	
Chi poteva in quel vegliardo *Who in that old man could* tanto sangue immaginar ? *imagine so much blood?* Chi poteva tanto sangue immaginar ? *Who could imagine so much blood?*	for this famous line Verdi's score demands individual stress on syllables of *immaginar.* Callas follows this. When the phrase is repeated, the same word expresses despair.
Di Fiffe il sire sposo e padre or non era ? Che ne avenne ? *The Lord of Fife, husband and father, was not he? What became of them?*	Lady Macbeth's mind wanders. These lines bear no special emotion.
E mai pulire queste mani io non saprò ? *Will I ever know how to clean these hands?* No, mai pulire io non saprò ? *No, I shall never know.*	first time sung in an outburst of anguish, the second time *"con dolore"* as marked in score, with a climax on *saprò.*

The Text	The Interpretation
Di sangue umano sa qui sempre. *There is human blood here always.*	a tone of subdued resignation.
Arabia intera *All Arabia*	*"con forza"* in the score.
Rimondar sì piccol mano *cannot purify this little hand*	*"cupo"* (darkly) in the score.
co' suoi balsami non può. *with its balms—it cannot.*	gradual dejection, with the final *non può* signifying utter hopelessness.
Ohimè! I panni indossa della notte! *Alas! Put on your clothes for the night!* Or via ti sbratta! Banco è spento *Go on, clean yourself! Banquo is dead*	she addresses the absent Macbeth in an almost normal tone, as if she had regained her control.
e dalla fossa chi morì non surse ancor. *and from his grave one who died cannot rise again.*	accent of deadly finality on *morì.*
A letto, a letto ... *to bed, to bed ...* Sfar non puoi la cosa fatta ... *What was done cannot be undone ...* Batte alcuno! Andiam, Macbetto, *Someone knocks! Let us go, Macbeth,* non t'accusi il tuo pallor. *be not accused by your paleness.* Andiam, Macbetto, andiam. *Let us go, Macbeth, let us go.*	she returns gradually to the distant dream world, trailing off with the score's "un fil di voce" (a thread of voice) to a high D flat before the concluding note an octave lower.

Surely, there are details to criticize from the point of view of vocal purity and perfect tone production. But do these objections really matter in the face of such a thorough comprehension of the personality portrayed, in the presence of musical recreation by a voice which, in the words of Teodoro Celli "contains a drama within itself?"

At the time the *Macbeth* excerpts were recorded in

London, during September, 1958, Callas also recorded the
final scene from Bellini's *Il Pirata.* The music contains
an important English horn solo which required a great
deal of rehearsing. To be able to concentrate on certain
passages, conductor Rescigno and horn soloist retired to
a small room while the rest of the orchestra was given a
break. Suddenly, the door opened, and in came Callas. At
first she listened intently. Then, as the two musicians
began discussing the passage, she added her views. Soon,
while the other two listened in astonishment, she delivered an expert treatise on Bellinian phrasings and
fioriture, accents on trills, the placements of breathing,
and the similarities between vocal and instrumental techniques. It was a typical discussion among musicians, in
straight technical terms only musicians appreciate. But
what Maria Callas had to say carried the authority that
is the result of dedicated study and thorough understanding of the style of the *ottocento.*

Returning the operas of this romantic period to currency after decades of complete disinterest is one of
Callas's main contributions to our operatic life. In many
cases she created her own interpretations—there were no
predecessors to be inspired by, no models to follow. Not
one vocal measure of Cherubini's *Medea,* Bellini's *Il
Pirata,* or Donizetti's *Anna Bolena* had appeared on records before Callas. The first *complete* versions of Bellini's
I Puritani and Rossini's *Il Turco in Italia* are also largely
due to her influence.

Interest in obscure operas is in itself not significant.
During her brilliant career, Renata Tebaldi has sung the
principal roles of Verdi's *Giovanna D'Arco,* Rossini's
L'assedio di Corinto, Spontini's *Olympia* and *Fernando
Cortez.* Every one of these can rival the Callas specialties
in the obscurity sweepstakes. But while these works, after

their beneficial exposure to Tebaldi's luminous tones, are now back resting among the cobwebs, interest in the Callas specialties continues to bloom—as long as Callas is willing to perform them.

Her relentless striving for perfection has elevated the standards of vocal performance. Callas has helped to make perceptive listeners aware of technical weaknesses which had long been overlooked or tolerated. She has even spurred others to more exalted efforts. Other sopranos may never admit this, but in opera's competitive domain the stimulating influence of a powerful rival cannot be underestimated.

Finally, and this is a contribution no one will deny, Callas brought new excitement into opera, created new and enthusiastic audiences. What if thousands go to see her as a result of front-page headlines, not knowing the difference between *Il Pirata* and *La Traviata,* and caring even less ? It is hardly likely that they will come away from the performance with the same lack of musical interest and information. Opera needs new mass audiences for its survival, new excitement and vitality. And when Cherubini's *Medea,* a work the Metropolitan has not deemed "safe" enough to program during its seventy-seven years of history, can attract 4,100 spectators on repeated occasions in Dallas, Texas, the influence of a personality who can make this possible takes on remarkable proportions.

This is the artistic portrait of Maria Callas, the singer with drama in her voice. Magical and irresistible to some, elusive or downright unacceptable to others. Yet, most of the strong objections seem to be emotional, rooted in artistic prejudices, or in a rejection of personality traits, true or imagined. Her artistic qualities evoke, more often than not, reluctant admiration.

Take the case of a noted man of music, whose insistence on remaining unidentified must be respected. Always remarkably cool to Callas, he complained with particular vigor about the Callas interpretation of *La Traviata.* "The whole conception is wrong. Too much tension, overacting. . . . The voice is uneven. You should have heard Toti dal Monte. Sure, she was not convincing in action, nor was she much to look at. But when you closed your eyes, what beauty in that voice, what charm and tenderness! Callas, for me, has none of these qualities."

"Have you tried listening to Callas with the eyes closed?"

"You must be joking," came the reply. "How can any one close his eyes when that woman performs on the stage!"

Epilogue (1985)

Manon
*In quelle trine morbide,
nell'alcova dorata . . .*

Puccini—MANON LESCAUT

A quarter of a century separates this book's first chapter from its Epilogue. Maria Callas has passed on to immortality—an immortality assured already in her lifetime (and of how many singers can this be said?). Gone, too, are many illustrious figures closely connected with her career who populate the pages of my chronicle: Walter Legge, Dario Soria, Tullio Serafin, Luchino Visconti, John Coveney, Carol Fox, and Lawrence Kelly. After all those years of bitter feuding, Evangelia and George Callas, Maria's parents, died unreconciled. Giovanni Battista Meneghini went to his grave protesting his love and loyalty to Maria. Her teacher, Elvira de Hidalgo, and many colleagues, partners of Maria Callas in memorable music-making, are no longer with us: Tito Gobbi, Mario del Monaco, Richard Tucker, Ebe Stignani, George London. And the "noted man of music" whom I quoted on page 337 twenty-five years ago can now be identified as the late Walter Toscanini.

My 1960 sense of foreboding—". . . vocal exhibitions in circus-like settings . . . will not uphold the high standards of art, to which the valuable years of an incredible career were dedicated" (p. 291)—proved all too justified. During the last few years of her career, Callas appeared in opera very infrequently and only in three roles: Medea (at La Scala, in 1961–62), Norma (in Paris, 1964), and Tosca (in London, Paris, and New York, 1964–65). She perpetuated her fascinating portrayal of Carmen on records, a role she should have realized on stage but never did.

There were times, particularly in the Zeffirelli-directed *Tosca* series in London, when the old magic held sway. Enthusiastic audience reaction was echoed by the English critics, who, generally speaking, were always more sympathetic to her art than their American counterparts. But the intense social whirl that Callas chose to embrace alongside Aristotle Onassis left her with little time and patience for the discipline of regularly planned and organized operatic seasons. Her art became a readily marketable "package" directed not so much toward the operatic faithful as toward a worldwide audience of celebrity-seekers. They thronged to London's Royal Festival Hall and similar arenas in Berlin, Copenhagen, Madrid, Amsterdam, the Far East, and—finally and tragically—New York's Carnegie Hall (March 5, 1974, a misguided joint appearance with Giuseppe di Stefano, another fading star whom the force of destiny cast in the role of Maria's intimate companion in those final years).

In 1962, when she had moved to Paris, she was probably the most talked-about woman in the world, seen at the chic spots and seemingly enjoying her reasserted Greek identity at the side of a man with whom she probably had some things in common but certainly not music, about which Onassis cared little.

In any case, by 1964 Maria Callas was no longer the most talked-about woman in the world. She could not compete for media attention with the widow of a beloved and assassinated American President. When, after a hugely publicized romance, Onassis married the former Jacqueline Kennedy on October 17, 1968, that event precipitated the final and tragic phase of Maria Callas: misguided artistic ventures and withdrawal into loneliness. Those years were tragic for Onassis, too. The much-ballyhooed marriage deteriorated; reverses shook his business empire; and, after the loss of his son in an airplane disaster, the adventurous shipowner died a broken man in 1975, the year that also claimed Maria's father and her close friends and artistic collaborators Luchino Visconti, Lawrence Kelly, and Pier Paolo Pasolini, the director of her only film, *Medea*.

In the second act of Puccini's *Manon Lescaut*, the heroine ponders her existence in luxurious Parisian loneliness:

> In quelle trine morbide,
> nell'alcova dorata,
> v'è un silenzio, un gelido mortal
> —un freddo che m'agghiaccia . . .
>
> (In those delicate lace curtains,
> in that gilded alcove,
> there is a silence, a mortal chill
> —a coldness that freezes me . . .)

Maria Callas died behind such delicate curtains, surrounded by exquisite art treasures and lavish furnishings in her apartment at 36, Avenue Georges Mandel. As her coffin was carried out of the small Greek Orthodox church where the funeral had taken place, attended by a few loyal friends, the

Parisian throng outside applauded and cries of "Brava, Callas" were heard.

Her remains were cremated. It all happened quickly and mysteriously, as though efficient unseen hands had been at work. In his touching account (*My Wife Maria Callas*, 1982) Meneghini pondered the possibility that Maria had taken her own life. Although recorded testimony by her maid and butler declares otherwise, that possibility cannot be ruled out altogether. Whichever way it happened, the end was heartrending. But can we imagine any other? Can we see Maria Callas in old age reflecting serenely on her tempestuous past? Lives that are lived with the unsparing intensity of Italian opera and Greek tragedy do not follow such patterns. The life of Maria Callas fits its own pattern. History will deemphasize the image of the tempestuous diva. As the most influential and significant operatic personality of her age, she will continue to inspire singers, to stimulate controversies, to excite and to mystify. That is what legends are meant to do.

GEORGE JELLINEK

New York, N.Y., 1985

The Callas Repertoire — 1960

	COMPOSER	OPERA	FIRST APPEARANCE
1.	Beethoven	*Fidelio*	Athens, 1944
2.	Bellini	*Norma*	Buenos Aires, 1949
3.	Bellini	*Il Pirata*	Milan, 1958
4.	Bellini	*I Puritani*	Venice, 1948
5.	Bellini	*La Sonnambula*	Milan, 1955
6.	Boito	*Mefistofele*	Verona, 1954
7.	Cherubini	*Medea*	Florence, 1953
8.	D'Albert	*Tiefland*	Athens, 1944
9.	Donizetti	*Anna Bolena*	Milan, 1957
10.	Donizetti	*Lucia di Lammermoor*	Mexico City, 1952
11.	Giordano	*Andrea Chénier*	Milan, 1955
12.	Giordano	*Fedora*	Milan, 1956
13.	Gluck	*Alceste*	Milan, 1954
14.	Gluck	*Iphigenia in Tauris*	Milan, 1957

COMPOSER	OPERA	FIRST APPEARANCE

15. Haydn ...... *Orfeo ed Euridice* .... Florence, 1951

16. Leoncavallo .. *I Pagliacci* .... (recorded) 1954

17. Mascagni .... *Cavalleria Rusticana* .... Athens, 1938

18. Millöcker .... *Der Bettelstudent* .... Athens, 1945

19. Mozart ...... *Abduction from the Seraglio*... Milan, 1952

20. Ponchielli ... *La Gioconda* .... Verona, 1947

21. Puccini ..... *La Bohème* .... (recorded) 1956

22. Puccini ..... *Madama Butterfly* .... Chicago, 1955

23. Puccini ..... *Manon Lescaut* .... (recorded) 1957

24. Puccini ..... *Suor Angelica* .... Athens, 1939

25. Puccini ..... *Tosca* .... Athens, 1942

26. Puccini .... *Turandot* .... Venice, 1947

27. Rossini ...... *Armida* .... Florence, 1952

28. Rossini ...... *The Barber of Seville* .... Milan, 1956

29. Rossini ...... *Il Turco in Italia* .... Rome, 1950

30. Spontini .... *La Vestale* .... Milan, 1954

31. Verdi .... *Aida* .... Rovigo, 1948

32. Verdi .... *Un Ballo in Maschera* .... Milan, 1957

33. Verdi .... *Don Carlo* .... Milan, 1954

34. Verdi .... *La Forza del Destino* .... Trieste, 1948

35. Verdi .... *Macbeth* .... Milan, 1952

36. Verdi .... *Nabucco* .... Naples, 1949

37. Verdi .... *Rigoletto* .... Mexico City, 1952

38. Verdi .... *La Traviata* .... Florence, 1951

39. Verdi .... *Il Trovatore* .... Mexico City, 1950

40. Verdi .... *I Vespri Siciliani* .... Florence, 1951

41. Wagner ..... *Parsifal* .... Rome, 1949

COMPOSER	OPERA	FIRST APPEARANCE
42. Wagner	*Tristan und Isolde*	Venice, 1947
43. Wagner	*Die Walküre*	Venice, 1948

Index

A CATALOG OF
SELECTED DOVER BOOKS
IN ALL FIELDS OF INTEREST

A CATALOG OF SELECTED DOVER
BOOKS IN ALL FIELDS OF INTEREST

CONCERNING THE SPIRITUAL IN ART, Wassily Kandinsky. Pioneering work by father of abstract art. Thoughts on color theory, nature of art. Analysis of earlier masters. 12 illustrations. 80pp. of text. 5⅜ × 8½.　　23411-8 Pa. $2.50

LEONARDO ON THE HUMAN BODY, Leonardo da Vinci. More than 1200 of Leonardo's anatomical drawings on 215 plates. Leonardo's text, which accompanies the drawings, has been translated into English. 506pp. 8⅜ × 11¼.
23411-8 Pa. $10.95
24483-0 Pa. $10.95

GOBLIN MARKET, Christina Rossetti. Best-known work by poet comparable to Emily Dickinson, Alfred Tennyson. With 46 delightfully grotesque illustrations by Laurence Housman. 64pp. 4 × 6¾.　　24516-0 Pa. $2.50

THE HEART OF THOREAU'S JOURNALS, edited by Odell Shepard. Selections from *Journal*, ranging over full gamut of interests. 228pp. 5⅜ × 8½.
20741-2 Pa. $4.50

MR. LINCOLN'S CAMERA MAN: MATHEW B. BRADY, Roy Meredith. Over 300 Brady photos reproduced directly from original negatives, photos. Lively commentary. 368pp. 8⅜ × 11¼.　　23021-X Pa. $11.95

PHOTOGRAPHIC VIEWS OF SHERMAN'S CAMPAIGN, George N. Barnard. Reprint of landmark 1866 volume with 61 plates: battlefield of New Hope Church, the Etawah Bridge, the capture of Atlanta, etc. 80pp. 9 × 12.　　23445-2 Pa. $6.00

A SHORT HISTORY OF ANATOMY AND PHYSIOLOGY FROM THE GREEKS TO HARVEY, Dr. Charles Singer. Thoroughly engrossing non-technical survey. 270 illustrations. 211pp. 5⅜ × 8½.　　20389-1 Pa. $4.50

REDOUTE ROSES IRON-ON TRANSFER PATTERNS, Barbara Christopher. Redouté was botanical painter to the Empress Josephine; transfer his famous roses onto fabric with these 24 transfer patterns. 80pp. 8¼ × 10⅞.　　24292-7 Pa. $3.50

THE FIVE BOOKS OF ARCHITECTURE, Sebastiano Serlio. Architectural milestone, first (1611) English translation of Renaissance classic. Unabridged reproduction of original edition includes over 300 woodcut illustrations. 416pp. 9⅜ × 12¼.　　24349-4 Pa. $14.95

CARLSON'S GUIDE TO LANDSCAPE PAINTING, John F. Carlson. Authoritative, comprehensive guide covers, every aspect of landscape painting. 34 reproductions of paintings by author; 58 explanatory diagrams. 144pp. 8⅜ × 11.
22927-0 Pa. $4.95

101 PUZZLES IN THOUGHT AND LOGIC, C.R. Wylie, Jr. Solve murders, robberies, see which fishermen are liars—purely by reasoning! 107pp. 5⅜ × 8½.
20367-0 Pa. $2.00

TEST YOUR LOGIC, George J. Summers. 50 more truly new puzzles with new turns of thought, new subtleties of inference. 100pp. 5⅜ × 8½.　　22877-0 Pa. $2.25

THE MURDER BOOK OF J.G. REEDER, Edgar Wallace. Eight suspenseful stories by bestselling mystery writer of 20s and 30s. Features the donnish Mr. J.G. Reeder of Public Prosecutor's Office. 128pp. 5⅜ × 8½. (Available in U.S. only)
24374-5 Pa. $3.50

ANNE ORR'S CHARTED DESIGNS, Anne Orr. Best designs by premier needlework designer, all on charts: flowers, borders, birds, children, alphabets, etc. Over 100 charts, 10 in color. Total of 40pp. 8¼ × 11.
23704-4 Pa. $2.25

BASIC CONSTRUCTION TECHNIQUES FOR HOUSES AND SMALL BUILDINGS SIMPLY EXPLAINED, U.S. Bureau of Naval Personnel. Grading, masonry, woodworking, floor and wall framing, roof framing, plastering, tile setting, much more. Over 675 illustrations. 568pp. 6½ × 9¼.
20242-9 Pa. $8.95

MATISSE LINE DRAWINGS AND PRINTS, Henri Matisse. Representative collection of female nudes, faces, still lifes, experimental works, etc., from 1898 to 1948. 50 illustrations. 48pp. 8⅜ × 11¼.
23877-6 Pa. $2.50

HOW TO PLAY THE CHESS OPENINGS, Eugene Znosko-Borovsky. Clear, profound examinations of just what each opening is intended to do and how opponent can counter. Many sample games. 147pp. 5⅜ × 8½.
22795-2 Pa. $2.95

DUPLICATE BRIDGE, Alfred Sheinwold. Clear, thorough, easily followed account: rules, etiquette, scoring, strategy, bidding; Goren's point-count system, Blackwood and Gerber conventions, etc. 158pp. 5⅜ × 8½.
22741-3 Pa. $3.00

SARGENT PORTRAIT DRAWINGS, J.S. Sargent. Collection of 42 portraits reveals technical skill and intuitive eye of noted American portrait painter, John Singer Sargent. 48pp. 8¼ × 11⅛.
24524-1 Pa. $2.95

ENTERTAINING SCIENCE EXPERIMENTS WITH EVERYDAY OBJECTS, Martin Gardner. Over 100 experiments for youngsters. Will amuse, astonish, teach, and entertain. Over 100 illustrations. 127pp. 5⅜ × 8½.
24201-3 Pa. $2.50

TEDDY BEAR PAPER DOLLS IN FULL COLOR: A Family of Four Bears and Their Costumes, Crystal Collins. A family of four Teddy Bear paper dolls and nearly 60 cut-out costumes. Full color, printed one side only. 32pp. 9¼ × 12¼.
24550-0 Pa. $3.50

NEW CALLIGRAPHIC ORNAMENTS AND FLOURISHES, Arthur Baker. Unusual, multi-useable material: arrows, pointing hands, brackets and frames, ovals, swirls, birds, etc. Nearly 700 illustrations. 80pp. 8⅜ × 11¼.
24095-9 Pa. $3.75

DINOSAUR DIORAMAS TO CUT & ASSEMBLE, M. Kalmenoff. Two complete three-dimensional scenes in full color, with 31 cut-out animals and plants. Excellent educational toy for youngsters. Instructions; 2 assembly diagrams. 32pp. 9¼ × 12¼.
24541-1 Pa. $3.95

SILHOUETTES: A PICTORIAL ARCHIVE OF VARIED ILLUSTRATIONS, edited by Carol Belanger Grafton. Over 600 silhouettes from the 18th to 20th centuries. Profiles and full figures of men, women, children, birds, animals, groups and scenes, nature, ships, an alphabet. 144pp. 8⅜ × 11¼.
23781-8 Pa. $4.95

25 KITES THAT FLY, Leslie Hunt. Full, easy-to-follow instructions for kites made from inexpensive materials. Many novelties. 70 illustrations. 110pp. 5⅜ × 8½.
22550-X Pa. $2.25

PIANO TUNING, J. Cree Fischer. Clearest, best book for beginner, amateur. Simple repairs, raising dropped notes, tuning by easy method of flattened fifths. No previous skills needed. 4 illustrations. 201pp. 5⅜ × 8½. 23267-0 Pa. $3.50

EARLY AMERICAN IRON-ON TRANSFER PATTERNS, edited by Rita Weiss. 75 designs, borders, alphabets, from traditional American sources. 48pp. 8¼ × 11.
23162-3 Pa. $1.95

CROCHETING EDGINGS, edited by Rita Weiss. Over 100 of the best designs for these lovely trims for a host of household items. Complete instructions, illustrations. 48pp. 8¼ × 11. 24031-2 Pa. $2.25

FINGER PLAYS FOR NURSERY AND KINDERGARTEN, Emilie Poulsson. 18 finger plays with music (voice and piano); entertaining, instructive. Counting, nature lore, etc. Victorian classic. 53 illustrations. 80pp. 6½ × 9¼. 22588-7 Pa. $1.95

BOSTON THEN AND NOW, Peter Vanderwarker. Here in 59 side-by-side views are photographic documentations of the city's past and present. 119 photographs. Full captions. 122pp. 8¼ × 11. 24312-5 Pa. $6.95

CROCHETING BEDSPREADS, edited by Rita Weiss. 22 patterns, originally published in three instruction books 1939-41. 39 photos, 8 charts. Instructions. 48pp. 8¼ × 11. 23610-2 Pa. $2.00

HAWTHORNE ON PAINTING, Charles W. Hawthorne. Collected from notes taken by students at famous Cape Cod School; hundreds of direct, personal *apercus*, ideas, suggestions. 91pp. 5⅜ × 8½. 20653-X Pa. $2.50

THERMODYNAMICS, Enrico Fermi. A classic of modern science. Clear, organized treatment of systems, first and second laws, entropy, thermodynamic potentials, etc. Calculus required. 160pp. 5⅜ × 8½. 60361-X Pa. $4.00

TEN BOOKS ON ARCHITECTURE, Vitruvius. The most important book ever written on architecture. Early Roman aesthetics, technology, classical orders, site selection, all other aspects. Morgan translation. 331pp. 5⅜ × 8½. 20645-9 Pa. $5.50

THE CORNELL BREAD BOOK, Clive M. McCay and Jeanette B. McCay. Famed high-protein recipe incorporated into breads, rolls, buns, coffee cakes, pizza, pie crusts, more. Nearly 50 illustrations. 48pp. 8¼ × 11. 23995-0 Pa. $2.00

THE CRAFTSMAN'S HANDBOOK, Cennino Cennini. 15th-century handbook, school of Giotto, explains applying gold, silver leaf; gesso; fresco painting, grinding pigments, etc. 142pp. 6⅛ × 9¼. 20054-X Pa. $3.50

FRANK LLOYD WRIGHT'S FALLINGWATER, Donald Hoffmann. Full story of Wright's masterwork at Bear Run, Pa. 100 photographs of site, construction, and details of completed structure. 112pp. 9¼ × 10. 23671-4 Pa. $6.50

OVAL STAINED GLASS PATTERN BOOK, C. Eaton. 60 new designs framed in shape of an oval. Greater complexity, challenge with sinuous cats, birds, mandalas framed in antique shape. 64pp. 8¼ × 11. 24519-5 Pa. $3.50

THE BOOK OF WOOD CARVING, Charles Marshall Sayers. Still finest book for beginning student. Fundamentals, technique; gives 34 designs, over 34 projects for panels, bookends, mirrors, etc. 33 photos. 118pp. 7¾ × 10⅝. 23654-4 Pa. $3.95

CARVING COUNTRY CHARACTERS, Bill Higginbotham. Expert advice for beginning, advanced carvers on materials, techniques for creating 18 projects—mirthful panorama of American characters. 105 illustrations. 80pp. 8⅜ × 11. 24135-1 Pa. $2.50

300 ART NOUVEAU DESIGNS AND MOTIFS IN FULL COLOR, C.B. Grafton. 44 full-page plates display swirling lines and muted colors typical of Art Nouveau. Borders, frames, panels, cartouches, dingbats, etc. 48pp. 9⅜ × 12¼. 24354-0 Pa. $6.00

SELF-WORKING CARD TRICKS, Karl Fulves. Editor of *Pallbearer* offers 72 tricks that work automatically through nature of card deck. No sleight of hand needed. Often spectacular. 42 illustrations. 113pp. 5⅜ × 8½. 23334-0 Pa. $3.50

CUT AND ASSEMBLE A WESTERN FRONTIER TOWN, Edmund V. Gillon, Jr. Ten authentic full-color buildings on heavy cardboard stock in H-O scale. Sheriff's Office and Jail, Saloon, Wells Fargo, Opera House, others. 48pp. 9¼ × 12¼. 23736-2 Pa. $3.95

CUT AND ASSEMBLE AN EARLY NEW ENGLAND VILLAGE, Edmund V. Gillon, Jr. Printed in full color on heavy cardboard stock. 12 authentic buildings in H-O scale: Adams home in Quincy, Mass., Oliver Wight house in Sturbridge, smithy, store, church, others. 48pp. 9¼ × 12¼. 23536-X Pa. $3.95

THE TALE OF TWO BAD MICE, Beatrix Potter. Tom Thumb and Hunca Munca squeeze out of their hole and go exploring. 27 full-color Potter illustrations. 59pp. 4¼ × 5½. (Available in U.S. only) 23065-1 Pa. $1.50

CARVING FIGURE CARICATURES IN THE OZARK STYLE, Harold L. Enlow. Instructions and illustrations for ten delightful projects, plus general carving instructions. 22 drawings and 47 photographs altogether. 39pp. 8⅜ × 11. 23151-8 Pa. $2.50

A TREASURY OF FLOWER DESIGNS FOR ARTISTS, EMBROIDERERS AND CRAFTSMEN, Susan Gaber. 100 garden favorites lushly rendered by artist for artists, craftsmen, needleworkers. Many form frames, borders. 80pp. 8¼ × 11. 24096-7 Pa. $3.50

CUT & ASSEMBLE A TOY THEATER/THE NUTCRACKER BALLET, Tom Tierney. Model of a complete, full-color production of Tchaikovsky's classic. 6 backdrops, dozens of characters, familiar dance sequences. 32pp. 9⅜ × 12¼. 24194-7 Pa. $4.50

ANIMALS: 1,419 COPYRIGHT-FREE ILLUSTRATIONS OF MAMMALS, BIRDS, FISH, INSECTS, ETC., edited by Jim Harter. Clear wood engravings present, in extremely lifelike poses, over 1,000 species of animals. 284pp. 9 × 12. 23766-4 Pa. $9.95

MORE HAND SHADOWS, Henry Bursill. For those at their 'finger ends," 16 more effects—Shakespeare, a hare, a squirrel, Mr. Punch, and twelve more—each explained by a full-page illustration. Considerable period charm. 30pp. 6½ × 9¼. 21384-6 Pa. $1.95

SURREAL STICKERS AND UNREAL STAMPS, William Rowe. 224 haunting, hilarious stamps on gummed, perforated stock, with images of elephants, geisha girls, George Washington, etc. 16pp. one side. 8¼ × 11. 24371-0 Pa. $3.50

GOURMET KITCHEN LABELS, Ed Sibbett, Jr. 112 full-color labels (4 copies each of 28 designs). Fruit, bread, other culinary motifs. Gummed and perforated. 16pp. 8¼ × 11. 24087-8 Pa. $2.95

PATTERNS AND INSTRUCTIONS FOR CARVING AUTHENTIC BIRDS, H.D. Green. Detailed instructions, 27 diagrams, 85 photographs for carving 15 species of birds so life-like, they'll seem ready to fly! 8¼ × 11. 24222-6 Pa. $2.75

FLATLAND, E.A. Abbott. Science-fiction classic explores life of 2-D being in 3-D world. 16 illustrations. 103pp. 5⅜ × 8. 20001-9 Pa. $2.00

DRIED FLOWERS, Sarah Whitlock and Martha Rankin. Concise, clear, practical guide to dehydration, glycerinizing, pressing plant material, and more. Covers use of silica gel. 12 drawings. 32pp. 5⅜ × 8½. 21802-3 Pa. $1.00

EASY-TO-MAKE CANDLES, Gary V. Guy. Learn how easy it is to make all kinds of decorative candles. Step-by-step instructions. 82 illustrations. 48pp. 8¼ × 11. 23881-4 Pa. $2.50

SUPER STICKERS FOR KIDS, Carolyn Bracken. 128 gummed and perforated full-color stickers: GIRL WANTED, KEEP OUT, BORED OF EDUCATION, X-RATED, COMBAT ZONE, many others. 16pp. 8¼ × 11. 24092-4 Pa. $2.50

CUT AND COLOR PAPER MASKS, Michael Grater. Clowns, animals, funny faces...simply color them in, cut them out, and put them together, and you have 9 paper masks to play with and enjoy. 32pp. 8¼ × 11. 23171-2 Pa. $2.25

A CHRISTMAS CAROL: THE ORIGINAL MANUSCRIPT, Charles Dickens. Clear facsimile of Dickens manuscript, on facing pages with final printed text. 8 illustrations by John Leech, 4 in color on covers. 144pp. 8⅜ × 11¼. 20980-6 Pa. $5.95

CARVING SHOREBIRDS, Harry V. Shourds & Anthony Hillman. 16 full-size patterns (all double-page spreads) for 19 North American shorebirds with step-by-step instructions. 72pp. 9¼ × 12¼. 24287-0 Pa. $4.95

THE GENTLE ART OF MATHEMATICS, Dan Pedoe. Mathematical games, probability, the question of infinity, topology, how the laws of algebra work, problems of irrational numbers, and more. 42 figures. 143pp. 5⅜ × 8½. (EBE) 22949-1 Pa. $3.50

READY-TO-USE DOLLHOUSE WALLPAPER, Katzenbach & Warren, Inc. Stripe, 2 floral stripes, 2 allover florals, polka dot; all in full color. 4 sheets (350 sq. in.) of each, enough for average room. 48pp. 8¼ × 11. 23495-9 Pa. $2.95

MINIATURE IRON-ON TRANSFER PATTERNS FOR DOLLHOUSES, DOLLS, AND SMALL PROJECTS, Rita Weiss and Frank Fontana. Over 100 miniature patterns: rugs, bedspreads, quilts, chair seats, etc. In standard dollhouse size. 48pp. 8¼ × 11. 23741-9 Pa. $1.95

THE DINOSAUR COLORING BOOK, Anthony Rao. 45 renderings of dinosaurs, fossil birds, turtles, other creatures of Mesozoic Era. Scientifically accurate. Captions. 48pp. 8¼ × 11. 24022-3 Pa. $2.25

JAPANESE DESIGN MOTIFS, Matsuya Co. Mon, or heraldic designs. Over 4000 typical, beautiful designs: birds, animals, flowers, swords, fans, geometrics; all beautifully stylized. 213pp. 11⅜ × 8¼. 22874-6 Pa. $7.95

THE TALE OF BENJAMIN BUNNY, Beatrix Potter. Peter Rabbit's cousin coaxes him back into Mr. McGregor's garden for a whole new set of adventures. All 27 full-color illustrations. 59pp. 4¼ × 5½. (Available in U.S. only) 21102-9 Pa. $1.50

THE TALE OF PETER RABBIT AND OTHER FAVORITE STORIES BOXED SET, Beatrix Potter. Seven of Beatrix Potter's best-loved tales including Peter Rabbit in a specially designed, durable boxed set. 4¼ × 5½. Total of 447pp. 158 color illustrations. (Available in U.S. only) 23903-9 Pa. $10.80

PRACTICAL MENTAL MAGIC, Theodore Annemann. Nearly 200 astonishing feats of mental magic revealed in step-by-step detail. Complete advice on staging, patter, etc. Illustrated. 320pp. 5⅜ × 8½. 24426-1 Pa. $5.95

CELEBRATED CASES OF JUDGE DEE (DEE GOONG AN), translated by Robert Van Gulik. Authentic 18th-century Chinese detective novel; Dee and associates solve three interlocked cases. Led to van Gulik's own stories with same characters. Extensive introduction. 9 illustrations. 237pp. 5⅜ × 8½. 23337-5 Pa. $4.50

CUT & FOLD EXTRATERRESTRIAL INVADERS THAT FLY, M. Grater. Stage your own lilliputian space battles.By following the step-by-step instructions and explanatory diagrams you can launch 22 full-color fliers into space. 36pp. 8¼ × 11. 24478-4 Pa. $2.95

CUT & ASSEMBLE VICTORIAN HOUSES, Edmund V. Gillon, Jr. Printed in full color on heavy cardboard stock, 4 authentic Victorian houses in H-O scale: Italian-style Villa, Octagon, Second Empire, Stick Style. 48pp. 9¼ × 12¼. 23849-0 Pa. $3.95

BEST SCIENCE FICTION STORIES OF H.G. WELLS, H.G. Wells. Full novel *The Invisible Man,* plus 17 short stories: "The Crystal Egg," "Aepyornis Island," "The Strange Orchid," etc. 303pp. 5⅜ × 8½. (Available in U.S. only) 21531-8 Pa. $4.95

TRADEMARK DESIGNS OF THE WORLD, Yusaku Kamekura. A lavish collection of nearly 700 trademarks, the work of Wright, Loewy, Klee, Binder, hundreds of others. 160pp. 8¾ × 8. (Available in U.S. only) 24191-2 Pa. $5.00

THE ARTIST'S AND CRAFTSMAN'S GUIDE TO REDUCING, ENLARGING AND TRANSFERRING DESIGNS, Rita Weiss. Discover, reduce, enlarge, transfer designs from any objects to any craft project. 12pp. plus 16 sheets special graph paper. 8¼ × 11. 24142-4 Pa. $3.25

TREASURY OF JAPANESE DESIGNS AND MOTIFS FOR ARTISTS AND CRAFTSMEN, edited by Carol Belanger Grafton. Indispensable collection of 360 traditional Japanese designs and motifs redrawn in clean, crisp black-and-white, copyright-free illustrations. 96pp. 8¼ × 11. 24435-0 Pa. $3.95

CHANCERY CURSIVE STROKE BY STROKE, Arthur Baker. Instructions and illustrations for each stroke of each letter (upper and lower case) and numerals. 54 full-page plates. 64pp. 8¼ × 11. 24278-1 Pa. $2.50

THE ENJOYMENT AND USE OF COLOR, Walter Sargent. Color relationships, values, intensities; complementary colors, illumination, similar topics. Color in nature and art. 7 color plates, 29 illustrations. 274pp. 5⅜ × 8½. 20944-X Pa. $4.50

SCULPTURE PRINCIPLES AND PRACTICE, Louis Slobodkin. Step-by-step approach to clay, plaster, metals, stone; classical and modern. 253 drawings, photos. 255pp. 8⅛ × 11. 22960-2 Pa. $7.50

VICTORIAN FASHION PAPER DOLLS FROM HARPER'S BAZAR, 1867-1898, Theodore Menten. Four female dolls with 28 elegant high fashion costumes, printed in full color. 32pp. 9¼ × 12¼. 23453-3 Pa. $3.50

FLOPSY, MOPSY AND COTTONTAIL: A Little Book of Paper Dolls in Full Color, Susan LaBelle. Three dolls and 21 costumes (7 for each doll) show Peter Rabbit's siblings dressed for holidays, gardening, hiking, etc. Charming borders, captions. 48pp. 4¼ × 5½. 24376-1 Pa. $2.25

NATIONAL LEAGUE BASEBALL CARD CLASSICS, Bert Randolph Sugar. 83 big-leaguers from 1909-69 on facsimile cards. Hubbell, Dean, Spahn, Brock plus advertising, info, no duplications. Perforated, detachable. 16pp. 8¼ × 11.
24308-7 Pa. $2.95

THE LOGICAL APPROACH TO CHESS, Dr. Max Euwe, et al. First-rate text of comprehensive strategy, tactics, theory for the amateur. No gambits to memorize, just a clear, logical approach. 224pp. 5⅜ × 8½. 24353-2 Pa. $4.50

MAGICK IN THEORY AND PRACTICE, Aleister Crowley. The summation of the thought and practice of the century's most famous necromancer, long hard to find. Crowley's best book. 436pp. 5⅜ × 8½. (Available in U.S. only)
23295-6 Pa. $6.50

THE HAUNTED HOTEL, Wilkie Collins. Collins' last great tale; doom and destiny in a Venetian palace. Praised by T.S. Eliot. 127pp. 5⅜ × 8½.
24333-8 Pa. $3.00

ART DECO DISPLAY ALPHABETS, Dan X. Solo. Wide variety of bold yet elegant lettering in handsome Art Deco styles. 100 complete fonts, with numerals, punctuation, more. 104pp. 8⅛ × 11. 24372-9 Pa. $4.00

CALLIGRAPHIC ALPHABETS, Arthur Baker. Nearly 150 complete alphabets by outstanding contemporary. Stimulating ideas; useful source for unique effects. 154 plates. 157pp. 8⅜ × 11¼. 21045-6 Pa. $4.95

ARTHUR BAKER'S HISTORIC CALLIGRAPHIC ALPHABETS, Arthur Baker. From monumental capitals of first-century Rome to humanistic cursive of 16th century, 33 alphabets in fresh interpretations. 88 plates. 96pp. 9 × 12.
24054-1 Pa. $4.50

LETTIE LANE PAPER DOLLS, Sheila Young. Genteel turn-of-the-century family very popular then and now. 24 paper dolls. 16 plates in full color. 32pp. 9¼ × 12¼. 24089-4 Pa. $3.50

KEYBOARD WORKS FOR SOLO INSTRUMENTS, G.F. Handel. 35 neglected works from Handel's vast oeuvre, originally jotted down as improvisations. Includes Eight Great Suites, others. New sequence. 174pp. 9⅜ × 12¼.

24338-9 Pa. $7.50

AMERICAN LEAGUE BASEBALL CARD CLASSICS, Bert Randolph Sugar. 82 stars from 1900s to 60s on facsimile cards. Ruth, Cobb, Mantle, Williams, plus advertising, info, no duplications. Perforated, detachable. 16pp. 8¼ × 11.

24286-2 Pa. $2.95

A TREASURY OF CHARTED DESIGNS FOR NEEDLEWORKERS, Georgia Gorham and Jeanne Warth. 141 charted designs: owl, cat with yarn, tulips, piano, spinning wheel, covered bridge, Victorian house and many others. 48pp. 8¼ × 11.

23558-0 Pa. $1.95

DANISH FLORAL CHARTED DESIGNS, Gerda Bengtsson. Exquisite collection of over 40 different florals: anemone, Iceland poppy, wild fruit, pansies, many others. 45 illustrations. 48pp. 8¼ × 11.   23957-8 Pa. $1.75

OLD PHILADELPHIA IN EARLY PHOTOGRAPHS 1839-1914, Robert F. Looney. 215 photographs: panoramas, street scenes, landmarks, President-elect Lincoln's visit, 1876 Centennial Exposition, much more. 230pp. 8⅜ × 11¾.

23345-6 Pa. $9.95

PRELUDE TO MATHEMATICS, W.W. Sawyer. Noted mathematician's lively, stimulating account of non-Euclidean geometry, matrices, determinants, group theory, other topics. Emphasis on novel, striking aspects. 224pp. 5⅜ × 8½.

24401-6 Pa. $4.50

ADVENTURES WITH A MICROSCOPE, Richard Headstrom. 59 adventures with clothing fibers, protozoa, ferns and lichens, roots and leaves, much more. 142 illustrations. 232pp. 5⅜ × 8½.   23471-1 Pa. $3.95

IDENTIFYING ANIMAL TRACKS: MAMMALS, BIRDS, AND OTHER ANIMALS OF THE EASTERN UNITED STATES, Richard Headstrom. For hunters, naturalists, scouts, nature-lovers. Diagrams of tracks, tips on identification. 128pp. 5⅜ × 8.   24442-3 Pa. $3.50

VICTORIAN FASHIONS AND COSTUMES FROM HARPER'S BAZAR, 1867-1898, edited by Stella Blum. Day costumes, evening wear, sports clothes, shoes, hats, other accessories in over 1,000 detailed engravings. 320pp. 9⅜ × 12¼.

22990-4 Pa. $9.95

EVERYDAY FASHIONS OF THE TWENTIES AS PICTURED IN SEARS AND OTHER CATALOGS, edited by Stella Blum. Actual dress of the Roaring Twenties, with text by Stella Blum. Over 750 illustrations, captions. 156pp. 9 × 12.

24134-3 Pa. $8.50

HALL OF FAME BASEBALL CARDS, edited by Bert Randolph Sugar. Cy Young, Ted Williams, Lou Gehrig, and many other Hall of Fame greats on 92 full-color, detachable reprints of early baseball cards. No duplication of cards with *Classic Baseball Cards.* 16pp. 8¼ × 11.   23624-2 Pa. $3.50

THE ART OF HAND LETTERING, Helm Wotzkow. Course in hand lettering, Roman, Gothic, Italic, Block, Script. Tools, proportions, optical aspects, individual variation. Very quality conscious. Hundreds of specimens. 320pp. 5⅜ × 8½.

21797-3 Pa. $4.95

HOW THE OTHER HALF LIVES, Jacob A. Riis. Journalistic record of filth, degradation, upward drive in New York immigrant slums, shops, around 1900. New edition includes 100 original Riis photos, monuments of early photography. 233pp. 10 × 7⅞. 22012-5 Pa. $7.95

CHINA AND ITS PEOPLE IN EARLY PHOTOGRAPHS, John Thomson. In 200 black-and-white photographs of exceptional quality photographic pioneer Thomson captures the mountains, dwellings, monuments and people of 19th-century China. 272pp. 9⅜ × 12¼. 24393-1 Pa. $12.95

GODEY COSTUME PLATES IN COLOR FOR DECOUPAGE AND FRAMING, edited by Eleanor Hasbrouk Rawlings. 24 full-color engravings depicting 19th-century Parisian haute couture. Printed on one side only. 56pp. 8¼ × 11. 23879-2 Pa. $3.95

ART NOUVEAU STAINED GLASS PATTERN BOOK, Ed Sibbett, Jr. 104 projects using well-known themes of Art Nouveau: swirling forms, florals, peacocks, and sensuous women. 60pp. 8¼ × 11. 23577-7 Pa. $3.50

QUICK AND EASY PATCHWORK ON THE SEWING MACHINE: Susan Aylsworth Murwin and Suzzy Payne. Instructions, diagrams show exactly how to machine sew 12 quilts. 48pp. of templates. 50 figures. 80pp. 8¼ × 11. 23770-2 Pa. $3.50

THE STANDARD BOOK OF QUILT MAKING AND COLLECTING, Marguerite Ickis. Full information, full-sized patterns for making 46 traditional quilts, also 150 other patterns. 483 illustrations. 273pp. 6⅞ × 9⅝. 20582-7 Pa. $5.95

LETTERING AND ALPHABETS, J. Albert Cavanagh. 85 complete alphabets lettered in various styles; instructions for spacing, roughs, brushwork. 121pp. 8¾ × 8. 20053-1 Pa. $3.75

LETTER FORMS: 110 COMPLETE ALPHABETS, Frederick Lambert. 110 sets of capital letters; 16 lower case alphabets; 70 sets of numbers and other symbols. 110pp. 8⅛ × 11. 22872-X Pa. $4.50

ORCHIDS AS HOUSE PLANTS, Rebecca Tyson Northen. Grow cattleyas and many other kinds of orchids—in a window, in a case, or under artificial light. 63 illustrations. 148pp. 5⅜ × 8½. 23261-1 Pa. $2.95

THE MUSHROOM HANDBOOK, Louis C.C. Krieger. Still the best popular handbook. Full descriptions of 259 species, extremely thorough text, poisons, folklore, etc. 32 color plates; 126 other illustrations. 560pp. 5⅜ × 8½. 21861-9 Pa. $8.50

THE DORÉ BIBLE ILLUSTRATIONS, Gustave Doré. All wonderful, detailed plates: Adam and Eve, Flood, Babylon, life of Jesus, etc. Brief King James text with each plate. 241 plates. 241pp. 9 × 12. 23004-X Pa. $8.95

THE BOOK OF KELLS: Selected Plates in Full Color, edited by Blanche Cirker. 32 full-page plates from greatest manuscript-icon of early Middle Ages. Fantastic, mysterious. Publisher's Note. Captions. 32pp. 9¾ × 12¼. 24345-1 Pa. $4.50

THE PERFECT WAGNERITE, George Bernard Shaw. Brilliant criticism of the Ring Cycle, with provocative interpretation of politics, economic theories behind the Ring. 136pp. 5⅜ × 8½. (Available in U.S. only) 21707-8 Pa. $3.00

THE RIME OF THE ANCIENT MARINER, Gustave Doré, S.T. Coleridge. Doré's finest work, 34 plates capture moods, subtleties of poem. Full text. 77pp. 9¼ × 12.   22305-1 Pa. $4.95

SONGS OF INNOCENCE, William Blake. The first and most popular of Blake's famous "Illuminated Books," in a facsimile edition reproducing all 31 brightly colored plates. Additional printed text of each poem. 64pp. 5¼ × 7.
22764-2 Pa. $3.00

AN INTRODUCTION TO INFORMATION THEORY, J.R. Pierce. Second (1980) edition of most impressive non-technical account available. Encoding, entropy, noisy channel, related areas, etc. 320pp. 5⅜ × 8½.   24061-4 Pa. $4.95

THE DIVINE PROPORTION: A STUDY IN MATHEMATICAL BEAUTY, H.E. Huntley. "Divine proportion" or "golden ratio" in poetry, Pascal's triangle, philosophy, psychology, music, mathematical figures, etc. Excellent bridge between science and art. 58 figures. 185pp. 5⅜ × 8½.   22254-3 Pa. $3.95

THE DOVER NEW YORK WALKING GUIDE: From the Battery to Wall Street, Mary J. Shapiro. Superb inexpensive guide to historic buildings and locales in lower Manhattan: Trinity Church, Bowling Green, more. Complete Text; maps. 36 illustrations. 48pp. 3⅞ × 9¼.   24225-0 Pa. $2.50

NEW YORK THEN AND NOW, Edward B. Watson, Edmund V. Gillon, Jr. 83 important Manhattan sites: on facing pages early photographs (1875-1925) and 1976 photos by Gillon. 172 illustrations. 171pp. 9¼ × 10.   23361-8 Pa. $7.95

HISTORIC COSTUME IN PICTURES, Braun & Schneider. Over 1450 costumed figures from dawn of civilization to end of 19th century. English captions. 125 plates. 256pp. 8⅜ × 11¼.   23150-X Pa. $7.50

VICTORIAN AND EDWARDIAN FASHION: A Photographic Survey, Alison Gernsheim. First fashion history completely illustrated by contemporary photographs. Full text plus 235 photos, 1840-1914, in which many celebrities appear. 240pp. 6½ × 9¼.   24205-6 Pa. $6.00

CHARTED CHRISTMAS DESIGNS FOR COUNTED CROSS-STITCH AND OTHER NEEDLECRAFTS, Lindberg Press. Charted designs for 45 beautiful needlecraft projects with many yuletide and wintertime motifs. 48pp. 8¼ × 11.
24356-7 Pa. $1.95

101 FOLK DESIGNS FOR COUNTED CROSS-STITCH AND OTHER NEEDLE-CRAFTS, Carter Houck. 101 authentic charted folk designs in a wide array of lovely representations with many suggestions for effective use. 48pp. 8¼ × 11.
24369-9 Pa. $2.25

FIVE ACRES AND INDEPENDENCE, Maurice G. Kains. Great back-to-the-land classic explains basics of self-sufficient farming. The one book to get. 95 illustrations. 397pp. 5⅜ × 8½.   20974-1 Pa. $4.95

A MODERN HERBAL, Margaret Grieve. Much the fullest, most exact, most useful compilation of herbal material. Gigantic alphabetical encyclopedia, from aconite to zedoary, gives botanical information, medical properties, folklore, economic uses, and much else. Indispensable to serious reader. 161 illustrations. 888pp. 6½ × 9¼. (Available in U.S. only)   22798-7, 22799-5 Pa., Two-vol. set $16.45

DECORATIVE NAPKIN FOLDING FOR BEGINNERS, Lillian Oppenheimer and Natalie Epstein. 22 different napkin folds in the shape of a heart, clown's hat, love knot, etc. 63 drawings. 48pp. 8¼ × 11. 23797-4 Pa. $1.95

DECORATIVE LABELS FOR HOME CANNING, PRESERVING, AND OTHER HOUSEHOLD AND GIFT USES, Theodore Menten. 128 gummed, perforated labels, beautifully printed in 2 colors. 12 versions. Adhere to metal, glass, wood, ceramics. 24pp. 8¼ × 11. 23219-0 Pa. $2.95

EARLY AMERICAN STENCILS ON WALLS AND FURNITURE, Janet Waring. Thorough coverage of 19th-century folk art: techniques, artifacts, surviving specimens. 166 illustrations, 7 in color. 147pp. of text. 7⅞ × 10¾. 21906-2 Pa. $9.95

AMERICAN ANTIQUE WEATHERVANES, A.B. & W.T. Westervelt. Extensively illustrated 1883 catalog exhibiting over 550 copper weathervanes and finials. Excellent primary source by one of the principal manufacturers. 104pp. 6⅛ × 9¼. 24396-6 Pa. $3.95

ART STUDENTS' ANATOMY, Edmond J. Farris. Long favorite in art schools. Basic elements, common positions, actions. Full text, 158 illustrations. 159pp. 5⅜ × 8½. 20744-7 Pa. $3.95

BRIDGMAN'S LIFE DRAWING, George B. Bridgman. More than 500 drawings and text teach you to abstract the body into its major masses. Also specific areas of anatomy. 192pp. 6½ × 9¼. (EA) 22710-3 Pa. $4.50

COMPLETE PRELUDES AND ETUDES FOR SOLO PIANO, Frederic Chopin. All 26 Preludes, all 27 Etudes by greatest composer of piano music. Authoritative Paderewski edition. 224pp. 9 × 12. (Available in U.S. only) 24052-5 Pa. $7.50

PIANO MUSIC 1888-1905, Claude Debussy. Deux Arabesques, Suite Bergamesque, Masques, 1st series of Images, etc. 9 others, in corrected editions. 175pp. 9⅜ × 12¼. (ECE) 22771-5 Pa. $5.95

TEDDY BEAR IRON-ON TRANSFER PATTERNS, Ted Menten. 80 iron-on transfer patterns of male and female Teddys in a wide variety of activities, poses, sizes. 48pp. 8¼ × 11. 24596-9 Pa. $2.25

A PICTURE HISTORY OF THE BROOKLYN BRIDGE, M.J. Shapiro. Profusely illustrated account of greatest engineering achievement of 19th century. 167 rare photos & engravings recall construction, human drama. Extensive, detailed text. 122pp. 8¼ × 11. 24403-2 Pa. $7.95

NEW YORK IN THE THIRTIES, Berenice Abbott. Noted photographer's fascinating study shows new buildings that have become famous and old sights that have disappeared forever. 97 photographs. 97pp. 11⅜ × 10. 22967-X Pa. $6.50

MATHEMATICAL TABLES AND FORMULAS, Robert D. Carmichael and Edwin R. Smith. Logarithms, sines, tangents, trig functions, powers, roots, reciprocals, exponential and hyperbolic functions, formulas and theorems. 269pp. 5⅜ × 8½. 60111-0 Pa. $3.75

HANDBOOK OF MATHEMATICAL FUNCTIONS WITH FORMULAS, GRAPHS, AND MATHEMATICAL TABLES, edited by Milton Abramowitz and Irene A. Stegun. Vast compendium: 29 sets of tables, some to as high as 20 places. 1,046pp. 8 × 10½. 61272-4 Pa. $19.95

REASON IN ART, George Santayana. Renowned philosopher's provocative, seminal treatment of basis of art in instinct and experience. Volume Four of *The Life of Reason*. 230pp. 5⅜ × 8.
24358-3 Pa. $4.50

LANGUAGE, TRUTH AND LOGIC, Alfred J. Ayer. Famous, clear introduction to Vienna, Cambridge schools of Logical Positivism. Role of philosophy, elimination of metaphysics, nature of analysis, etc. 160pp. 5⅜ × 8½. (USCO)
20010-8 Pa. $2.75

BASIC ELECTRONICS, U.S. Bureau of Naval Personnel. Electron tubes, circuits, antennas, AM, FM, and CW transmission and receiving, etc. 560 illustrations. 567pp. 6½ × 9¼.
21076-6 Pa. $8.95

THE ART DECO STYLE, edited by Theodore Menten. Furniture, jewelry, metalwork, ceramics, fabrics, lighting fixtures, interior decors, exteriors, graphics from pure French sources. Over 400 photographs. 183pp. 8⅜ × 11¼.
22824-X Pa. $6.95

THE FOUR BOOKS OF ARCHITECTURE, Andrea Palladio. 16th-century classic covers classical architectural remains, Renaissance revivals, classical orders, etc. 1738 Ware English edition. 216 plates. 110pp. of text. 9½ × 12¾.
21308-0 Pa. $11.50

THE WIT AND HUMOR OF OSCAR WILDE, edited by Alvin Redman. More than 1000 ripostes, paradoxes, wisecracks: Work is the curse of the drinking classes, I can resist everything except temptations, etc. 258pp. 5⅜ × 8½. (USCO)
20602-5 Pa. $3.50

THE DEVIL'S DICTIONARY, Ambrose Bierce. Barbed, bitter, brilliant witticisms in the form of a dictionary. Best, most ferocious satire America has produced. 145pp. 5⅜ × 8½.
20487-1 Pa. $2.50

ERTÉ'S FASHION DESIGNS, Erté. 210 black-and-white inventions from *Harper's Bazar*, 1918-32, plus 8pp. full-color covers. Captions. 88pp. 9 × 12.
24203-X Pa. $6.50

ERTÉ GRAPHICS, Erté. Collection of striking color graphics: *Seasons, Alphabet, Numerals, Aces* and *Precious Stones*. 50 plates, including 4 on covers. 48pp. 9⅜ × 12¼.
23580-7 Pa. $6.95

PAPER FOLDING FOR BEGINNERS, William D. Murray and Francis J. Rigney. Clearest book for making origami sail boats, roosters, frogs that move legs, etc. 40 projects. More than 275 illustrations. 94pp. 5⅜ × 8½.
20713-7 Pa. $2.25

ORIGAMI FOR THE ENTHUSIAST, John Montroll. Fish, ostrich, peacock, squirrel, rhinoceros, Pegasus, 19 other intricate subjects. Instructions. Diagrams. 128pp. 9 × 12.
23799-0 Pa. $4.95

CROCHETING NOVELTY POT HOLDERS, edited by Linda Macho. 64 useful, whimsical pot holders feature kitchen themes, animals, flowers, other novelties. Surprisingly easy to crochet. Complete instructions. 48pp. 8¼ × 11.
24296-X Pa. $1.95

CROCHETING DOILIES, edited by Rita Weiss. Irish Crochet, Jewel, Star Wheel, Vanity Fair and more. Also luncheon and console sets, runners and centerpieces. 51 illustrations. 48pp. 8¼ × 11.
23424-X Pa. $2.00

YUCATAN BEFORE AND AFTER THE CONQUEST, Diego de Landa. Only significant account of Yucatan written in the early post-Conquest era. Translated by William Gates. Over 120 illustrations. 162pp. 5⅜ × 8½.   23622-6 Pa. $3.50

ORNATE PICTORIAL CALLIGRAPHY, E.A. Lupfer. Complete instructions, over 150 examples help you create magnificent "flourishes" from which beautiful animals and objects gracefully emerge. 8⅛ × 11.   21957-7 Pa. $2.95

DOLLY DINGLE PAPER DOLLS, Grace Drayton. Cute chubby children by same artist who did Campbell Kids. Rare plates from 1910s. 30 paper dolls and over 100 outfits reproduced in full color. 32pp. 9¼ × 12¼.   23711-7 Pa. $3.50

CURIOUS GEORGE PAPER DOLLS IN FULL COLOR, H. A. Rey, Kathy Allert. Naughty little monkey-hero of children's books in two doll figures, plus 48 full-color costumes: pirate, Indian chief, fireman, more. 32pp. 9¼ × 12¼.
24386-9 Pa. $3.50

GERMAN: HOW TO SPEAK AND WRITE IT, Joseph Rosenberg. Like *French, How to Speak and Write It.* Very rich modern course, with a wealth of pictorial material. 330 illustrations. 384pp. 5⅜ × 8½. (USUKO)   20271-2 Pa. $4.75

CATS AND KITTENS: 24 Ready-to-Mail Color Photo Postcards, D. Holby. Handsome collection; feline in a variety of adorable poses. Identifications. 12pp. on postcard stock. 8¼ × 11.   24469-5 Pa. $2.95

MARILYN MONROE PAPER DOLLS, Tom Tierney. 31 full-color designs on heavy stock, from *The Asphalt Jungle, Gentlemen Prefer Blondes,* 22 others. 1 doll. 16 plates. 32pp. 9⅜ × 12¼.   23769-9 Pa. $3.50

FUNDAMENTALS OF LAYOUT, F.H. Wills. All phases of layout design discussed and illustrated in 121 illustrations. Indispensable as student's text or handbook for professional. 124pp. 8⅛. × 11.   21279-3 Pa. $4.50

FANTASTIC SUPER STICKERS, Ed Sibbett, Jr. 75 colorful pressure-sensitive stickers. Peel off and place for a touch of pizzazz: clowns, penguins, teddy bears, etc. Full color. 16pp. 8¼ × 11.   24471-7 Pa. $2.95

LABELS FOR ALL OCCASIONS, Ed Sibbett, Jr. 6 labels each of 16 different designs—baroque, art nouveau, art deco, Pennsylvania Dutch, etc.—in full color. 24pp. 8¼ × 11.   23688-9 Pa. $2.95

HOW TO CALCULATE QUICKLY: RAPID METHODS IN BASIC MATHE-MATICS, Henry Sticker. Addition, subtraction, multiplication, division, checks, etc. More than 8000 problems, solutions. 185pp. 5 × 7¼.   20295-X Pa. $2.95

THE CAT COLORING BOOK, Karen Baldauski. Handsome, realistic renderings of 40 splendid felines, from American shorthair to exotic types. 44 plates. Captions. 48pp. 8¼ × 11.   24011-8 Pa. $2.25

THE TALE OF PETER RABBIT, Beatrix Potter. The inimitable Peter's terrifying adventure in Mr. McGregor's garden, with all 27 wonderful, full-color Potter illustrations. 55pp. 4¼ × 5½. (Available in U.S. only)   22827-4 Pa. $1.60

BASIC ELECTRICITY, U.S. Bureau of Naval Personnel. Batteries, circuits, conductors, AC and DC, inductance and capacitance, generators, motors, trans-formers, amplifiers, etc. 349 illustrations. 448pp. 6½ × 9¼.   20973-3 Pa. $7.95

SOURCE BOOK OF MEDICAL HISTORY, edited by Logan Clendening, M.D. Original accounts ranging from Ancient Egypt and Greece to discovery of X-rays: Galen, Pasteur, Lavoisier, Harvey, Parkinson, others. 685pp. 5⅜ × 8½.

20621-1 Pa. $10.95

THE ROSE AND THE KEY, J.S. Lefanu. Superb mystery novel from Irish master. Dark doings among an ancient and aristocratic English family. Well-drawn characters; capital suspense. Introduction by N. Donaldson. 448pp. 5⅜ × 8½.

24377-X Pa. $6.95

SOUTH WIND, Norman Douglas. Witty, elegant novel of ideas set on languorous Mediterranean island of Nepenthe. Elegant prose, glittering epigrams, mordant satire. 1917 masterpiece. 416pp. 5⅜ × 8½. (Available in U.S. only)

24361-3 Pa. $5.95

RUSSELL'S CIVIL WAR PHOTOGRAPHS, Capt. A.J. Russell. 116 rare Civil War Photos: Bull Run, Virginia campaigns, bridges, railroads, Richmond, Lincoln's funeral car. Many never seen before. Captions. 128pp. 9⅜ × 12¼.

24283-8 Pa. $6.95

PHOTOGRAPHS BY MAN RAY: 105 Works, 1920-1934. Nudes, still lifes, landscapes, women's faces, celebrity portraits (Dali, Matisse, Picasso, others), rayographs. Reprinted from rare gravure edition. 128pp. 9⅜ × 12¼. (Available in U.S. only)

23842-3 Pa. $6.95

STAR NAMES: THEIR LORE AND MEANING, Richard H. Allen. Star names, the zodiac, constellations: folklore and literature associated with heavens. The basic book of its field, fascinating reading. 563pp. 5⅜ × 8½.

21079-0 Pa. $7.95

BURNHAM'S CELESTIAL HANDBOOK, Robert Burnham, Jr. Thorough guide to the stars beyond our solar system. Exhaustive treatment. Alphabetical by constellation: Andromeda to Cetus in Vol. 1; Chamaeleon to Orion in Vol. 2; and Pavo to Vulpecula in Vol. 3. Hundreds of illustrations. Index in Vol. 3. 2000pp. 6⅛ × 9¼.

23567-X, 23568-8, 23673-0 Pa. Three-vol. set $36.85

THE ART NOUVEAU STYLE BOOK OF ALPHONSE MUCHA, Alphonse Mucha. All 72 plates from *Documents Decoratifs* in original color. Stunning, essential work of Art Nouveau. 80pp. 9⅜ × 12¼.

24044-4 Pa. $7.95

DESIGNS BY ERTE; FASHION DRAWINGS AND ILLUSTRATIONS FROM "HARPER'S BAZAR," Erte. 310 fabulous line drawings and 14 *Harper's Bazar* covers, 8 in full color. Erte's exotic temptresses with tassels, fur muffs, long trains, coifs, more. 129pp. 9⅜ × 12¼.

23397-9 Pa. $6.95

HISTORY OF STRENGTH OF MATERIALS, Stephen P. Timoshenko. Excellent historical survey of the strength of materials with many references to the theories of elasticity and structure. 245 figures. 452pp. 5⅜ × 8½. 61187-6 Pa. $8.95

Prices subject to change without notice.

Available at your book dealer or write for free catalog to Dept. GI, Dover Publications, Inc., 31 East 2nd St. Mineola, N.Y. 11501. Dover publishes more than 175 books each year on science, elementary and advanced mathematics, biology, music, art, literary history, social sciences and other areas.